PARENT, TRAPPED

PARENT, TRAPPED

Voices of Parenthood from Behind Bars

Taj Mahon-Haft, Ph.D.
&
Gin Carter, M.S.

Humanizing Publications
A Division of the Humanization Project
Virginia
www.thehumanizationproject.org

© 2021 by Taj Alexander Mahon-Haft and Virginia Lintecum Carter
All rights reserved.
No part of this book may be reproduced, in any form, without written permission from the publisher.

Requests for permission to reproduce selections from this book should be emailed to:
gin@thehumanizationproject.org.

PAPERBACK ISBN: 978-1-7377975-0-0
EBOOK ISBN: 978-1-7377975-1-7 (ebook)

Library of Congress Control Number: 2021916874

Published in the United States by Humanizing Publications, a division of the Humanization Project, Christiansburg, VA.

2022

To: Sarah –
Thank you for your help and understanding!
With love,
Gin

Dedicated to D and all children who have parents behind bars.

Thousands of years ago, a native Mesoamerican culture called Toltec talked about the magnificent gift that humans have received. No other animal in the animal kingdom, except humans, has the ability to speak and to write.

Keeping this in mind, when we speak we need to honor this gift by speaking in an impeccable manner. Each writer in this book honors the Toltec tradition and has chosen their words with great love and care.

- Jack Doxey

Foreword

Invisibility.

This is an idea that has enchanted people for millennia - from the ancient Greeks who represented their Olympian Gods as being able to appear at will to Harry Potter's "Cloak of Invisibility."

But, there is a sinister side to being invisible. An invisible person would be powerless in so many respects. Not being seen by others, this person could suffer hardships or pain that would easily be ignored.

There are many in our society today who truly are invisible; though, in fact, they can be seen by anyone with a will to do so. This book invites the reader to meet some of these invisible persons who happen to be parents, too. The reader will see what they say and be given a unique opportunity to understand the pain, frustrations and hopes of those who are no longer seen by society because of incarceration.

The authors understand the world of invisible persons, and though they have suffered because of that knowledge gained by the experience of one of them being behind bars, they have successfully worked to change things for the better for others. One important feature of this work is that it ends with a chapter which offers an incisive and practical set of recommendations for changing a system that has caused such human tragedy.

Parent, Trapped is a ground-breaking work. It is one that may well become a classic in sociological and criminological studies as it allows the reader to enter a world rarely seen by most persons. It reminds one of the truth of these words of the second century (B.C.E). Roman playwright, Terence: "I am a person and think nothing human is foreign to me."* And, it challenges us to keep in mind that "real change will occur when we take direct action" to make our society more just and compassionate in dealing with those who are vulnerable.

William J. Cook, Jr., Ph.D.
Emeritus Professor, Criminal Justice
WESTFIELD STATE UNIVERSITY

Homo sum, humani nihil a me alienum puto.

Preface

Growing up, I never wanted to have children. In fact, I was adamantly against it. I was an environmentalist before most kids even knew what that word meant and I attributed—as I still do—most of our world's problems to overpopulation. But that all changed years ago when I went to visit one of my best friends from college. It was the first time I had met his son who was about 4 at the time. Seeing them together for a few days made me realize, if I could have a child like that and a relationship with my child like that, I would want to have kids.

Fast forward over a decade later, and I am proud to say, that friend is now my partner, his son, who is now almost 16, will someday be my stepson, and hopefully, we will be able to have a child of our own—once we are done with this whole prison thing that is.

Years ago, he wrote a letter to his son, after being wrongfully incarcerated, and I helped him put it together into a keepsake book filled with pictures of the two of them, family, and friends. At that time, we thought, "what if other people behind bars could do this for their children too?" This book you are now holding in your hands—or reading on a screen—is the result of that musing. I am happy, as I write this, that you will get to see even a small glimpse of the amazing father-son relationship that changed my mind about having children.

When my best friend got locked up, I knew nothing about prison. Sure, he had worked in criminology and sociology and would tell me about those things, but I was off saving coral doing conservation work and a lot of it really didn't sink in. Now though, through the experience of him being behind bars and me jumping in to help with his ongoing work, I have gotten to see the effects of mass incarceration first hand. I now have friends—genuine friends—who are in prison and who have gotten out. I have friends who have loved ones behind bars. I have many friends who work in criminal justice reform. I can tell you, it is amazing the number of genuinely good people affected by our criminal justice system.

Please, let go of whatever ideas you have had about people behind bars and just read this book and the letters within it with an open mind. You will not find the words of "criminals" or "evil" people, but I know, you will find the words of parents who genuinely love their children and have wonderful things to say to them.

Most of the content in this book was written over a year and a half ago, and it has taken me quite some time to compile and edit it. Why? Because it really hit me emotionally reading all these heartfelt words from parents who are trapped away from the world, held in little boxes where they are not allowed to fully love their children. It was hard for me to work on it. Maybe it was just too close to home, having the original letter and much content of the book written by the man I love, him held in one of those boxes, also, away from my arms. So I will warn you, this is a heart-wrenching book. But it is also a beautiful book, full of love and kindness.

Most of the letters in this book were handwritten, meaning I had to type them all. That being said, any errors, I can assure you, are mine, not theirs. Also too, as you proceed, I elected to put Taj's letter to his son—originally a single piece, but here broken up to bind the other letters together—in a handwriting font. I trust that it is not distracting, but just meant to distinguish the original letter from the other letters and Taj's writing meant directly for you, the reader.

Also, there is a lot of reference to data and information regarding what is helpful for families behind bars, especially in Part 2 of the book. Please know we chose not to put citations in the book, as it would bulk up what is meant to be a heartfelt book. That being said, Taj is a PhD sociologist and criminologist, so the statements in the book are not unfounded and are based on years—even while in prison—of him keeping up with criminal justice and sociological data and papers. If you would like to read his most recent paper—written from behind bars—which contains references to many other papers, you can find that information at the back of this book.

I encourage you, please open your heart as you turn these pages, and if this book speaks to you, please share it with others, and of course, if you want to help more directly, please reach out to us at the Humanization Project.

In solidarity and love,
Gin Carter, M.S.
The Humanization Project

PART 1
Letters

To my brightest, kindest, strongest D:

Lots of sweat and crumpled drafts have gone into this letter. It is meant as a gift that keeps giving, a compilation of my knowledge and experience and love, passed on in words and intended to provide some foundation for your life. I hope it's useful, I hope you like it, but most of all I hope it means something to you.

Everything I say below I offer as if I may know something, but I could be wrong. What you do with this is for you to decide.

The only thing that I am completely certain about is that I love you wholeheartedly. No distance or time or hardship can ever dent my devotion to you and your wellbeing, son.

As far as everything else goes, I confess a lack of knowledge and wisdom in many realms. If I had to fix the engine, we'd be walking, that's for sure! But I do have—according to some people at least—the following qualifications: I am a lifelong student of fatherhood, an avid devotee of friendship and love, a doctor of understanding society—that's sociology—and a newly-minted member of street life.

There are so many things that I want to say to you about my being here now, away from you, to reassure you and help you understand how unjust and plain wrong my conviction was. And that it was, deeply so. I will answer any questions you ever have open and honestly. But what is important in this situation is not me; it's you! You are the best part of me, my greatest pride and hope. So this letter is focused not on me, but on helping build your beautiful, bright future.

This letter is the chance for me to organize and make useful the billions of ideas that swirl around my brain for and about you. It's not that you are the only topic on my mind while I'm here. Not quite. But I'd say that my mind finds its way to good vibes, inside jokes, stories, lessons, or something relating to you approximately once a minute. If you do the math, that makes about 1440 times per day. I speak of you so often with my friends here that they not only know your name, someone asks me how you are almost daily.

Anyway, in order to not ramble aimlessly forever on these topics, I am going to break this letter into the following three parts:

1. Love
2. Support
3. Lessons

But first, a bit about Loss...

Loss

First, they take our freedom. Lock us up in a steel and cement bathroom with bunkbeds and another grown adult. Sharing that same 65 or so square feet all the time. We cannot even open and close the door at our discretion nor flush the toilet as often as needed. Everything needs permission and often assistance from a guard who doesn't care. Live almost all of life in this cell and the big pod shared by 50-90 others. To go outside the building is on their schedule and needs approval. To go more than 100 yards means hours shackled, hands and feet. My drive to my first prison was 13 hours on a bus, the entire time with cuffs so tight on my wrists and ankles that my hands and feet were swollen and numb for four days and their bite still visible in my skin. This is our new normal.

Next, they take our identity. Shave our heads 'til we all do look alike. Dress us first in unicolor jumpsuits or pajamas until we graduate to the exact same blue chambray shirt, elastic-wasted generic jeans, and white underwear and T-shirt as everyone else. Turn in every item we own. Only a few state-approved items are available for purchase, the same few that everyone else can have at exorbitant prices. No longer do we have a name, only a number to which we answer.

Next, they take our voice. When we want to cry, to share, to connect, we cannot. We are taught quickly–even though I've found it untrue–not to trust anyone here with us. There is no counseling here except when we say we're a threat to ourselves, and that means time in the turtle suit or naked in solitary, not real treatment.

When we write about our lives and experiences, no one typically listens. The stamp marking our letters out as prison-born make most strangers disregard anything therein. We cannot even readily talk to our family and friends "on the streets." Entry jobs here pay $18-25 per month and calls are a buck apiece, emails about 40 cents, and a stamp 55 cents.

When we have an internal issue, we get either ignored or complete lip service. Paperwork is typically provided with brush off responses or lost entirely.

Then comes the loss of affection. Even the friendships we dare make here are founded in the land of distrust. We may get brief bro pats, but no real hugs. The lexicon of the place is steeped in negativity and criticism, from the top down. Positive reinforcement, kind words, and hugs are rarer than honesty from politicians. What is life without affection?

But, to varying degrees, we can and adjust to all that. Far worse is the loss of our loved ones from our daily lives, especially our children.

When I first found myself locked up, all I could think about is how much I missed my boy and how much I worried about his well-being. I had organized my entire life around being his dad. Since the day he was born, we were inseparable. We had faced reading, swimming, and steep hikes together and he was my best buddy. Now, I could not even talk to him on demand, let alone see him or share laughs and adventures. As much as this hurt me, I could only imagine how much he was hurting and confused, only seven years old when this happened. My heart was broken for him and about him that very first day. I often found myself lost in thoughts that cascaded to tears that flooded until I was wrought for hours in heaving sobs.

I have rebuilt myself enormously since then, working through depression and dismay, overcoming the structural obstacles to the system. We have maintained a great connection emotionally and we now talk as much and as openly as any 13-year-old does with his dad. He remains my greatest pride. Yet to this day, my heart breaks for him and about him every single day.

Just imagine suddenly not being able to do all the little things that a parent does with your child, even as you continue to feel all those parental feelings and urges. It is slow motion torture.

And the same holds true with my parents, as I reflect on the same from the other side. We are closer now than ever before, yet I watch them age and cannot help. I cannot celebrate their honorary birthdays. Rather than finally helping them as they deserve and we all desire, I must again ask their help and patience. I know how much it hurts them to see me here and that stings, too, on top of missing these prime years.

As those relationships are filtered through steel bars, there comes too a loss of the purpose that they bring. No matter who you are, being a parent is a defining characteristic. Taking care of our children may not be the only thing that we do and we may all do it slightly differently, but in all its forms it is a fundamental part of who we are. Being a parent is a primary status and shapes our time and goals. When this is the norm and it is suddenly taken away, it leaves a huge gap in our lives.

My biggest fear since I first got locked up was what would happen to my son. I went from doing everything to help him and spend time with him to feeling like I could do nothing at all for him. I wrote and called all I could, but the way it changed left me feeling directionless, my primary function in life gone. I'm a sociologist too, so I know all about the statistical odds further stacked against him. He's incredibly strong, thriving now, despite that, but he bears the scars of a childhood of lost opportunity and security for I cannot do my daily job properly. A sense of helplessness haunts me even as I do all I can.

Much research has found that maintaining purpose is central to resilience in any traumatic situation. Since the Holocaust, this has been examined in the sciences and found true repeatedly. A recent study of the lives of those thriving most despite being behind bars found that having a purpose that involved helping others was the universal common ground among positive prison leaders.

Additionally, nearly everyone able to do well in this

setting described bonds with their kids and loved ones outside as central to their purpose. Yet the system, even while recognizing the value of these bonds, is designed to limit them as much as possible.

Though better than nothing, ephemeral and distant are phone calls, emails and letters. Likewise they typically require waiting in line for hours and are completely censored and surveilled. We no longer even get color family photographs in the mail here. Instead, they make a black and white Xerox copy of any mailed in and we get that. The letter better not be more than 2.5 pages, too, or it will be returned.

The best thing available are the visits. Weekends only here, 8:30 a.m. to 3 p.m., and only one of the days. Our family must drive hours usually, then submit to typically rude, demeaning full searches and scans and long lines. Once inside, we get but a brief hug and a kiss at the beginning and end. Try to hold hands during and our visit will be terminated. Try it again and we lose visits for an extended time. We must dress in a backwards beige onesie, and there are only candy bars allowed in the vending machines. Most places, the visitation rooms are overcrowded, so the next groups in will typically force us out after only an hour and half or so, no matter how far our family comes. Until I got lucky and made it to a less crowded spot, my amazing, devoted partner, Gin, would leave home at around 8 a.m. and not return until around 4 p.m. to spend just 90 minutes together, braving nasty comments and endless waiting. Once, as we first got together, she got kicked out after 59 minutes after coming from Hawai'i to Virginia to see me.

Often overlooked is how it is not just us behind bars who lose. Thanks to mass incarceration, the Annie E. Casey Foundation estimates that 5.1 million of today's parents will spend time locked up before their kids are adults. With each parent behind bars having about two kids, that means over 10 million children will have to know this stress. In this state, Virginia, it is about one of every 14 kids, and one of nine African American children. That means the average classroom has between two and four kids who'll at some point face this traumatic obstacle. Sadly, too, this greatly elevates the risks of those kids eventually being incarcerated—by six or seven-fold. Their families are 65% more likely to have a hard time paying the bills, according to one recent study. College opportunities usually seem to fade away, too.

But it is not those statistics that matter. It is the kids. Imagine the trauma these young people must feel when one of the people they love and trust most suddenly disappears. No more hugs, no more stories, no more help with homework, no more solid presence. Lives are disrupted, finances made fretful, leaving less time for bonding with the remaining parent and less chance to simply be a kid. How can a young person truly live carefree, as they all deserve, when a parent has been ripped from their world unceremoniously and usually for years? What innocence is lost and replaced by a constant sense of anxiety over what might fall apart next?

Likewise, everyone behind bars had parents themselves. Imagine the trauma in the other direction when your child goes off to where a parent can do nothing for them except, if lucky, send a few dollars for the occasional phone call or commissary junk food. Imagine how it must feel to have a child locked up.

So this book must start with loss, for that is where everyone begins when time starts ticking behind bars. But we are so much more than that loss, all of us here.

But what this book is really about is people and relationships. For that is what is attacked, challenged, and lost when we incarcerate. And the most powerful impacts are where it comes to the parental bonds that are so essential to all our lives. So this book is about parents and children impacted by jail and prison sentences. It is about how we respond, about how we feel, about how we make the most of difficult situations, and how we are, above all else, people. Just like anyone else.

This book is not a diatribe about how terrible the criminal justice system is. Nor is it meant to claim that everyone behind bars is perfect nor every conviction unjust. It is simply meant to provide a voice to the muzzled and awareness for the majority. This book is meant to celebrate the human beings behind bars and their very human experiences.

In my own prison experience, beyond striving constantly to maintain my own relationships, especially with my son, D, I stand determined to make a difference, to make use of this time, to be a voice for the voiceless. Before my own incarceration, I was already a vocal critic of the current criminal justice system, shouting and teaching about the racist, classist impacts. I already made a point to highlight to every student how the stereotypes on the screens are absurd, how there is no difference between "criminals" and "regular people" except who got caught and punished. There are degrees, certainly, but no adult Americans have not broken at least some minor laws.

Yet I stand now, enlightened by my time behind bars. Woke, if you will, though I prefer we don't. I seek more than ever to make a difference now because what I have learned during my time down is that many of my college students and old college buddies broke many more laws than people with whom I now break bread in the chow hall. The backgrounds of the men I've come to know here are often different than my own. It's a very diverse group, contrary to stereotypes. Dungeons and Dragons is the second most popular hobby here, after basketball, and it includes all backgrounds.

One of my biggest lessons is how I was not right enough in my concern for the human impacts of mass incarceration. Everyone here is a meaningful person, even if I don't agree with everyone, and that is the biggest lesson yet. Hopes, dreams, goals, feelings, hobbies, strengths, and, yes, weaknesses. Human beings who, treated with respect and kindness, almost always provide the same.

What I realized during this time also, though, is that all my years of research and all the facts in my arsenal won't change things. Most people are not convinced by that. Stereotypes are too prevalent and data is not a convincing language to the majority of Americans.

What is needed is a shift in mainstream awareness about the impacts of mass incarceration. As long it is seen by the majority of everyday Americans as an issue affecting others—one dimensional criminal stereotypes—meaningful change will not happen. However, if everyone out there could just see that it is three-dimensional people stuck behind bars for years and decades and lifetimes, away from their communities and families who also suffer, real change may advance. Those with convictions must be seen as more than that label, for no one is only their worst mistake. If we want to be treated humanely behind bars, we must be recognized as human.

The best way to get there is to speak the language of the day. In today's world, personal stories are the currency of attention. The personal rules. The personal sells. This is why influencers make money. People respond to other people. We are hardwired to connect empathetically with other individuals.

As I have opened up about my own constant striving and challenges to keep deeply connected with D, I have heard so many similar stories. These new friends, some of the best people I've known in a life across country and classes, have shown me that parental bonds are universal. Everyone knows what it's like to have parents and most adults have kids. And these guys—and the women behind bars I've met indirectly—have shown me how many good and even great parents are doing all they can with very limiting and limited resources while behind bars.

What better way, it suddenly dawned on me, to show the depths and contours of humanity behind bars than to let the voices of parenthood speak for themselves?! The greatest distance between stereotype and reality I've encountered is between the widespread projection of worthless dads and moms locked up, not caring, and the men and women I've met here. Nearly every parent here is doing the best they can. So we decided to highlight these voices to show the world the truth of these parents, trapped, and their children along with them. Their voices speak to experience. Their voices speak to the common ground we all share. Their voices speak to humanity. Their voices speak to all our children.

Still, in collecting these voices of parents trapped behind bars, loss must be understood. These letters were solicited without any direction except that each writer begin with, "I may not be there in person now, but above all else, I want you to always know..." We found, in some of the most tragic cases, parent-child bonds have come to be defined by loss because of a lengthy incarceration.

While many of these men and women have made mistakes, it should be noted that none are anywhere near evil. None, in my experience, are even dangerous to others at this point. Yet these parents and these children continue to suffer these stresses on the very bonds that are most essential to a strong community. At what point do we question the value of these lengthy sentences?

Letters on Loss

"It's like everybody had a say so in the matter except the one man who chose life for her. The one man who just wanted to be a part of her life. I may not be Destiny's biological father, but Destiny is the manifestation of my love as a father."

André Dixon

The things in life that we experience are supposed to make us stronger, but for some it can make us weaker especially when that experience hits close to home like a baby born out of the womb, so innocent and sweet, into a world filled with chaos and confusion only feeling the love of a mother and father shielding them from all.

Regardless of the circumstance that brought us together, from the close abortion of us almost giving up—only if it wasn't for a father's love, a father's wanting, who made a fatherly decision to keep that child when our world was filled with chaos and confusion—we persevered through the unknown with help from others. My family giving their all for a child loved so dearly, who became a part of them.

Then for me to hear the devastating news of that child not being mine crushed my heart, it broke my spirit and had my soul drowning in tears, but with my love for her, I still wanted to be in her life. I spent days shedding tears with my family, because my mother lost a granddaughter, my sister a niece, me a daughter and our son was affected by this also, but our love for her is greater than what you can understand. To this day her baby pictures still hang on the walls of our hearts. I gave her life. I didn't allow for my son to be given up for adoption and I wasn't going to give our Destiny up for abortion.

To me Destiny is more than a word meaning fate or a

predetermined course of events. Through the course of nine months I bared witness to the growth and development of Destiny. From her little heartbeat, to her kicking in her mother's stomach and then on that day in April of 2000 my Destiny became flesh.

See, naming her Destiny was more than a name to me, it symbolized how we almost gave up on a precious life, but the father in me wouldn't allow us to. If I wasn't with her mother that day at the clinic, Destiny wouldn't exist to this day, so Destiny meant the love and bond of us not giving up, because she was destined to be.

For three years she was my princess. Even after hearing that she wasn't mine, I forgave her mother, I didn't care about the past. I was more worried about our future as father and daughter. Nobody took into account my feelings and how much I was hurting, torn apart by the situation. It's like everybody had a say in the matter except the one man who choose life for her. The one man who just wanted to be a part of her life.

I may not be Destiny's biological father, but Destiny is the manifestation of my love as a father. As a father making that life-or-death choice and not having you as mine, nobody will ever know my pain. On the inside I cry tears of hurt and sadness, but also of joy and happiness, because I made the right decision, for you to breathe the air I breathe and for you to see life as you see it through your own beautiful eyes. Tears of a father.

André Dixon

"Energy's merely the effort that we place into things to see them accomplished. Energy can never be destroyed, it only transforms.

♥

Wayne A. Thomas, Jr.

*On May 20th, 2017—her 22nd birthday—my daughter was shot by her children's father—2 days before my birthday. I actually received this news on my birthday by way of my mother, who relayed it through a close friend. Neither wanted to be the one to sadden me with the bad news. However, thankfully, both wounds weren't life threatening. The one lodged in her arm, shattered her bone causing her to have surgery, while the other embedded within her thigh left an unforgettable flesh wound. Through it all, I still have my daughter. Hearing this news instantly took me to what I felt to be the very place I'd consciously stored every ounce of what I knew would someday soon bring calm to her and I both upon consolidation: My Freedom—The Cellar—fighting the urge of possibly ruining the moment in my attempt to crack the seal, and selfishly pour out everything I saved for just that occasion.

My only child and daughter was shot by a guy that she claims still loves her because within the moment of her despair, he took off a piece of his own clothing to slow down the bleeding of her wounds, pleading for her not to die.

Of course me being her father utilizing every means I still have to see her protected, she—my daughter—took the side of a so-called-man who for whatever reason attempted to take her life, over the very man who gave her hers. For a long time after that visit, when I tried to protect her and convince her to leave the man who shot her twice in jealousy, she did not speak to me, after a lifetime of closeness.

***

Dear Shynekia,

As I push this pen to design for you the many pictures from my illustrated point of view, I'm hoping that at least one of my illustrations marinates with you like an aged old wine, leaving you with an unforgettable sense of how time and patience manifest within and throughout all things and decisions.

I've kept so much bottled up over these years feeling that you were too young to reciprocate receptively all that I felt was necessary to express to you as a commemoration or honor of just being your Father, however 21 years, and 2 granddaughters later, having to go through long-term frustrations of me—your father—not being able to be there as you would've liked him to; which I often feel made way for this dilemma that you & I are now going through. There is no better time than now to pop the cork on all that I once set aside for later.

Just this scenery Baby Girl, everything within life deals with time and reparations. It's said that time heals all wounds, however within the same breath, neither are we promised tomorrow. I can only assume that your decisions revolve around me and how my physical absence affected your growing up, and how maybe you don't want that for your children.

Baby, I commend you for exercising your experiences as a supplement in order to replenish what's been depleted from your life, however never lose or let go of purpose. Energy's merely the effort that we place into things to see them accomplished. Energy can never be destroyed, it only transforms. No different than this metaphoric bottle that I spoke on throughout the opening of this letter. I'm hoping that my time and energy enhances your views, and stimulates all of my efforts in regards to the many untold truths stemming from me being where I am.

"I may not be there in person now, but above all else I

want you to always know that I am your father, I am always here to assist you, and most of all, I love you.

Sincerely,
Daddy

> "This is my promise to you, Kirstyn, I will do everything in my power to be humble about my problems, and stay above them, and out of here."

♥

T.F.

This is a letter to my lovely daughter, such a sweet young woman, just beautiful inside and out–I love you.

When I think of how wonderful you have always been all of your life, so smart and strong, I feel so blessed to have the privilege of having even a little of the fatherhood that honestly I feel I don't deserve. I say that because I was not there over the years. As you know I have been battling the disease of addiction for most of my adult life. Not to hide behind an excuse, but the struggle is so destructive and real, it needs to be mentioned.

There have been tough times over the years, I think more for you and the rest of the family than myself, and I can only imagine because it's been so hard here. I want you to know that not a day goes by that I don't think of you and your wellbeing, I care so much for you. I thank God for the good and honest relationship that you and I have now, even if it's over the phone or a very uncomfortable visit in a state-issued backwards jumpsuit, that is redundant, and them taking all real food from the vending machines which makes no sense, except as yet another tool of Mass Punishment. I am sorry that you have to go through what you do when you come to visit. Yes I know they–VA-DOC– do seem to be anti-family as of late–thank you Virginia. I'm so sorry for that.

I do want to make that very point of mostly uneducated, unqualified VA DOC personnel, often picking up where the sentencing judges left off to impose even more punishment, when all their real role is to maintain safety, health, and housing. Seriously, these days the VA-DOC acts as if the confinement from family and society doesn't go far enough. Furthermore my dearest Kirstyn, I'm so very sorry that I will never have any chance of parole due to the state of Virginia abolishing it in 1995 and then passing Truth in Sentencing to get more bodies to fill their new federally funded prisons–that is correct, living breathing human beings were given inflated sentences for the purpose of making money. I don't understand all of it, but even a man as myself can see corruption.

This is my promise to you, Kirstyn, I will do everything in my power to be humble about my problems, and stay above them, and out of here. Thank you for seeing the good in me, and hanging in there. It means so much. You mean so much to me. Thank you for letting me use your letter as a platform to mention some important issues for many forgotten people.

Love always,
Dad

"I can't change the past, but I can learn from it to try and make a better future, and I've been doing everything I can from where I'm at to better myself physically, mentally, and educationally so I can be the Dad that she should've had all along."

❤

Joey "Dubs" Morrison

December 20, 2018

Bailey–age 9,

Hey, how's my precious girl doing? I want you to know that I love you very much and I miss you each and every day that goes by, and just because I'm not there doesn't change that fact. I hope you have a very Merry Christmas and a Happy New Year. I know you still don't want to speak to me yet but just know that I'm here for whenever you're ready to talk. It's hard to believe that soon you're going to be 10 years old already, you're growing up so fast. I hope things are going well in school, you're a smart girl so I know you can make good grades. Have fun during your holiday break and don't give your Mom a hard time. ;) I love you more than you know, don't ever forget that or think otherwise. Much Love and Positive Vibes!

Love Always,
- Dad

April 10, 2018
Bailey,

I just want you to know that I'm always thinking about you and that I miss you so much. I wish you would speak to me when I call but I know that you will when you're ready. I know it's impossible to make up for the time I've missed by not being there for you and for that I am truly sorry, but when I get home I will do any and everything I can to work towards that. I know how you feel because my Dad wasn't there for me either when I was growing up and I should've learned from his mistakes but I didn't. I had to learn the hard way too and in the end I not only hurt myself but you and your brother Charlie as well. Just know that I still love you very much and I always will, no matter what.

Love Always,
-Daddy

*Poem I wrote in a self-made birthday card for my son, Charlie. April 21, 2018
    Charlie,
    What a day
    Oh what a day
    To my little boy I have this to say
    I wish you a great big Happy Birthday
    You are now seven years old
    No telling what the future holds
    It's a special day made just for you
    May all your birthday wishes come true
    Oh what a day
    What a day.

Love Always,
-Daddy

*A P.S. to an email I sent my daughter's Mother. May 18, 2018
P.S. My regret is that I haven't been the father that Bailey so rightfully deserves. I can't change the past, but I can learn from it to try and make a better future, and I've been doing everything I can from where I'm at to better myself physically, mentally, and educationally so I can be the Dad

that she should've had all along. I don't expect you or anyone else to have complete faith in me right now. I have to earn that from everyone, I have to change people's perception of me and show that I am capable of change, capable of being the parent I should've been from the start.

-Joey

Untitled
    Life is akin to the open sea and our actions are like the vessel,
    Our choices can help keep us afloat or sink us under a trusses;
    Places like these give many a man plenty of time to think,
    Either ways to help him stay afloat or just more ways to sink;
    I intend to float because I'm sick and tired of being a statistic,
    And depending on what course you take life can be simplistic;
    Just toe the line and do what I must but all only within reason,
    Wanting a decent life for me and mine isn't committing treason;
    With you by my side helping with steps along the way,
    Many things can be accomplished each and every day;
    All we must do is work together for a common goal,
    Separated we are weak but together we're unstoppable;
    WE need to stick to the plan and keep our noses to the grind,
    So we can make something better and leave our old lives behind;
    There will be times when things are rough and we will have to row,
    There'll also be periods of smooth sailing where the wind begins to blow;

So when the wind picks up I'll grab the help and sail us to the East,
Because that's where the sun rises and each new day is a treat.

-Joey "Dubs" Morrison

3/16/18
Untitled
    I would be just as lost without y'all,
    as a novice lost at seas,
    drifting along with the currents,
    and not able to go alee.
    I would be just as lost without y'all,
    as an astronaut lost in space,
    stranded amidst the emptiness,
    and planets laid to waste.
    I would be just as lost without y'all
    as an adventurer without a guide,
    buried amongst the wild animals,
    and with nowhere left to hide.
    I would be just as lost without y'all
    as lost as lost could be,
    and I sit around and think about it...
    Would y'all be just as lost without me?

- Joey "Dubs" Morrison
12/19/17

Love

This has to be first because it is the most important thing in the world, the most important thing about you and me. Also, love is the most powerful thing in life. It is the only thing not constrained or limited by time, distance, gravity, or money. Can't be bought. Does not fade with years. Floats through endless skies to touch people worlds apart.

Specifically, I want you to know that you are never alone, always surrounded by love—it is the central guiding force in my world. I've long been a bit of a hippie, shouting love as a priority. But the day you were born, my heart and mind opened up wider, bringing an understanding and depth of love I'd never heard of or imagined. It's only gotten stronger and deeper every day since. It sounds silly, but it's true: I love you more with every word or breath that escapes your body. No matter the miles, time zones, or walls and bars between us, please never doubt that. My love for you, Son, is unconditional, boundless, and expanding. Nothing can ever change that or diminish it even slightly. It is longer than forever, bigger than the universe. It grows grander with every memory, phone call, letter, and shared laugh.

I can never say it properly; there are no words, but your wellbeing is always my top priority, so I try to do anything I can think of to demonstrate my fatherly love. Sometimes it is probably cheesy and excessive, but in this situation I am simply seeking to provide you confidence in that love with the words and limited actions I can share.

As a quick aside, please know always that you are blessed to be loved by many good people. Your mom, obviously. Also all of both sides of your family and every single one of my friends. Even those folks you barely get to see love you deeply. Wherever you go in the U.S., you are near someone who loves you blindly.

All this love for you is no mystery—it is because you embody love. You are full of it. You exude it from your pores, breaths, smiles, words, and deeds. It's evident to me every day in your every action. Your genuine adoration of your dogs. Your kindness towards your little sister. Your consideration when your mom feels ill. Your thoughtful words, written and stated, to me. Your eternal motivation to provide smiles and laughs to your friends. Your tears for other people suffering in any way. Everything you do shows love.

This makes sense, too. After all, love is essential to your identity, the main theme in your carefully chosen name. D means "lover of the earth," and it honors the goddess of the harvest festivals and celebration. Karma is the way that all the energy you put into the universe comes back to you, a cycle that rewards positive, generous, selfless living. And you embody both names so naturally. That love in your character swells me with pride, though it does not surprise me at all.

Collectively, then, all this is why I implore you to please hang in there through this trying, sad, unjust separation. Rely on love, breathe it, nourish from it on your darkest days. I know it's tough—incredibly so, maddeningly so—and many days feel like it will never end. But it will. I promise. Remember what Nikki Giovanni told me: It will all be ok in the end. If it's not okay, it's not the end.

When things get tough, cling to love and consider this: every day that passes brings us one day closer to being able to hang out and do whatever we want for as long as we want.

This is what I focus on, and it's the only thing that's worked. Hope for our future together times, my love for you, and your love for me have kept me going on the darkest days. You are the light at the end of my tunnel. When my world just kept crumbling and I did not understand and I lost all hope and wanted to give up on everything, the biggest thing to keep me going was our connection. I exercise to give more days to hang with you after I'm out, huffing and sweating up and down hours of the same steel stairs. I continue to teach and conduct research because they are right and mean something to me, but when I need to motivate myself out of bed at 6 a.m. with guards blowing whistles, administrators not caring, and students not showing up, I think of you. Doing these things ensures that I am still helping and living a life of which you can be proud. I write poems and journal to strengthen my connection with our future, our past, and even our today.

    Keep looking forward and envisioning even better times than we've shared before, even as you cherish those priceless memories and ongoing conversations. We will be full-fledged father/son life adventurers again, and it will be glorious! There are so many things we will still share, and I treasure the taste of hope on each such vision produced during my workouts, daydreams, and nightly slumber.

    Love should always be your guide, too. Even beyond the awesome love I have for you, that many people grace upon you, and that is fundamental to your being, always prioritize love in your decision and all realms of life. Never fame. Certainly not power. Absolutely not money. Love first, forever.

    To explain this, I'd like to interject a quick poem, "true wealth":

when we see a color, it's a gift
all the laws of physics can offer our eyes
fire engines do not have red, they reflect it
dandelions do not possess yellow but share it

*our senses perceive white not because glaciers keep the light
but when they give us sun's every hue
    share every shade of the spectrum
    along with warmth and Vitamin D unseen
wealth does not possess things either
rich does not live in a bank's account
but rather within the reflection
of all our lives have offered others
love is not owning someone
but sharing with them life
true fortune cannot be held, controlled
like light and white
it must be spent with people to be worth a dime
real riches are how we seed the senses
    of copilots, passengers, and passerby
wealth is how you spend your energy
    brightening, coloring lives encountered
all the world' grandest treasures
are keys to other's memory banks
sure social elite are the dazzling acrobats
    happily inhabiting recollected smiles
    across decades and oceans*

   Point being, a rich life is one where you give and impress yourself positively on the lived experiences of other people. This entails living to love the world.

About two years ago, this project began without me realizing it. Continuously striving to connect with D, I was also continuously discussing how to do so best with my circle of confidants. He was getting older, and I'd already been gone long enough for it to seem to him like much of his life. Talk about a heart-breaking thing to have my child express.

We spoke daily then, but I knew he would be growing out of that soon and we wouldn't have the daily casual interactions to build off when teenager took over his scheduling priorities. Plus, somehow he was already way, way cooler and more popular than I ever was growing up, so I knew I would soon be relegated to second place, behind the biological imperative of independence. Plus, he still was clearly attacked in moments by sadness from our separation.

In all those moments, I needed him to know what was really important. I needed him to be able to plug into at least some semblance of our bond in times when he needed me but I was not at that second able to call. When he makes the team, and when he doesn't. When he can't figure out algebra. When he gets his first girlfriend. When she becomes his first ex. I needed to be able to offer what was special about our bond—all communication and acceptance and blackberry picking and water guns permanently ready in the trunk of the car—even when I was not going to be there in person.

Over a few months then, I picked at this idea. What do I say when I cannot be there in person in important moments? What is the elixir down to which distills my fatherhood? Countless ideas swirled and morphed. Many of them became snippets.

When it was all said and done, though, I realized that it all boils down to one thing first and foremost: Love. Everything else grew organically from there.

Together, Gin and I ended up turning my words into a photo album with my letter to him as its foundation. It begins with love, elaborates upon it, and shows images thereof. He adored it then and still does now. He told me recently that he still looks at it when he misses me most, even now. What a powerful compliment! Thirteen-year-old boys don't read loving sentimental stuff from their dads! Unheard of!

Next, this book will continue with the beginning of my letter to him, starting with love. When I first completed it, I was nervous and wanted some input. My family read it, and they were apparently quite touched by it. I shared it with some friends at my last prison, and it got many of them talking and writing too.

In the process, it suddenly dawned on me: what if we all did this?!

Through my own endless discussion of and bragging about D with my peers here, I have been blessed to deeply discuss parenthood with many parents behind bars. Without a single exception, every single one starts and ends with how much they love their children. Just like all parents everywhere.

As we compiled these letters, that overwhelming love became clear in what everyone wrote. In many cases, that is the primary focus of these letters, so those are the ones highlighted in this section. That love is professed in many ways, but it is quite telling how central love is to what everyone says to their children.

It also exemplifies a lesson that has been quite surprising to me within these walls and fences. I knew that there were many decent people behind bars. What I was unaware of was how much love would be displayed—if not always expressed so directly—between those so readily dismissed by many as "heartless cons."

I have recently been enjoying giant bear hugs from a great friend called Bear. He is a tremendous artist, and he has painted me a few pieces just to have because we share great walks and meaningful talks. The most recent piece had an inscription on the back reading, "To my stalwart and steadfast friend, whose rooted wisdom helps me to lay down some of my own." We only met 18 months ago, but in this place designed for despair, shared creativity and idealism have made true friendships. We're the two furriest people here, so the hugs are intentionally hilarious—and also kind of like Velcro. Laughter and learning keep misery at bay, and that matters here more than anywhere. In foxholes and prisons the strongest bonds are forged. He will be my friend long beyond our release dates, I know.

 I have witnessed a man convicted of murder risk his fingers to save a frog from a lawnmower. We were all walking during the door break to our classrooms, library spots, and jobs while the grass crew was out mowing. Suddenly, Joe almost fell over bending down so quick, reaching in front of the oncoming mower, pushed by someone zoning out entirely. He walks with crutches permanently after prison medical negligence almost caused foot amputation, yet he was determined. He was the only one who saw the perfectly camouflaged tree frog, and he managed to catch it just before the blades did, dropping his crutches in the process. Everyone stopped, and he hopped across the grass to put it by the wall, out of danger. No fanfare, but nearly everyone here has a special spot in their heart for even the lowliest creatures who join us. Guys really coddle and feed the occasional mouse, just like Shawshank. Nothing like confinement to instill a deep love for nature's right to freedom and life.

 I have watched a former Blood offer up his spot in a three-hour phone line so the weakest guy in the pod could call his family on Christmas. Three phones were being shared by 86 people. Even without power politics and affiliations, not everyone had a chance to make one twenty-minute call. In many places, someone needs to be part of some crew to have easy access to any phone time. Yet that day, perfectly permitted by prison norms to call three or four times, a good man named Adib gave up his turn to ensure an old man had at least one chance. They weren't friends. "It's just right, man," he said when I asked. "Everyone has family and his matters as much to him as mine does to me." And though not perfect, he was one of the leaders that helped us ensure no one got left out entirely from the phone in one pod in the most gang-affiliated building in most of Virginia's DOC.

In fact, it seems to me that there is just as much love in the hearts of the people I've met behind bars as anywhere else I've been. Many have not always been shown or, as a result, shown love as it could and should be. But who has always been as loved and loving as they wish in retrospect?

Yet the place where that love is most readily, emphatically shown is to and about our kids. My favorite part of my visits with my partner, Gin, are the kisses and the laughs, of course. Yet both of us get distracted from all our lovey-dovey reverie whenever a guy comes in and gets to see his child. The brief pause to savor and take in. The glowing look on both faces, everyone smiles like the first dawn. They embrace like hugs are nirvana. For a moment, the weight of distance melts away.

The best group I've been part of during my time was the Therapeutic Support Group. Ten to twelve guys, with intermittent turnover around a core group, working on ACT and CBT programs to help us all cope and thrive amidst ugliness. It was less about the type of therapy and more about leadership–the incredible Dr. Rodney, genuinely caring and challenging and fighting for this one group of ten, the only actual therapeutic programming for over 1000 guys there–and the members. We sincerely listened and deeply shared. We worked through each of our tougher challenges together over a couple years.

The most inspiring moment in that group, across rivers of tears and truths so deep and scarring they could reach the earth's core, was the only all day "conference" we held. The group decided, with just one chance to spend the whole day together, we must make it a seminar on fatherhood. We emerged puffy eyed, hugged repeatedly, knowing we had all learned about fatherhood from people we likely never would have spoken to were it not for prison. Whole lifetimes and generations separated by bars and barbed wire, yet Dr. Rodney came the next week and told us that her boss, a highly recognized psychiatrist who came to teach left telling her how impressed he was with our parental love and priorities.

The common, singular focus so many of these letters place on the centrality of love for our children shows the true power of these bonds. There are universal truths of parenthood, and they transcend circumstances and even mistakes. It shows emotional awareness and gentility. It shows us that love can shine bright enough in a parent's heart to be a beacon visible in the darkness beneath the deepest dungeons with no windows or doors. This focus on love belies the stereotypes, spotlighting the basic kindness that our children bring out in all of us.

Letters on Love

"You dug into that soil so saturated with the seat of animosity, bitterness and apathy to uproot those decaying woods. In its place you all have planted fields of love that perennially bloom, seasoning the air with kindness and humor, honesty and charity, modesty and bravery, smiles and goofiness. I love the way each of you are a complete galaxy, not lacking anything, yet, you are all unlike each other save one exception–loving."

♥

Dustin Lee Russel

My Dear Macyn, Ethan, and Cayden,

I may not be there in person now, but above all else, I want you to always know I love you, I am proud of you and you are worthy. You are each good enough, in time though, you will each develop into being great enough.

The three of you have shown me that despite my circumstances I am worthy of love in its purest form. You have awakened belief in me for the condition of our truth as a society. You see so much violence and negativity on the news that desperation begins to unfurl its roots into the landscape of the mind producing tainted forests distorting the view of what is to come. Then you three came along. You dug into that soil so saturated with animosity, bitterness and apathy to uproot those decaying woods. In its place you all have planted fields of love that perennially bloom, seasoning the air with kindness and humor, honesty and charity, modesty and bravery, smiles and goofiness.

I love the way each of you are a complete galaxy, not lacking anything, yet, you are all unlike each other save one exception–loving. Soooo loving. How you randomly hug

your mother, Macyn. How you, Cayden, dance with your mother in public. Ethan, how you fix your mother oodles of noodles the exact way she likes without her asking. How each of you are self-sacrificing for the benefit of those around you.
You have allowed me the honor of your love and it has exploded my night sky with neon after glow. You are illumination, a brightening, and enlightenment to my spirit and this world is much more mushier for all that you are.

   As a parent, you want the best for your child. As a bonus parent, it is not different. You hope they are kind, selfless, respectful, loving, charitable, creative caretakers of their environment. Strong-willed, resilient, hopeful, happy, goofy, super-heroic, capable of flight, and impervious to peer pressure. You want their bruises and scrapes to be healed on sight, but you also want them to learn from their mistakes the first time and not the fifty-leventh time. :)

   At 14-years-old, Ethan and Cayden, you are the same age I was when I was influenced to be in a situation that horrifically cost a man his life. I did not kill him, yet I did not stop him from being killed. Nor did I speak against the idea of him being killed. Your voice is important, your voice is needed, your voice can change the world. But it won't if you live life quietly. I wanted to fit in as a kid and I pray that inclusion never motivates any of you. Let your voice be strong, filled with love, and true to who you are. Be yourselves, be creative, be unique. But above all, be love. Our Christ-like love will never steer you wrong. God first, family second, community third. Take care of your mother. Love her completely and know she is our gift from God, amazon and beautiful, as she is. I love you All...

Second most and in a weird way,
Dustin Lee Russell

> "I always tell you at the end of our visits as well as the end of our phone calls, 'I love you, I love you more than anything.' And you reply with, 'I know dad you tell me all the time!' I tell you because I don't ever want you to forget it."

♥

Darrel Lashawn King

Dear Son,

I may not be there in person now, but above all else I want you to always know that I love you more than anything. I've never loved the way I love you my son. Never think that I didn't want you or that I didn't want to be there. I made a lot of mistakes in life, a lot of which made me who I am now, enough that I'll be able to help you navigate through the mistakes you'll make in life. Because we all make mistakes.

I also want you to know your worth. Society, unfortunately, will make you feel less than or unequal because of our skin, where you live, how much money you have, who your family is, etc., so always, no matter what, always know that you are a king in every way. Be strong and be you, nothing wrong with being different, it takes strength to be different. Never let anyone treat you or take you as weak, always show your strength and let your light shine.

I always tell you at the end of our visits as well as the end of our phone calls, "I love you, I love you more than anything." And you reply with, "I know dad you tell me all the time!" I tell you because I don't ever want you to forget it.

Darrel L King

> "....if I had ten hearts and lived a thousand lives I would still feel as though I couldn't love you as much or for as long as I need to. And if I never get to show you these words in the flesh you will always know that they exist within me."

❤

D.L. Jackson

I may not be there in person now, but above all else I want you to always know that I, your dad, has loved you since the day your existence inside your mother's womb became known to me. I was right alongside your mother learning things in preparation for your arrival into this world. At sixteen years of age, I had to become a man, a man that would be able to provide and protect this little lady from the bad of a foreign region to her. I made a vow, took an oath to do all that is humanly possible to ensure your place on this Earth is secure. And though I fell short in making myself available for you physically, I kept my word about keeping you safe. With the odds against me, I was able to achieve my goal to some extent from behind these walls.

Now, twenty-five years later, I continue to hold you as dear to my heart as I did that first day in the hospital when you opened your big brown eyes and stared up at me. I will never forget that day for as long as I live. You are a grown woman now, and I am a very proud father. Would I change anything? Sure, I would. If I had things my way, I would have spent every waking moment by your side. You are still daddy's little girl, but I missed the opportunity to let you see firsthand how a man should treat a woman. In doing so I took a grievous gamble that you would learn to expect more than what money can buy. Luckily for me, you managed to make good choices for yourself—knock on wood.

The worst is behind us these days, your dad will be

home soon. I imagine the smile on your face being even more grand than they were when you would hug me in the visiting rooms of prisons past. And just so that you know, if I had ten hearts and lived a thousand lives I would still feel as though I couldn't love you as much or for as long as I need to. And if I never get to show you these words in the flesh you will always know that they exist within me.

I love you my royal being,
Dad

"Regardless of prison confinement nothing will deter or prohibit my love for my only son and daughter. Thank you or accepting and communicating with me as your father and not holding me hostage to my past transgressions."

❤

Jerome A. Beale

3/25/19

I may not be there in person now, but above all else I want Anthony and Alysia to always know my longing for them will never dissipate. After visually seeing the physical birth of you and your sister, the thought of estrangement from my offspring was non-existent. In fact, living a life apart or separated from the obligation of loving and caring for my little ones at no time popped in my mind. I viewed myself as a consistent and reliable father, so to be physically not present for the past 18 years is tremendously silencing. The pride and ego of once being an indestructible father continually takes a back seat to the reality of incarceration with each passing day. Frustration, anxiety, and tension all take turns eating away at fatherhood. Fighting against the notion of negligence and irresponsibility is hard.

    Anthony and Alysia think about it!! How do I explain the subtraction of nearly two decades from your personal lives? I simply don't have a suitable answer to give. However, in trying to shed greater light on the magnitude of my absence, I'll make my point through a numerical method since numbers can be used to establish a truth. Let's see, I missed so far 6,570 days from you and your sister's life. I also missed 18 birthdays, 18 Christmases and Thanksgiving holidays, 18 family reunions, 8 high school proms, 2 graduation ceremonies, driving lessons and license attainment, track & field events, basketball games, planned trips and an assortment of other things. When reflecting on everything I've missed, it's only fair just to accept responsibility and pray for reconciliation. No child should be deprived of a father's continual presence. I've failed in this regard.

At this point, unconditional forgiveness is all I can hope from you. Really, the both of you don't owe me anything because I chose to leave society by my actions. So, over the past 18 years, my only recourse was to try and help persuade the two of you to see me in a positive manner. I tirelessly wrote letters to you and your sister throughout your entire period of attending elementary and high school. Even to the present moment, I'm still practicing this habit. I've prepared diaries, sent countless cards, arts and crafts, and mailed financial gifts. These tangible items were used to testify of my personal existence and to debunk the myth of a father as a fictitious person that's hidden by prison walls.

Regardless of prison confinement nothing will deter or prohibit my love for my only son and daughter. Thank you for accepting and communicating with me as your father and not holding me hostage to my past transgressions. My love is indisputable for my biological children. Right now, success for me is having the opportunity to be in the presence of your lives and sharing life experiences. The goal is to see you all flourish and blossom into productive adults and one day loving parents.

Love Dad,
Jerome A. Beale

> "There is something else I want you to know—when I have a bad day or I'm sad—I think about all the good times we had, and it puts the biggest smile on my face."

♥

Terrence Harkness

Tesslee,

Hey, my beautiful princess. How are you? I miss you so much! I hope you know I love you more than anything in the world! I want you to know I'm sorry I'm not home with you right now. I never want you to think I don't love you, and don't think about you every day—because I do. I also want you to know I'm here for you, and you can talk to me about anything. I also want you to know I'm so proud of you—for being so smart, caring, and because you're my beautiful daughter!

There is something else I want you to know—when I have a bad day or I'm sad—I think about all the good times we had, and it puts the biggest smile on my face. Do you remember when you would ride on my motorcycle and pop wheelies going down the road. I really miss those days.

I can't wait to get out and see you again so we can have fun, hang out, and get us some new four wheelers! Do you know how special your letters you send me are? They put the biggest smile on my face. I love the drawings you drew of us! I love to brag how smart you are, and I show them to my friends because I'm so proud of you! Well my beautiful little princess, let me get this letter wrapped up. I love you to the moon and back! XOXO hugs and kisses!

Love your
one and only Dad
P.S. Your smile makes this world so much better!

"Either way, time is passing by, and before you know it, we will be together again. In the meantime, keep doing what you can to continue forward. Take care and use your time to the maximum. Always think before doing anything, and follow the sign of your hearts."

❤

Alcides

Hola Hijos,

Los saludo con mucho cariño. Deseo que cuando lean ésta carta se encuentren muy bien todos en general.
    Les cuento que por la gracia de Dios, yo me encuentro muy bien; así que no hay nada de que preocuparse. Todo por aquí esta muy bién, excepto por el motivo de estar alejado de ustedes, hace este lugar no muy agradable. Pero ni modo, el tiempo va pasando y al rato estaremos junto de nuevo. Por lo tanto, sigan haciendo lo que puedan hacer para continuar hacia delante. Cuidense mucho , y aprovechen el tiempo al máximo. Piensen siempre antes de hacer cualquier cosa, y sigan la señal de sus corazones.
    De mi parte, les cuento que estoy haciendo lo más posible para mantenerme lo más saludable posible para cuando salga poder disfrutar de una vida normal junto a ustedes, si Dios lo permite. Y una de las cosas que me mantienen con mi espíritu en alto es el saber que ustedes se encuentran bien. Así que ya les digo. Espero que sé encuentren muy bien, y no se préocupen que yo estoy bien gracias a Dios. El hecho que me encuentre encarcelado y lejos, no significa que no esté con ustedes espiritualmente.
    Cuidense mucho, y portensen muy bien. Saludes a todos, y no se olviden que los quiero mucho.

Hasta luego, su Papá.
Alcides

* * *

Hello sons,

I greet you with love. I hope this letter finds you all in general with good health.

    By the grace of God, I am well, so there is no need to worry. Everything around here is fine, except for being away from you makes this not be a very pleasant place. Either way, time is passing by, and before you know it, we will be together again. In the meantime, keep doing what you can to continue forward. Take care and use your time to the maximum. Always think before doing anything, and follow the sign of your hearts.

    For my part, I am doing the most I can to keep myself as healthy as possible, for when I leave, we can enjoy a normal life together, if God permits. One of the things that keep my spirits up is knowing that you are doing well. So I tell you, I hope you are doing well, and please do not worry about me since I'm fine, thank God. The fact that I'm incarcerated and far from you does not mean I'm not with you spiritually.

    Please take care and behave. I send greetings to everyone and remember that I love you.

Until next time your father,
Alcides

"Always know that you are my motivation and the reason I changed my life! 'Love is a verb.'"

❤

Troy "Ketch" Ketchmore

To: Tre'qwane, Afrika and Yasine

I may not be there in person right now, but above all else, I want you to always know that I love you more than I love myself! I'm so sorry I wasn't there when you needed me in your life, my mistakes forced you to grow up faster than you had to, and you did so without ever blaming me or complaining. Thank you for the respect you have always shown me over the years I've been gone, you have never once judged me, as a matter of fact, 'til this very day you still call me Daddy! It warms my heart and it breaks my heart to hear that word coming from you because that's what I fight so hard to get home to you to be—a great daddy—but to hear that word come from you and to live with the fact that for 24 years I robbed you of the reality of daddy in the form in which daddy truly counts, reminds me every day that I owe you and I must do whatever it takes being to pay on that debt.

Going forward my purpose is to reconnect with you (the three aspects of myself) and bond until we become one again. I know each of you are all grown up, however, since you didn't ask to come here it's my job to be daddy until death parts us. Always know that you are my motivations and the reason I changed my life! "Love is a verb."

Sincerely,
Troy Ketchmore
DADDY

> "No amount of time nor distance can affect the love I have for you. I thank God for you, my son, an extension to a better part of myself."

♥

Kermit Williams

I MAY NOT BE THERE NOW, BUT ABOVE ALL ELSE I WANT YOU TO ALWAYS KNOW:

I loved you before you took your first breath, my son, an extension to a better part of myself. I'm all too aware that my absence could not have been easy for you during your young life, but I've never been too far away that you could not have access to my love, knowledge, and advice.

To say that I've only lived with the regret of what my own hands brought forth could never reach the level of regret I feel for not being the example of a father that you could be proud of.

I know that I've missed some of the most important moments of your life, and if I could do it all over again, I would have chosen a different path. But never think for a moment that because I have not been there in body, that I have not been there in mind.

However, I'm here now, and my hope is that we can build a foundation of love, trust, honesty and respect shared between a father and his son.

No amount of time nor distance can affect the love I have for you. I thank God for you, my son, an extension to a better part of myself.

I love you,
Dad

> "I want you all to know that 'I am chained,' but my 'love will never be chained.'"

♥

T.L. Halloway

"Love from Beyond"

I was there for you when you first entered into this world. The dates will never slip my mind. On December 6, 1995, the doctor said that you would never make it through the night. So, twenty-four years later, you are my miracle, TT. On November 16, 1998, I was anxious to see you and unsure if you were a healthy child. Twenty-one years later, you blessed me with my first granddaughter. On August 31, 2004 my third princess was born and what a miracle that you turned out to be. It was daily cardiac medications, monitoring and uneasy nights, but a ray of sunshine. On October 12, 2004, well well, my pooka calmed the storm of life. A beautiful bonding of joy and life, that caused me to humble myself further. Of course, last but surely not least; on January 3, 2012 my final queen Halloway arrived. A bundle you were with the perfect hair, smile, and the completion of team Halloway.

I never meant for me to never be there when it means the most to you all. Missing birthdays, graduation, prom, pregnancy, illness, and many other things, I want you all to know that "I am chained," but my "love will never be chained." I want you to always know that I am your dad, and I will always love you. I think about you every day, and pray that God's blessings will find you always. I am continuing to strive to be the dad I have always been to you, even now from behind bars. I will always call you, pray for you, think about you, and do everything that I can to get back to all of you. Always remember, I was there to hold you at birth, and I will be there to hold you now.

* * *

Love always,
Dad

Team Halloway
Tierra Simone - "TT"
Tatyana Nicole - "TA"
Janay Kempey-Faith - "Nay Nay"
Ariana Patrice - "Pooda"
Jaelyn Noel - "J-Rock"
"A love that can't be chained"

"You and I did so much together and it's those times that get me through my rough times."

♥

Mario Jennings, Jr.

To Lindsey,

I may not be there in person, but you are always in my heart and mind. I've replayed the days we spent together and the smiles and laughs we had. I knew the day you were born and when I saw you open your eyes, I knew then as I know now that I love you. You and I did so much together and it's those times that get me through my rough times. I think about what gets you through your rough times. I can't tell you enough how it breaks my heart that I'm not there for you. I know it's really got to be hard for you at times as well. We want to be together going to places to do nothing at all. God only knows how I wish I could change all of it. You are the best thing in my life then and now.

    Always know I love you and not a day goes by I don't think of you.

Love,
Dad

"It seems as if seeing you prosper has inspired me to examine myself more in order to continue my growth."

♥

S. Taylor

Cedric,

I know I've said this time and time again, but I just can't say it enough. I am so proud of you son, and the man that you've become. This world is so full of so-called macho men that can't see past their own egos in order to express that most needed proclamation to our young men now-a-days. And it goes beyond all spectrums, don't get me wrong, there are some real stand-up guys out there also, but I can only look through my eyes and talk of what I've experienced.

    I never thought I'd be a better father to you while incarcerated, but it's somewhat true. I guess this was the only thing that was going to slow me down so life could catch up to me. During all this you've taught me a lot about myself that you noticed while I was around, things that I didn't think mattered at first. But now I see that they were keys to molding you into the man that you have grown to be. And that makes me more proud to know that you've taken the good you have seen in me and used it to your benefit and growth. Those components are your foundation. Continue to build on them. And when your growth seems stunted, examine yourself to find other avenues to build on. Son, you mean so much to me. It seems as if seeing you prosper has inspired me to examine myself more in order to continue my growth. That's right, it never stops. We can always improve on the men we are to get to the men we want to be. Love you son.

Dad

* * *

PEACE!!!   Perseverance
    Education
    Acceptance
    Community
    Evaluation

> "Thoughts of getting to know you and you knowing me are what gets me through. Since your birth you've been the best part of me."

♥

B

From B to B,

I may not be there in person now, but above all else, I want you to always know...there's not a day that goes by where I'm not thinking of you...

Over the years I have watched you grow from afar, with that I have mixed emotions, some of sadness, but great emotions of proudness of the young lady you're becoming. Your mother has done a tremendous job in giving you all you need to be the smart, joyous, beautiful young girl you are. The emotions of sadness I spoke about are simply this...I feel sad because I'm not there to help you, to grow with you. Please believe me I never planned it to be this way. I made a poor choice and the consequence of that choice was far greater than I could imagine: being taken out of your life. That's why one thing I want you to always understand deeply in life is, "choices and consequences." Babygirl you always have a choice...but there are consequences to those choices whether good or bad...you may be too young to understand this now, but as you get older, I'll be sharing this very lesson with you!

Thoughts of getting to know you and you knowing me are what gets me through. Since your birth you've been the best part of me.

During my absence I don't want to you ever feel like I don't love you, because that's so far from the truth. I love you with all the breath in me.

Continue to obey your mother. Continue to allow your love for God to grow. Continue to talk to Him, your prayers

go from your heart to God's ears.
    And always know if you get lonely for me close your eyes and open your hand, babygirl I'm right here...

I love you...
Dad

> "When I get to talk to you, I always feel much better. I know you're busy, Kristy, between work and the kids, but you always find time to talk to me."

❤

Louis P. Lindsay

My Dearest Daughter,

How are you? Let Hailey know I said congratulations on passing high school.

Now the choices become more limited, college, work, or the military become her way of thinking. The raising that you instilled in her will be put to the test.

I honestly believe she'll choose the army so that she can travel, and she'll specify on one trade or schooling. I'm extremely proud of you, Kristy and all my Grandchildren.

Take care of that knee. Believe me, you want everything working great or be prepared to be pushed around in a wheelchair or a hospital bed. Just kidding kiddo. You're in great shape, and mentally and spiritually, you're in harmony.

When I get to talk to you, I always feel much better. I know you're busy, Kristy, between work and the kids, but you always find time to talk to me.

Soon, honey, just a few more years, and then I can come see you in Nevada. I'll probably not be able to recognize them.

Soon you'll have another birthday. I believe it will be your 40th, but you act and behave like a wise woman that's been around for ages. I don't think you got that wisdom from me.

I love you, my daughter, and I'll call you this weekend after church.

Your Papaw

"...but what I failed to mention then, is now being delivered from my chest, though you didn't weigh a lot, it was enough to knock me off the #1 spot."

♥

La Torres

The Moment That Changed My Life Forever

"Wake up! Wake up! Wake up!" were my mother's words when she shook my comatose body. I was stretched out asleep on the foot of my bed. When I opened my eyes, a blurry image of my mother was hunched over me with a smile. As I set up sluggishly, my mother quickly sat down beside me. "What's going on with her this morning?" I thought as I wiped out the cold from my eyes. Before I could even ask her "what's up" my mother shared why she was in a jolly mood. "It's a boy," she said softly, "and he's six pounds and six ounces." Reflecting my mother's expression, elation filled my body with energy. I was a 15-year-old dad now. "I can't wait 'til after school," was what I thought.

    On the night before, I sat inside MCV hospital holding on to my son's mother's hand. My mother, best friend Rico, and I had waited hours for my son's mother, Katie, to go in to labor. Rico—a chubby Puerto Rican with long curly hair—was anxious to see his godson, and my mother was ready to welcome her fifth grandchild. However, Katie's contraction levels fluctuated from low to medium. Though the nurses were convinced Katie was going to deliver that night, anticipation weighed heavy on my eye lids. I fought sleep because I did not want to miss the birth of my first child. Unfortunately, it was a school night so my mother insisted that we call it a night and go home.

    When our school bell rang, Rico and I paid for bus fair to the hospital. As I strolled at a fast pace on the shiny, off-white tile floors, my baby face raised eyebrows of curiosity in the main lobby. My joyful behavior was obvious, so people wanted to know what the hype was about. Remembering what floor to go to, Rico and I ignored the receptionist and hopped on the elevator.

While I was on the elevator, my emotional roller coaster had shifted from excitement to nervousness. The closer Rico and I got to the floor, the more sweat dripped from my pores. Rico—who was also experiencing similar emotions—had detected my uneasiness; however, I concealed my unstable nerves with jokes and laughter.

After Rico and I got off the elevator, we began to look for my son and his mother. Minutes into our search, we came to a frustrating halt. "I can't remember what room it was," I said. Rico shrugged his shoulders. A nurse with a clipboard noticed our distress, and offered to help us. "I've been waiting on you!" the nurse exclaimed after she learned who I was. The nurse handed me a document—the birth certificate—to sign, then led Rico and I to Katie's room.

The very instant I walked inside the room, my mother made me the center of attention. "There goes the daddy everybody," my mother said aloud to the dozen or so relatives and friends. Everyone embraced me with "It's a boy" balloons, bubblegum cigars, and hugs. With no sight of my son, I immediately locked eyes with my son's mother who sat upward on her bed wearing a medical gown. "You just missed him. One of the nurses took him to run a few tests," Katie said. My son's mother was exhausted, yet she kept up with her company's upbeat tempo. "I'll go and get him after they're done daddy," the nurse said with a flirtatious smile. My son's mother checked me with a "don't play with me" look in her eyes. Catching my son's mother's vibe, I turned down the nurse's advances with a nonchalant nod, then I went to hug and kiss Katie.

Waiting for my son to return, I lasted only a few minutes before my patience broke. I abruptly stood up and demanded to see my son. "I want to see him, where is he?" I said aloud. After getting no solid response from anyone in the room, I took matters into my own hands. I left the room, with Rico behind me, and went to find the nurse who had flirted with me. When I saw the nurse, I asked her to take me to see my son. Without objection, she signaled for me to follow her. We stopped outside one of the nursery's windows. "There he is," the nurse pointed to a incubator-like bed where my son rested quietly. "He looks just like you, papi," Rico said. Staring at the most beautiful creation I had ever seen, tears flooded my eyes. "That's my Jr.," I mumbled. From that day going forward—whether it was good or bad—I lived for my son.

"6 Pounds 6 Ounces"

There's nothing more valuable
in the eyes of a father
nor is the love less doubtful
that I feel as a father
the sight of my offspring
shifted the gears of my heart
I would scramble and put up a fight
like you reflected of me from the start
as I stared at you
the love grew by the heartbeat
though you could neither see me nor them
hope you felt the love while you quietly slept
amazed I was by your size
lol you couldn't be any lighter
but the moment you opened your eyes
hasn't been a day more brighter
the blessing that comes from within
how grateful could I be
love and protect you to the end
is how thankful I should be
your adorable smile and grin

had the strongest effect
but what I failed to mention then
is now being delivered from my chest
though you didn't weigh a lot
it was enough to knock me off the #1 spot.

    I know that we've been distant for quite some time now. I haven't had the chance to be there for you but that doesn't mean I don't love you. Honestly, there's nothing in this world matters most to me than you. Though, the years have been blank, my heart's full of love for you. Since day one I loved you with all my heart, and the love will never stop growing. You are my motivation, my purpose and my everything. I Love You, Jr!

> "I also want you to know that you have to love in order to live efficiently. I say that because love is the utmost highest level of communication between people."

♥

Kelby Sheppard a.k.a. Sincere Power Supreme Lox God Allah

I may not be there in person now, but above all else, I want you to always know...

That I wish I was there in person now because if I was, I would not just tell you, but show you, to learn from your mistakes. A lot of older people always say to younger people, "I want you to learn from my mistakes." But I see my mistakes as a collection of missteps that I made due to my decisions and my circumstances. I need you to take your own steps and missteps so you can learn your own way and influence your own next decisions and circumstances. As much as we are the same, we are ultimately different and have totally different realities. As much as I can influence your reality, no one has more influence over your reality than you!

    I also want you to know that you have to love in order to live efficiently. I say that because love is the utmost highest level of communication between people. In life, it always takes two or more people. Sure, you can get it down on your own or by yourself, but what is it all worth without someone to share it with? Plus more/many hands make for less/lighter work. Share the load with the love. Love is the essential glue that binds/bonds you with whoever you chose to share with. You can't share without communication. Love is that communication.

    Lastly, I want you to know that I love you and no matter where, how, or why I am, that will never change. To my wife, my siblings, my children, my family, my friends:

thank you.

> "Everything that I do throughout the course of a day includes thoughts of you."

♥

Kevin Neal

To my beloved daughter:

I may not be there in person now but above all else, I want you to always know this is not a situation that I chose! My absence has nothing to do with you and everything to do with several decisions that I made.

    The place that I'm at is called the penitentiary. The name was changed to the Department of Corrections. The root of penitentiary is penitent. Penitent means feeling or expressing sorrow for sin or wrongdoing and disposed to atonement and amendment; repentant; contrite. In language that you can understand, the penitentiary is supposed to make you sorry for the crime that a person is locked up for. But, what if a person is innocent of the crime that he or she is alleged to have committed?

    Like I said, me being locked up has nothing to do with you, but everything to do with my choices. I love you very much and would see and talk to you every day if I could. Just like I used to do when I was at home. Everything that I do throughout the course of a day includes thoughts of you. I wonder what you did that day? What time you woke up? What time you went to bed? What makes you happy and what makes you sad?

    The only thing that gives me peace of mind is knowing that this will not be permanent. I enjoy the time we spend together during the visits, but I would rather be there with you so that we can be together. Until then, I love you.

Love,
Dad

> "When you can put smiles on random people's faces and change the atmosphere, let's me know God is real."

♥

Ma'Kayle Avrion Sheppard

Dear Zy & Kayla,

Even if you hadn't come into this world as my children, you'd still be the most beautiful beings I've ever seen. Sometimes I think to myself: Ghee while, your mother and I made really cute kids. You constantly turn heads when we're grocery shopping. I don't feel like speaking to strangers today, I'm just here for eggs and bacon. When you can put similes on random people's faces and change the atmosphere, let's me know God is real.

    God has to exist 'cause you have Angel-like spirits. When I look at the news I'm deeply saddened because of this world I brought you into. The thought that there could be billions of other kids like you out there impacting the lives of people like me, there just might be hope. With you, there were never dull moments. We turn the hood's public park with the broken swing set into Disneyland.

    I never truly realized who I was until I saw how miserable I am without you. I'm so sorry for being careless with my decision making that has taken me away. My selfish actions robbed you of precious years of experiencing a father figure you can call your own. With that being said, just worry about what little kids worry about. There's always a light at the end of the tunnel. Trust the process, and I promise I'll come back better than the hero you already believe I am.

> "Knowing that you were out there "bringing the sunshine" and making the world a brighter place has inspired me so much. It has given me the strength to maintain the calm, patient demeanor one needs to thrive in environments like these."

❤

Michael K. McNew

Dear Channyn,

I may not be there in person now, but above all else I want you to know that I have always been, and will always be proud of the wonderful, intelligent, beautiful, funny, and compassionate woman you have become. Though it has been painful to watch from afar, our phone conversations, letters, and visits have allowed me to see you grow from a bright and inquisitive cherub into the magnificent angel you are today. (The angel who has set numerous records on the Kick-Ass-O-Meter. :))

Note 1: The standard North American Kick-Ass-O-Meter tops out at score of "10". The records set by Channyn K McNew broke the scales at "13".

Note 2: The Russians have tried over the years to create KAOM's that reached "15"...and we all know how well that turned out.

Knowing that you were out there "bringing the sunshine" and making the world a brighter place has inspired me so much. It has given me the strength to maintain the calm, patient demeanor one needs to thrive in environments like these. Please keep in mind that this period of tribulation will soon be over and we can continue with our lives. I can be the father I always wanted to be, the father I should have been from the beginning, the father you deserve.

* * *

I love you. BooYah!!! (fist bump hand there)
Daddy

> "...your letters to me and your want to have a relationship with me or asking to be my lil' girl, is what helped me want to take that fake mask off to be real and let me be the one who paves the way to define who I am by my true actions."

❤

Frederico Jimenez-Pyke

Hola Mi Angelita.

You are always on my mind and in my everyday thoughts and I want you to know that your papa loves and cherishes you ever since you blessed this world with your arrival. Even though I may have not been there in person, I want you to know and understand I've been there watching you grow up from behind these lonely walls.

 Me going away was my fault, not yours. I made poor choices that caused me to not be there for you like a real dad is supposed to. You asked me once was it because of you I left or wasn't around. Hearing that broke my heart and broke through my tough guy armor that I built around my heart, so, no! Mija, you or your mom or brother and sisters have nothing to do with me not being around. I allowed my environment to choose my course in life. You already know I was heavy in the "gangster lifestyle" false hopes and dreams. I let my status or misguided growth in the ranks to curb my judgment on everything I did. My actions took me away from you, which for you that pains me and I have to live with, and that person that I was back then was not capable of being a father or doing anything right. My reputation that I have out there is one that used to define me. However, your letters to me and your want to have a relationship with me or asking to be my lil' girl, is what helped me want to take that fake mask off to be real and let me be the one who paves the way to define who I am by my true actions. So I have to give you my utmost respect and thanks for inspiring me to get out of the gang, take the chance on being "vulnerable." Nothing but peace and many doors that were once closed have been opened.

I want you to know that no matter where we are in our lives, me in here, you out there, I will always be there to protect you. I love you, mija and you are in my thoughts and in my prayers, today, tomorrow, and yesterday. Siempre y para siempre.

Tu papa,
Frederico
I love you through the stars to the moon and back.
Fé y Esperanza

Support

And with that unconditional, endless love comes support. Complete and total.

Because support is the practical embodiment of love, I promise you that I will do all I can to assist, encourage, and provide for you always, in all ways.

Because respect and acceptance are the fundamental foundation of true support, I promise you both eternally. You can be, tell me, or do anything. No matter where you go, what you seek, who you are, I will be on your side, Son. Just be true to yourself and honest with me, and I will never judge you, always do all I can to prop you up and elevate you.

Because love and this judgement-free support are what I believe to be a father's duty, I offer those to you unconditionally, permanently. I see it that way based on great parental examples, great self-reflection, and lengthy study of people. Based on that, I promise you I'm fully dedicated to living so as to reflect my love for you, doing all I can to maximize your health, strength, and mind. In all your days, live with the confidence that you have my utter support, respect, and acceptance.

It breaks my heart 100 times a day, every time I think to do some little in-person things for you and cannot do so immediately. Helping you remains my top priority. And I can still constantly provide for you emotionally, verbally, and in many small practical ways. Ask me for anything, share anything, and I'll do all I can to help. I'll stand in line for days to use a phone, ask favors of gangsters, and spend every cent to call, write, show you support.

Yes, there will be things I cannot do at that moment, but I still want to be involved in your daily needs and thoughts. Once this nightmare ends, you can count on even more resources for me to work with, but even in these limited circumstances now, please share your feelings, your requests, your requirements. I can always offer ideas and a kind, supportive ear, and often much more. You have eternal access to pick my brain, sir.

In short, D, turn to me always, even now. I'm always on your side.

That's an important point for life in general, when you need anything, do not be afraid to ask those you can rely on. Even here, there's much I can do to help. More than that, though, while it's important to be an independent person, no one can succeed entirely alone. Plus you're still young and growing up requires people's help. This brings to mind a tasty bite of wisdom that my buddy, Nelson, shared when I was resisting asking anyone for assistance when I first arrived in prison: "Nothing wrong with needing help. If we could do everything by ourselves, we wouldn't need each other." And wouldn't that be a travesty, if we weren't social.

You also have that same all-encompassing support from so many other people. In fact, you're the most widely supported young man I have ever known, from the family you see regularly all the way through friends and relatives you last met as a baby. From coast to coast, even Hawaii, you've got countless great folks who will do anything they can to help you out when you have a need—or even a strong desire. So please don't hesitate to ask them, even out of the blue. I will always help ask around, too, of course, but the door's always open to you. Your entire family, Gin, Sam, Trish, and many other friends support me this way, and they have all promised me to do the same for you. Forever. It's the first thing I asked people when I found out I'd be gone a while.

It doesn't matter how long it's been since you've talked with them, but I do still encourage you to keep in touch with those you love. You won't now—it's tough at your age, naturally—but keep it in mind as you grow. To build the type of powerful, wide-ranging support I'm blessed with for yourself with new people I advise you to live according to a motto I made up and adopted at Virginia Tech: It's All About the People!

Whenever anyone debated any decision, be it social, leadership, or school related, I would say that to encourage everyone to prioritize people. Meeting good people involves a touch of luck, but fostering the bonds that nourish lifelong support and acceptance is a reflection of the interactions you have. Live in a way that clearly puts people above possessions, greed, pride, and self. That way you will stay surrounded by great people offering devoted support. It's all worth it too, because the best things, places, and adventures are meaningless without good friends with whom to enjoy them. It is with people that we share the laughs and smiles that highlight our best memories.

Consistent, selfless, unrequested support. That's the glue of community, the foundation of its importance in our lives. Despite all the dysfunction and deliberate, designed despair and deprivation, prison is a community. Within, we support each other way more than the average person thinks.

I have seen multiple groups collect and dole out charitable soap, toothpaste, Ramen, and instant coffee when the state won't provide even hygiene products for the indigent. Sometimes this is organized around faith, sometimes not, but it is always self-motivated and unofficial. I have seen guys regularly give twenty or thirty percent of their $35 monthly paychecks for this purpose.

Even without an official group, we watch out for the downtrodden. When Mr. Ford, an elderly fellow dying of cancer and with no family, suddenly lost his job after a petty infraction for trying to poop with a privacy shade halfway covering his window, he never lacked for anything. A proud man, he refused all offers, so commissary fairies—cousins of the tooth fairy—would instead show up with peanut butter, crackers, and coffee when he was out. All his favorites, anonymously.

My own entire time behind bars was altered by the support of a stranger. Scott, a guy long ago convicted of two homicides that were really self-defense, chose not to be bitter but kind. He introduced himself on the volleyball court one of my very first days and took the time to let this nervous guy just hang and show my true self. Later, he sat beside me for hours after a concussion I got on that same volleyball court, risking his own precious job to demand I receive treatment and speak up officially when they at first denied it to me. I was never unconscious, but blacked out for a while and then suddenly came to in the shower, with no idea why I was in prison, how long I was stuck there, or the phone numbers of my family. Talk about terrifying! So Scott sat with me and problem solved, gently listening and questioning, until I gradually regained myself. He even organized an overnight watch to check on me until I finally saw someone medically.

    Scott also opened the doors that led to me regaining my own purpose and confidence. He made a point to introduce me to every good man he knew on the compound, connecting me in a way that got me jobs, friends, and respect that rebuilt my life. He was one of the first subjects in an ethnographic research study I conducted while there, and he made all the logistics possible. Now that he's finally out, he's remained a good friend, far beyond the prison walls and limits.

    The boundaries of prison community support extend beyond expectations. Most guys here are intimidated by legalese and have little education, even when often quite intelligent. Most cannot afford lawyers to fight the many unjust cases, yet the system in this state inherently presumes against anyone filing themselves with unprofessional language. In steps Kevin, a legal savant, self-taught, with a record of victories. He knows case law relevant in Virginia better than any lawyer I've met and worked himself as a respected paralegal. When he meets anyone in need, he helps for free, doing endless consultation and writing that is worth tens of thousands. Never asks a dime and teaches as he does it, even as he comes from the streets and lacks his own privileges.

I have been lucky enough to be part of three separate educational organizations begun unofficially for us, by us. Despite administrative foot dragging and active resistance, I've been invited by Lord Prince, Justice, Maurice, Ketchmore, Truth, G, and a handful of other men, some of the best leaders I've ever met, to help build up the educational and social capital where the system keeps failing. DOC loves to pay lip service to rehab and education yet never has enough seats in any programs, leaving this a wasteland of human warehousing—until we step up ourselves. Most official proposals get shot down, even those written professionally. Either way, invites are extended with fist bumps in passing and meetings are held in laundry rooms and on the yard. Growing roses in concrete from the grassroots, I've been lucky to be a part of. Often these efforts extend beyond these walls. Positive Offenders Implementing New Thinking has recently expanded its efforts. Even while continuing to educate ourselves in practical ways using voices that don't judge or condescend, the leaders have added a food drive for homeless shelters and a voting awareness campaign for underserved home neighborhoods.

Many people behind bars find purpose in helping peers and neighbors. But no greater purpose exists than supporting our kids. That is central to our identities as parents, just as it is yours. So when we speak of and to them, love is where we often begin and matters most, yes. But just loving our children is not enough. Being able to do for them, that's the gift that's in the giving.

That is why, contrary to many public presumptions, folks here are far from dead beat dads and moms. Most of us bend over backwards to find ways to support our kids. In that great small group fatherhood seminar I attended, the number one concern expressed was about feeling hindered in our ability to do so from here, of feeling, being, and being perceived by our kids as distant and uninvolved. So we worked on a number of solutions, many very creative. Support for our kids is the difference between being donors and dads, so we were determined to find every opportunity.

Through all my dialogue on this topic, I have seen an inspiring array of solutions.
I knew a guy at Greensville, Geoffrey, but he went by G, and every year he bought his son some nice kicks to start the new school year. G said he wanted him to stay in school like he hadn't. If his son has something nice so he can feel proud going, he figured, he'll be more likely to go. This may not sound like much, but he made 45 cents an hour, so he would set aside about a third of his paycheck all year just to make this possible.

Another buddy, Joey, grew up with virtually nothing, his own father locked up. He was determined, even during a ridiculous sentence for minor drug possession, not to let that hinder his son like he had felt growing up. So when his son's mother ended up in an abusive relationship that she hid from Joey, he couldn't let that slide. Without even having a job here, any internet access, or the straightforward honesty of his son's mom he figured out what was going on and got his son in the custody of his own mother. He found a way to offer safety that he had been deprived, even from here.

It's often the little things our children miss as they grow. Hence, Alex had his aunt send him and his son matching books for years. Then, when they'd get on the phone, they didn't just chat. They read together before bed, first mostly Alex with the voices he made so well that made his boy love story time. Then, as he got older, in turns, taking turns with each of the voices.

Another guy I know, Spike, every month sends his ex-wife an unrequested $50 with a thank you note. The money ensures his child has a phone to always be able to connect. It seems small until we learn that his salary is $54 per month. He gives all he makes just to make sure his kid can hear his voice.

Beauty, but honestly, I continue to be challenged by a sense of helplessness in supporting D. I know intellectually I do all I can. My family, friends, and partner all commend my efforts. They also all do a great deal to stay involved themselves, driving for days, spending thousands, and being as present as distance allows. I'm intensely appreciative. We are family.

Yet it never feels like enough. I'm proud of how engaged I am, how supported he is. Yet it is not what it was, what I wish, or what he deserves.

This is an ongoing challenge for me emotionally, but it also drives me to never let pass a single chance to be there for him.

That is why I write two or three letters a week and have my entire time here, even has he lives in a modern era where responding via snail mail isn't even conceivable. Still, he has said that the letters matter, so I include stories, advice, questions, and articles from sports and science.

That is why I have called him every single chance I've had since this began. When it started, he answered every time, and now that his social life is full and he would often rather keep playing ball or goofing off, I still ring him before trying anyone else. He will always know that sound means I'm there for him, even when I'm not.

That is why I have created endless discussion prompts, to ensure he ever felt engaged and interested. We considered and discussed Zobmondo's hilarious "Would you rather..." questions, then shifted to making up our own hypotheticals. I've made a crossword puzzle of extended family trivia to prompt him to connect with everyone. I keep up with his favorite athletes and artists. Anything for him.

That is why I find a way to send him a small but symbolic $20 via his grandmother every month. Even if I have to eat more "meat rock" and less ramen, at least he's getting something to have fun with from me and talking to her.

It is also why in my own letter to him, the first thing after expressing my love had to be a reminder of just how supported he is. Even across barbed wire and time zones, I can, do, and will offer the same understanding and advice, along with every bit of practical support humanly possible. This is my priority.

Likewise, for so many of us parents, even while we're trapped. The brilliance of these letters is how they highlight the way that parents behind bars prioritize supporting our children creatively and diligently. To do so, we make a dollar out of fifteen cents, birthday cards from reclaimed scraps, and art from cement and steel and loneliness. These letters demonstrate the committed, endless support that transcends circumstance and reflects the indefatigable power of wanting to help our kids in every way possible, regardless of self or circumstance.

We may be stuck here at the moment, maybe even for some really irresponsible reasons. But parenting continues and the duties of that role become often even more pronounced in our identities when we are limited and apart against our will. We do all we can with what we've got and who we are to help our children live beyond our absence.

Letters on Support

"Stay strong, be brave, and know that wherever you go and whatever you do, I will always be very proud of you. Always pursue your dreams and remember that you're braver than you believe, stronger than you seem, smarter than you think, and twice as beautiful as you ever imagined."

♥

Joe "Truth" Parker

Raising children from prison is one of the absolute hardest things to do. I can't speak for the "sperm donors" who fathered a child or children with a woman, and played no part in the raising and upbringing of that child, or even the ones who at least gave up some form of financial child support (most times reluctantly and court ordered). Im speaking from a father's perspective of one who actually played a dominant or substantial role in that child's or children's upbringing and lives.

Prior to incarceration, my first job and main priority was to care for, and raise my children. Both physically and financially as well as emotionally. I was present and "hands on" on large scale in their growing years with the exception of my youngest, who wasn't even one year old when I came to prison. Even then, I fed him, changed diapers, held him when he cried, played with him, put him to sleep, attended all doctor visits, clothed him, and made the same sacrifices for him, that I did for my other three children, when they were babies.

Aside from all the stresses, turmoils, and problems physically, mentally, and emotionally we may face as incarcerated men, I find that the hardest thing for me is coming to grips with and/or dealing with, not being able to be the father I was or am able to be to my ever needing, forever growing, forever changing, forever learning children. I miss them dearly and on the daily.

Since my incarceration, my role as a father has been reduced to being a good listener, consoling, inspiring, giving advice, sharing knowledge and experience, and mentoring them through phone conversation, email, and short visits. I strive to still be a teacher of some sort to my best efforts, and I can only hope my influence upon them helps them to make the right choices in life. I dream and long for the day to be reunited with them and be the father I have always been.

Donna (21), Destiny (19), Jahkel (14), Jahmai (8),

"I may not be there in person now, but above all else, I want you to always know…"

That you are the source of pride in my life. I want you to always feel my presence and know that I love you with all my heart. In no way shape or form, can words describe the amount of love and space in my heart for you. You are everything good in my life. You are the special blessing that's always brought joy and happiness in my life from the day you were born and have grown beyond my greatest expectations.

I miss you immeasurably. I've missed out on so many of the greatest moments of your life: birthdays, holidays, graduations, high school, college, boyfriends, girlfriends, learning to drive, sports and academic achievements, and countless other milestones and merry makers. Moments that cannot be relived or done over for me to see nor take part in, but will always be stamped and engraved in my mind as unforgotten thoughts for me to rethink often of what I've missed out on. Through pictures and conversations, I use my imagination and somehow play out those events, time and time again in my head and mind. I want you to be happy in your life and know that there is nothing you can't do.

Remember that your life has no boundaries or limitations, and as long as you do what is right, no one can ever stop you from being you. Stay strong, be brave, and know that wherever you go and whatever you do, I will always be very proud of you. Always pursue your dreams and remember that you're braver than you believe, stronger than you seem, smarter than you think, and twice as beautiful as you ever imagined.

    I will treasure you always and love you forever. You mean the world to me. You are without a shadow of a doubt, my greatest achievement in life and I am more proud of you than you will ever know.

Your Father

"I always told you, 'if you are in the right, I will have your back, and if you are in the wrong, I will ensure that you are judged fairly.'"

♥

Derrick Andrey Wade

Claudia,

We have finally reached the half-way point in this journey, so I wish to reflect on a few points of interest or concern. First and foremost, you're becoming the woman I knew would be great at every aspect of life. You were an honor roll student from first grade till your graduation 10 years later. I was away from grade nine through the present, but with your mother's help I've followed all points of your life. Since you were first born, everyone assumes you're the favored child. You simply made life easy by doing as you were told, and being respectful to everyone.

Do you realize that the closest you were to trouble was when you were 12 years old? That was when that little boy (Steven) decided to touch you on your behind. You promptly kicked him. We thought you had killed him, with the way the teachers were acting and you were crying so hard. I always told you, "if you are in the right, I will have your back, and if you are in the wrong, I will ensure that you are judged fairly." I still can't believe his family sued me for his medical bills. At that time, I had never heard of retrieval surgery. It was worth $650 for him to learn to keep his hands to himself. It never dawned on me or your mother that you quit soccer over that incident.

I'm sorry that I missed your junior and senior proms, but with your uncles standing in for me, I'm sure your dates were terrified enough (not really, your uncles are weenies who adore you and would never embarrass you).

Currently you're seeking a degree in political science,

which is weird given your views on the last four heads of state. 1, Clinton—"a brilliant economist yet a scumbag pervert." You were born during his 2nd term, you can only go off of what you've read. 2, Bush—"a greedy, selfish individual." His 2 terms didn't affect you much; it put us adults in a bad recession. 3, Obama—"A good looking liberal super softee." This might have been influenced by your mother, she was always saying how good looking and soft he was. I'm not giving you credit for saying that, I'm blaming your mother. 4, Trump—"A bigoted egomaniac." I will let you have that one, only because you voted in his election. I'm gonna blame you if he gets a second term.

No matter which path in life you take, I will love and support you as you have done me. There is no part of the day or night that I am not thinking of you. When all of you (mom, James, you) leave from a visit, it causes as much pain for me as it does for you. Remember, I am responsible for my actions. I won't allow you to blame yourself. We have to look forward to finishing this journey. I hope to come home to grandchildren. You better not be holding your life up waiting for me. God willing, we will make amends for lost time. The memories of you growing up sustain me every minute we're apart. You are my heart and soul, sweetheart. I love you.

Always in my thoughts,
Dad
P.S. Keep an eye on your brother. He may graduate in my lifetime (smile).

> "You all are the reason when I wake up every morning, no matter where I am, I feel blessed."

❤

B. Chism a.k.a. Bae-Zeus

I may not be there in person now but above all else I want you to always know that you are my universe. Amani, Zyasia, Makayla, and Zadea, you are my life. You all are the reason that when I wake up every morning, no matter where I am, I feel blessed. Your grandma Vera has passed away, but she went to heaven knowing she left 4 beautiful girls on this earth. She saw something special in you all. She saw a light shining within you. I'm going to do everything in my power to keep that light aglow.

When I was born it was like a blockbuster movie had started. The name of this movie was "My Life." I was the main character of the movie. Whether I was the hero or the villain, the movie was about me. The day Zadea, Makayla, Zyasia and then Amani were born, I was no longer the main character. You gals became the stars. I became the writer, the producer, and the director of this movie called "My life" or "Our Life." I have to make sure that this movie is a success. I have to make sure that the main characters overcome all obstacles. I have to make sure that this movie has a happy ending. You all are the most important thing in "My Life." Without you in it, I cease to exist.

The world can be harsh and unfair. Your father is a victim of this "harsh reality." A lot of people give up hope and surrender to the wicked ways of the world. The main reason why, is because we feel that we can't save the world or even change it. I realized through you 4 girls, that in order to change the world, you have to change the course of the future. There is only 1 way to do that. We have to change the hearts and the minds of the children. You are the future. You are the world. Everyone on this planet is somebody's child. Love is the key. We have to teach love and understanding. Not hate and confusion.

The problem has been passed from generation to generation. As time changes the next generation changes. In most cases it changes for the worse. The issue is that our elders are so disappointed in how the ones after them turn out, that they just give up hope. Instead of teaching them and leading them on a more positive and righteous path, they look down on them and scold them. They will never learn that way. It is human to err. You can't punish a child when they make a mistake. They'll never understand right from wrong. You have to explain the error in their action. Cause and effect. Help them to understand. Love is the highest level of understanding. Teach the children love, respect, honesty, and teach them how to forgive. Not how to compete or how to envy the next person. It breeds hate. When we fail, we give up hope. Sometimes life seems like a big competition or contest. But we have to realize that if you are doing your best and you know you were righteous at heart when doing so, there is no competition. If we fail, try again. Don't give up hope.

So, parents of the world, no matter what the situation is, never give up on your child. I will never give up on my daughters. I will always be with you no matter how far apart we are from each other. Why? Because you are the best part of me.

Love,
Daddy

"I want you to know that I believe in you and will support you, as your father. I will always be honest with you even when I know you may not want to hear it. I want you know that you can talk to me about anything and be honest about everything."

♥

Cyrus Havens

Greetings Baby Girl,

I pray that this letter finds you smiling, doing better today than you were yesterday, and overall as well as can be expected.
 Akeelah, I write you all of the time but 99% of the time I keep the letters because the communication between us is nonexistent with the exception of the times your mother has you on or around your birthday.
 A friend of mine and his wife came up with an idea to give people with situations and circumstances like mine and incarcerated individuals all over a chance to show the world that we are more than the negative thoughts people have about us and bigger and brighter than the stereotypes placed on us and the boxes they place us in. He asked me to write you a letter as long or as short as I want completing the following: "I may not be there in person now, but above all else I want you to always know..."
 Akeelah, I may not be there in person now, but above all else I want you to always know that I am your number one fan, and I always will be. I want you to know that I love you and think about you every day, and that I never stopped exhausting all avenues to be a part of your life and put my best foot forward to keep any form of communication between us open. I want you to know that I believe in you and will support you, as your father. I will always be honest with you even when I know you may not want to hear it. I

want you know that you can talk to me about anything and be honest about everything. Akeelah, I want you to know that I take full responsibility for my actions which caused my incarceration and my absence in your life, but I need you to know and understand that I did what I thought was right at the time with you and your mother's best interest in mind. Good intentions with bad actions are still wrong and is a lesson I learned the hard way but none-the-less a lesson learned.

Know that I will never jeopardize any of my freedoms again especially knowing that losing you is the end result. When you and I are reunited I promise not to live just for making up for lost times but to invest in our future creating memories as we grow along. Akeelah, you are a beautiful young lady, smart, talented, with an infectious smile and one of the best things that has happened to me.

You and I have a lot of questions to ask and answer, stories to share, things to experience together and overall some catching up to do, and I can't wait. I miss you. I love you, and until we meet again, peace, love, & blessings.

Love always,
your dad Cyrus Havens.

P.S. Everybody that came with you can't go with you. Believe in yourself & know that you are here for a reason, so go win on purpose with purpose. If you do what you can, God will do what you can't, and worrying only gives a small thing a big shadow.

> "Feeding you, burping you, changing you, bathing you, and even putting you to sleep was always a challenge but I did it like the proud father I am. From the day I get out of here I know it will be a challenge to reconnect with you, but it's going to be my mission to rebuild that father-son relationship."

♥

Lazaro

I may not be there in person now, but above all else I want you to know that I always love you and no matter what I always will love you, Benjamin. I know that I missed some of the most important moments of your childhood or more specifically your infant years, but I always knew what happened because your grandparents–my parents–kept me up to date on everything. I have not forgotten the many times I changed your diaper leading up to your first birthday. Since the day you were born, I cherished every moment I spent with you. Feeding you, burping you, changing you, bathing you, and even putting you to sleep was always a challenge but I did it like the proud father I am.

From the day I get out of here, I know it will be a challenge to reconnect with you, but it's going to be my mission to rebuild that father-son relationship. I will teach you whatever sport you're into, or I will teach you an instrument, or I will do whatever it is you want to do. I will always be there for you when you need help or advice. I will not only be your dad but also your best friend when you need one. I will make sure you don't commit the same mistakes I committed in my life. You, Benjamin, will always be my motivation to do better in life and to strive for success. I want you to always remember this, don't let anyone tell you that you can't succeed in life. You can do whatever it is you want to do or be in life.

Parent, Trapped

I love you Benjamin,
your dad, Lazaro

> "I'm with you in your dreams. Moreover, I'll always stand behind you 100% of the time no matter how right, wrong, or indifferent. Daddy will always be with you."

♥

Slaughter

Makalay S.,

I may not be there in person now, but above all else I want you to always know I'm with you in your dreams. Moreover, I'll always stand behind you 100% of the time no matter how right, wrong, or indifferent. Daddy will always be with you. I know you are going through a lot of change at the moment and dad's not there, but baby girl there's nothing to fear, I'll always be there. So dry your tears, I'm always here.

XOXO Love,
Daddy

Makayla - my lil soldier,

I may not be there in person now but, above all else I need you to know how much I truly care for you. I will always stand behind you no matter your choices in life, just like your grandmother and grandpas were there for me. I've made a lot of bad choices in my life and they are still on my side just like I am for you. My heart will always belong to you. I'm so glad that I have a kid as smart and wonderful as you. I know I'm not the smartest man in the world but your mom is my better half for that. I'm just glad I was able to have two beautiful kids with a woman that is as good of a mom as her. She can even cook a lil bit too. Honey I just need you to remember you can be anything and everything you ever wanna be and much more. Always keep your eyes

and mind open. Never settle for anything else than great because that's what you are. I love you to the moon and back.
Love,
Daddy

> "So please be the best man that I couldn't be & remember my support & love will always be there for you whether you need it or not."

♥

J. Lyfe Yeoman-El

Dear Marquise!

3/18/19 A.D.

I may not be there in person now, but above all else I want you to always know I love you! I always have & I always will. I know I haven't been there but that doesn't mean that I haven't thought about you. I think about you every day. I think about what's your favorite sport? What your favorite team? What's your favorite color? I think about a lot of things. Mostly all the things that I missed are what haunt me the most. I often think about how to apologize to you & would you even accept my apology for leaving you? I have made a lot of mistakes in my life & I am paying for it dearly! But most of all, you shouldn't have to pay that price with me. Now, for that I am deeply sorry! I wish that these words would reach you in a place that I am probably not welcomed because if I can leave you with anything, the only thing that I would like for you to take forward in life is that please don't make the same mistakes that I did. Always believe in yourself and don't become discouraged when you fall down. Just pick yourself up and continue to chase your dreams. You will always have my support even if it's from afar. I love you! & will always continue to do so. So please be the best man that I couldn't be & remember my support & love will always be there for you whether you need it or not.

Love Alwayz!
Sincerely,

J Lyfe Yeoman-El

> "I want you to know that I've made a lot of mistakes in my life. but you are not one of them."
>
> ♥
>
> Ronnie Davis, Jr.

Dear Haleybug,

I may not be there in person now, but above all else I want you to always know that I have never left you, I have always been in your heart as you are in mine. There is not a single second that escapes me that you are not loved, thought of, missed or wishing I was not behind these bars and razor wire but with you teaching you how to ride a bike, fish, cook a mean steak on the grill, drive a car and so on. I know one day this will be behind us and we can pick up the pieces together but until that day, I want you to know that I've made a lot of mistakes in my life, but you are not one of them. I love you and miss you with all that I am and look forward to rebuilding our life together and being there for you. I love you!

Your Dad,
Ronnie Davis, Jr.

"Neither of you has ever been without me. I was there when you both entered the world, and I will be there for you until the journey is finished."

♥

Peter Simpson

Peter and Jermaine,

I may not be able to be there in person now but above all else I want you to always know, I will always be there for you. Sooner or later we will be together again. In tough times I think of you guys, the responsibility I have as a father, not just to be able to talk about a problem but to say "follow me" and solve the problem. I have to be above the many situations that can cause me to lose more of my freedom and stay focused on what is important—the family I have. I will not give up. I will see you both again.

    We have come a long way. Grandma's parents sent her away to Barbados for a short time when she was two and a half years old. The short time turned into twenty-six years. She and I talked recently about the anger and resentment she had to deal with related to people in her life and how they treated her. I try not to be angry about what people in my life did or didn't do.

    The family I tried to build had been hurt and abused for their existence. Anger, hurt, and violence was what they knew. Even good treatment didn't register. I diagnosed the problem. You know what reacting to something in the present as if it was occurring in the past is called? Mental illness, and it is a disease. Nobody gets mad when a person has heart disease, but we do get mad when they know and then eat bacon by the pound.

    It wasn't anyone's fault but after they knew they were sick, then acted out, it was disappointing. That's where I am with that situation.

Neither of you has ever been without me. I was there when you both entered the world, and I will be there for you until the journey is finished. In all things and at all times, I want you to respect yourselves and protect yourselves. You will look in the mirror at the end of the day when you are washing—you see a man. To be a King you have to wear the crown and behave like a King. Get wise counsel.

Love,
Pops

I am Peter Simpson. I am son, brother, friend, uncle, great uncle, hero, college graduate, single parent, basketball player, coach, Registered Nurse, teacher, researcher, student and more, but most of all father. The thing that will change all of that for you is that, according to the treasonous, slave, Jim Crow, segregation, and the mass incarceration state of Virginia, I am also an "offender".

If you read the book "Situations Matter," you will see that our attitudes and beliefs, even our behaviors, are more pliable than we—I—thought.

As a single parent I experienced this firsthand. First there was shock. Black guys aren't single parents, they all run away and leave the single mom, right? No, there are actually single dads. Then as it sunk in, the attitudes changed to, well that's OK. Let's just help the guy.

My youngest, Jermaine, is a daddy's boy. He wanted to do everything I did. I am a crazy, obsessed fisherman, so at a year and a half or two years old Jermaine was sitting on my leg watching the sunfish, bream, swimming in the shallows. He was entranced with the water and fish. "Fishies, fishies," he said, but it came out more like "pishies, pishies." Gotta love him.

At about three or four, before he went off to school, we went to the lake. I wanted to fish and so did he. I got him a thin six-foot stick and a piece of fishing line. His bait was an eighth ounce jig with a small power grub. He dropped his lure into the sunfish beds. I tried to fish but he was catching sunfish too fast.

After about three or four fish I gave up. I put down my rod and just sat down on my tackle box and released the sunfish after he caught them. Twenty-four sunfish later we had a memory for life. He never let me forget that he out fished me on that day.

Later as he got into pre-teen years, I taught him the fullness of chasing fish. We talked about the weather, water quality, depth, cover, structure, bait fish and more. He took the bait casting rod out of my hand one day. I told him I hadn't taught him to use it yet. His reply? Daddy, I've been watching you for years. He cast that rod like an expert, thumbed down the spool speed at the end of the cast and all. He beamed with pride, "guess you've got to get me one of these."

One day we had really favorable fishing conditions: full moon, stalled front, clear water conditions and it was Father's Day. We caught over a hundred bass in a day with off and on showers, clouds and periods of sunshine. We caught fish on every lure in the tackle box. From surface baits, minnow baits, spinner baits, crank baits, jigs, worms, and grubs. It was awesome. It was the best Father's Day of all time.

As he grew older, he grew into a kind, lovable person. He walked down the hallway at middle school hugging, giving high fives, rubbing heads and shouting to friends and teachers. Imagine my surprise when I got a call from the middle school about Jermaine beating up some other boy. I jumped into the F-150 and went right up there. I found him in the principal's office. He didn't seem upset or rumpled, like he had been fighting. I asked him to explain himself. It turns out the other boy was teasing one of Jermaine's friends. She had leukemia, the chemo made her lose her hair and she was wearing wigs. The other boy involved teased her until she cried. Jermaine insisted he stop. The other boy told Jermaine to mind his business. Jermaine told him, "walk away now." Some disrespect and cursing followed, and the young man learned not to pick on sick girls. I asked the principal if my son's account of events was correct. We all know the drill: do not answer the question, quote some obtuse policy. Well, I took him out of school and we went out to the diner for pancakes and sausage. He was so shocked, he asked me, "you're not mad pops?" I said no, you did that guy a service, picking on sick girls can get you into serious problems.

We moved to Virginia in 2003 or 2004. By High School he was taller than I am. He now stood about six three or four. I'm a little above average at six feet and about two hundred twenty pounds.

He had good success in school and at sports. He played for the Swift Creek Association Sharks basketball team and did well. He went on to play for the Manchester High School basketball team. Another young man I coached for the association also went on to the Manchester High team. Jermaine's ability at fishing also grew, on one of our outings he had his bait casting outfit at Swift Creek Reservoir. We were fishing under the bridge on Genito Road. There was a shout, some splashing and a four to five pound bass was hoisted in celebration. That's my boy.

Jermaine graduated in '08, was working out the transition from high school to adulthood and we had a family tragedy. Today, he sells cars in Rockland County, New York. He is successful enough to have made it onto television. He, his older brother Peter, and the rest of my family have been a great support to me during these years of incarceration.

The means the Commonwealth attorney used to convict me were criminal. It is really simple. If a person told you they were not at a particular place at a particular time and then later told you they were there at that particular place and time and saw everything that happened, you would think they were lying at one time or the other, right? Well, when the Commonwealth wants to convict someone, college educated people will believe any story that gets them a conviction. Even if the "witness" has these opposite stories recorded under oath by a court reporter. I'm still fighting the conviction. But that's another story.

My name is Peter Simpson and I am many things. First, I am a survivor. As an African American, living in the United States, that should be obvious to anyone who can read, write, or even watch the news. My first struggle was surviving my family's failed structure. The story goes, my grandparents sent my mother to Barbados to escape the hardship in America. They lived in Brooklyn, New York.

The people who were taking care of my then ten-year-old mother cashed in her return ticket back to the U.S. My mother was trapped in Barbados for twenty-six years.

I was one of what I thought were three children born to her during that time. My mother returned to the U.S. and sent for us when I was five years old. We flew to the U.S. in 1959, to live in Brooklyn for a year. We then moved to Haverstraw, New York.

From the time I can remember until after I had my first son, I had no contact with my father. This left me with deep feelings of loss and abandonment, that I wasn't important. Even when I was a little boy, I swore that if I ever had kids I would never leave them. The behavior of my mother's boyfriend with jealous girlfriends and an alcoholic, abusive stepfather later, made my decision to be a good father deeper than ever. Although it was a negative image, I knew I didn't want to be like my dad.

I did high school at Spring Valley High, went to college at Utica College in upstate New York at age 17. I didn't do well. I quit school, went to work at a grocery store, made manager then had some life and marriage issues. I fought through that and went back to school at Dominican College in Blauvelt, New York and graduated in '97.

I was twenty-six, had my own apartment, Peter Jr's mom was beautiful. I was finally a father. We moved from an apartment to a house on Roosevelt Avenue in Spring Valley, New York. Little Peter had the best of everything and I loved that little boy better than life itself. I dropped him off at grandma's, came home from work and took care of my little guy. I fed him, burped him, changed him, walked him in the stroller and beamed with pride. I wanted all the best in life for him, I wanted him to know me.

Peter had the best life a boy could have in a small town in New York. He had two good parents. He lived in a nice house, had the resources for success. His favorite was letter go round, it was a game for children on the first home computer. He could read when he first went to school. He didn't learn to walk on time. My proud mother, took her first grandchild to the doctor. After counting three aunts, three uncles, three cousins and a dozen family friends the doctor gave his medical opinion. He said, "If I had more than twenty people carrying me around, I wouldn't walk either." Well, shortly after putting the beloved boy down, he walked, ran, jumped and played just like little boys all do.

Parents do come with issues. My wife, Lynette, also had abandonment issues with her father. We had a challenge to the marriage and she left me before I could leave her. According to her family history of a father "going to the store" and disappearing forever, men leave. So I wound up separated from my son when he was about five years old. I had pain and up and downs that I need a full-length book to go into but I came out ahead.

After I was stable, I got a call one day. It was my now ex-wife, she wanted me to come get my son. It turned out she had unknowingly married the biggest drug dealer in the area and wanted her son safe. I jumped in the car and drove through a bad snowstorm to get my boy. Then we settled in for the long haul.

After living with his grandmother, then with me and a girlfriend, we got an apartment. Now we were a family of three. I had finished a four-year nursing college and made good money. We also had a little brother for Peter, Jermaine. Jermaine's mother and I never lived together. After his birth, she had some problems and I tried to help. I got custody of my second son after several court visits and allegations of abuse.

They were both daddy's boys but Peter was a gamer and golfer. Jermaine was a basketballer and a fisherman. We went out to the reservoir for a mixed trip. Jermaine and I would cast for bass at rocks, channels and points. Peter would sit in a lawn chair and play his video game next to a rod baited with corn for the huge carp that lived there. A hundred yards out we heard Peter shouting, we ran back towards him and saw him change from gamer to fisherman. He whipped that fifteen-pound carp with a little coaching. Some guys from Europe, Poland or somewhere, came by. They asked how we caught the carp, what we used, would we show them. We had a great time. We shared our simple method of throwing handfuls of corn, that sink to the bottom. Then unweighted hooks sweetened with a couple kernels of corn tricked the fish, brilliant in its simplicity.

I taught both my guys to be decent, to follow the law, to help family, to help people in need. Peter finished community college, Jermaine did not, but I consider them both successful. They both have good jobs and are productive. Neither one of them has ever been in any trouble with the law. They are only one generation removed from what most people would call a tragedy. But here we are doing the best we can.

> "Be an educated man because they can always trap your body, but they can never trap your mind. Always do the right thing and you'll never go wrong. You are a king. Always carry yourself as one."

❤

Kareem A. Landers

I may not be there in person now, but above all else I want you to always know: First of all, peace young King. What I want you to know is, I'm so very proud of you, and I am so proud to be your father.

You are the best thing that has ever happened to me in my life, you are the breath that I breathe, you are the reason why I live. Son, little do you know, you are the reason why I'm still here living today. I was on a bad path in my youth, before you were born, I really didn't care if I lived or died.

When you were born you changed the whole narrative to the story of my life, you gave me reason, purpose for living. Son, everything that I do, I do it for you, to ensure that you have or live a better life than I did. When I build with you, it's not to beat you down but to build you up, to pass the knowledge and wisdom that I have on to you so that you will know and understand that you don't have to make the wrong choices that I made as a youth. So that you don't have to go through the negative things that I've been through, so that you will be the one to bring about the change that our family needs to be successful and prosper in life, so that you can break the cipher of incarceration that my father, his father, and now me have been in for so long. You are the key to unlocking the door of endless possibilities that life has to give, so that you can be a better man, a better human being than I am.

I've done a lot of wrong in my life and Kamaree you gave me reason to do right, son, and I love you with every ounce that I have in me more than I love myself. I miss you with each passing day that I'm away from you, from your football games, school, etc. I can't make up for lost time but what I can do is be your father, and your best friend and try my best to be the beacon of light that will guide you through this thing called life. I promise I'll give it all I got, and do the best I can to be that for you. I want you to know that I do all I can for you from behind these walls. I stay on you so hard because I care about you so much and want you to live your life with purpose, with principles, but most of all, I stay on you because I don't want you to ever have to go through the things I've been through in my life, never have to experience being in prison because this is no place for any man, woman, or child to ever be in or have to go through.

    Always cherish your freedom, and respect it. Don't ever take it for granted. I leave you with this: live your life to the fullest, have fun, be a righteous man, a respected man. Make your life count for something. Be an educated man because they can always trap your body, but they can never trap your mind. Always do the right thing and you'll never go wrong. You are a king. Always carry yourself as one. I love you my son, always and forever. Be the author of your own book. Write your own history. Never let anyone determine what you are or what your future will be.

Peace King,
Your Father,
Kareem Landers

Lessons

Live life fully, my boy. Harvest and savor every ounce of joy and excitement. You only live once, so don't leave anything behind. Live as much as possible now, get the most out of every day—you can catch up on sleep and rest when you're done being alive.

Why? Because as Dave Matthews says: "I can't believe that we would lie in our graves, wondering if we spent our living days well. I can't believe that we would lie in our graves, dreaming of things that might've been."

Because, in short, life is measured in memories. Not in dollars or power. Not in fights won, Facebook friends, or trendy clothing, either. No one finds themselves on their deathbed, wishing they'd spent more time in an office cubicle or posting anonymously. Those things do not stand out at the end. In a life inevitably cluttered by repetitious events, traffic jams, paperwork, and mindless meetings, avoid the mundane. What people wish for at that moment far too often is that they spent more time doing great things with great people. That is what stands out in life, so maximize your memorable experiences.

We are defined by memories; those we hold, share, and inhabit in others are our life's essence. When I meet people, one of the first things I share with them—besides stories about you—is typically a tale involving the 50 states or 11 nations I've visited along with the countless friends and lifelong memories I've made along the way. Those memories define and reflect who I am, way more than my educational attainment or income. Despite being here now, I can still say I've lived a fantastic life thanks to those memories and experiences. You too, already, have a life reflecting touchdown receptions, finding giant shark's teeth in clay cliffs, slip-n-slide human bowling, and so much more. So chase dreams, love, and moments, always.

To make as many priceless memories as possible, you should always advocate and admire adventure, in all its forms. The resulting awe, wonder, and thrills are like steroids for memories, for defining your life and character. So much of my life is embodied in close encounters with grizzlies, bison, and moose; in swimming with sharks and barracudas; in jumping from freaky-small planes; in scaling local peaks on a whim. So much of you consists of cracking geodes on mountain trails, splashing in frigid waterfall pools, and tackling epic waterslides as soon as you're tall enough to try. None of that can ever be taken away.

But adventures are not just adrenaline rushes. Always pursuing adventure means going all in for the things that excite you in any way. It can be reading great books, like your past adventures with "the BFG" and "the Forbidden Library," or mine with "the Dark Tower" or "Game of Thrones" series. It can be personal challenges overcome or sights you've always wanted to see. When you come to a fork in any road, take the adventurous route.

Stalk serendipity. Shamelessly pursue every happy coincidence and once in a lifetime experience. Many chances at adventure require you to be spontaneous. Like a wild stallion, galloping past, they are rare and fast and unpredictable. To make the most of such encounters, always be willing to harness that chance and ride into the unknown.

Nurture wanderlust, too. Take the scenic route, with regular unmapped hikes from unplanned pit stops, both literally and figuratively. Cherish wandering towards new places and trying new things, both physically and mentally. Go where chances for memory or adventure take you. The journey is often way better than the destination, offering great truths and delightful surprises.

Often this requires doing things that are not strictly rational or according to plan. Life's not a race, so that's okay. Had I not been willing to take a poetry class—which, beforehand, I thought I'd hate as a topic—even though I was—then—studying architecture, I never would have met Nikki Giovanni, become a—mediocre—writer, found my teacher calling, or even moved to Washington. And she and I are still friends decades later.

This notion also relates to money: don't be too careful or rational. Likewise, work. Be a responsible, bill-paying, productive member of society. Duh! But always with a balance. Savor life's pleasures regularly, just not too much. Don't ever make money a primary goal. It is a tool; a dollar is just a concept. It's only a piece of paper until you do something with it. I recommend spending it primarily on experiences, not things—besides essentials. Save appropriately, but be sure to turn money into good times, especially when young. You can have way more fun with $500 at 23 than 73!

All of this adventuring is not automatically easy, I know. It requires going out of your comfort zone and conquering fears. It's a process. Fears of rejections, embarrassment, and pain used to stop me cold. But they can be overcome, and they should. You will be happier and healthier if you do. I can't dance, and I don't know Spanish. But one of my favorite memories ever is dancing with Marigot to Chilean folk music that we didn't understand one bit of at a country club in a desert almost half a world away.

Also, you must live to laugh. Laughter bonds you to people and cements memories permanently. Any adventure becomes unforgettable with a good dose of belly laughs. I know you don't find me particularly funny, but a big reason I have such wonderful support is a foundation of shared laughter with good people over the years. Victor Borges said, "Laughter is the shortest distance between two people." Laughing together builds bridges that span differences. Here, I laugh together with Muslims, Christians, atheists, gangbangers, and hackers. As a result, we now call each other friends. Scientifically, laughter is priceless, offering huge doses of endorphins—the body's feel good chemicals—and positive psychological effects.

    To fully pursue memories, adventure, and laughter requires some risk, though, even some pain. But scars are just more stories, funny or thrilling, to share with new people, currency for new friends. Scars are also the trophies of a life lived fully, skin shined and toughened, gleaming in the glow of companionship and smiles. This pursuit will produce some discomfort along the way—that is what the next poem is about. Despite any pain, for my money "the juice is worth the squeeze." When you put yourself out there fully, the reward far outweighs the costs.

The inevitable penance
    for the opportunity to bask
    in radiant golden burgundy swirls
    catalyzed by gulps of undiluted bliss
must be intermittent spells of anguish
    child of vulnerability and pursuit
    birthed howling but breathing
    from between vulnerability's legs
The chase of all that life can offer
costs periodic swells of pain
unmilled to those choosing
to dance and skirt around risk
that jig of adversity avoidance

that polka of solely safe decisions
complacent worshippers of utter rationality

But that self-protective jitterbug
must be danced eternally along,
while those that live footloose
dumping caution for a night with chance
even their occasional throes of hurt
match the beat of life's bass line
and spotlight their natural rhythm
forever shimmying til dawn
a dance partner always within reach

    Now I would like to offer you some other little tidbits that I believe are useful and important to consider as you grow. No common theme, just the leftover morsels of advice that may help you navigate the world, based on my experiences and learning.
    The most important suggestion I have for you is this: as you go through life, make sure you are giving more to the world than you are taking from it. This is especially true when it comes to people and nature. If you can go through your days confident that you are providing more than you are asking from those around you, you'll know you're having a good life. I mean this in terms of your personal interactions. Having to receive food, shelter, and such growing up doesn't count as taking—that's totally appropriate.
    From all I know of you, too, you are already on a great path with this, embodying it early on. So often I hear of how you give time, thought, effort, and even tears when your mom's sick, your sister's hurt, your friend's upset, or your pet's in danger. This speaks volumes about your high character and makes me very proud. Keep living so well!

An addition to this initial suggestion: do not ever be afraid to be too nice or too generous! Lots of people say they don't want to be taken advantage of when they're kind, which makes sense—I guess!—but which is also an easy excuse not to share and help others. Try instead to err on the side of generosity and trust. If the worst thing anyone can say about you is that you are too nice and let people take advantage of your kindness, then you should be very, very proud.

This is why it's a good policy to help everyone less fortunate than yourself. Any time I see someone without a home asking for change, I give them any I have and offer food, too. Sure, they might use it for booze or drugs. But it is just as likely or more likely to not be the case. Many good people end up needing spare change at some point. A buck or two means little in my life, but it may mean a huge difference in theirs. Besides, even if it is for addiction, they're still a human being. If their life is so bad that they see their best option as putting up with all the insults they get approaching stranger, then the least I can do is help a touch.

Now, as much as I wish your life to be problem-free forever, that's impossible. Everyone encounters problems of many types. There are also many different ways to get past whatever problem you face. Go through it, attack it, or avoid it. Over or under it, perhaps around. Overpower it, juke it out, or outrun it. The important thing is that you realize that all problems you encounter are really just obstacles on your path. You can always get beyond that obstacle! Just don't give up. Don't ever give up.

As for how to tackle any specific problems, decide for each the best approach. Don't come at every issue the same way. Some require brains, others brawn, others heart. The important thing is that you face it and choose your strategy to match the situation.

Do not just ignore the problems and hope they'll go away. Patience is absolutely a virtue, and some concerns require a gradual approach. But just waiting forever, indefinite patience, is rarely—if ever—a useful strategy for any serious obstacle in a crisis. Enslaved people waiting patiently to be freed magnanimously by slavers died patiently.

Choose your battles, though. Fight only when there's no choice, and always fight with ideas and words unless you're physically endangered. When you fight, figuratively or literally, you have to expect to take some punches.

Up to this point, I have consciously focused on positive ideas but to fully complete this, I need to include a final thought on two things to avoid. They are what I've come to consider the only two wasted emotions: jealousy and regret. They are natural, but I implore you to do all you can to train yourself out of them. It is possible. And worth it, too, because all they do is bring pain, frustration.

Jealousy is the worst feeling, if you ask me, poison for you and those around you. It provides nothing for society except injury and injustice. It's entirely counter-productive for you, too, on multiple levels. Jealousy simultaneously keeps you from moving forward while eroding principles and joy.

First, jealousy is problematic because it actually stands in the way of you getting what you want. It encourages you to destroy others instead of building yourself. For every drop of energy or second of time you spend envying others' things or success, you've lost that amount to achieve the same for yourself. Jealousy is like quicksand—when you're stuck there, no matter how much effort you exert, you cannot ever move forward and keep getting sucked in deeper. You never have to take from others to get what you want—you are naturally extremely bright, talented, and charismatic! The quickest simplest way to get to your goals is to do what you need to do to earn them. I will always have the utmost confidence in your ability, and you have my support.

Jealously is also like acid, eating away at the mortar that holds together the bricks of your personal foundation, leading you to act contrary to your own interests and values. Lots of guys here—of those actually "guilty"—are here because they hurt someone or took something when feeling jealous. Lots of people I know outside of here believe that the worst things they've done were motivated by jealousy.

This is especially true when it comes to romance. Acting jealously is the worst way to treat and to keep alive a relationship with someone you love. At least as far as love goes, we live in a free society: if that person wants to be with you, they will be. If they are with you, then trust that they want to be. When you instead accuse or threaten someone you love, all that does is push them away and make you harder to love. It shows the worst side of you. Plus, if you act jealously, even if your relationship continues, you'll never know if they are with you out of love or if you threatened or guilt-tripped them into it. Thus, you can't appreciate the love you have when jealousy wins.

After jealousy, regret is the other wasted, useless, counter-productive emotion. I say that even now, even here—though I confess that this situation has challenged my past self-training on this. Despite my overall innocence of charges against me, I did not take the situation seriously enough at first and handled it poorly in a number of minor ways that added up to make it much worse in the end. They mostly weren't things I could've known at the time, but I still spent my first two years here dwelling miserably on my mistakes and what I've lost. I was defying my own long-running, hard-fought dedication to avoiding regret—

until I gradually realized that it was hindering me from being productive and positive, which are necessary to stay true to myself and the people I care deeply for. So now I'm more convinced than ever that regret is pointless and debilitating.

Bad stuff happens to everybody, you see, multiple times in life. Everyone makes mistakes and poor decisions. Learn from them, absolutely, but always move forward. Don't make them again, but getting stuck on crappy events that happened to you or involve you solves nothing and keeps you from growing.

Since you can't change the past ever, keep heading ever onward, leaping, running full speed ahead. That way, even if you stumble or fall, your momentum keeps your body and head going in the right direction. Often you will land in even greater success and opportunity, so long as you are always headed enthusiastically forward.

That is why a conservative approach to the world is almost never the way to go. Conservative means keeping things the same, sitting still. Progressive, on the other hand, means seeking progress and improvement. Individually and collectively, we must change and adapt to make life better. If you look at history, the path to species survival and human social advancement is invariably one of progressive solutions, finding new ways to do things. This is particularly true for reducing violence, increasing economic sharing, and growing diversity, tolerance, and inclusion. Move forward, D, be on the side of progress.

One last thing: try to hold yourself to slightly higher standards than you hold others. It will keep you from judging and, more importantly, from being a hypocrite. It also makes you easy going and forgiving, great social traits.

"I hope you go up state and learn your lesson," more than one judge has callously intoned. Punishment and misery are implied to be some kind of magic conduit to following all the laws. Having come from a life as an activist criminologist, I thought I knew most of what there was to know about the need to end mass incarceration, especially having had a couple of friends locked up in my younger years. Turns out, I was wrong.

There are too few mirrors within these walls and too few folks willing to look even where they're found. Yet those who seek can find, and some deep self-reflection clarifies perspective, even when limited to 4" x 6" warped plastic safety mirrors.

Some of the biggest lessons I've learned in life occurred in prison—just not in the sense that most people would think. I learned that there are lessons to be learned everywhere, even in our nightmares. I learned that lessons can be learned from anyone, too, and often surprise us when we least expect them.

This book, in fact, is the fruit of some of my deepest epiphanies. First of all, that it is through our shared humanity that we connect and progress. Having arrived knowing endless reams of statistics about the inequalities and deprivations of incarceration, I was floored still by the people that I got to know. Not one fit a stereotype or even a simple demographic background. Dungeons & Dragons games at my current spot include multiple languages, ages, zip codes, education levels, and racial and ethnic identities. So many fascinating people I've gotten to know, having found ourselves face to face after paths tragic, adventurous, spiritual, and everything in between. I always spoke passionately about the need to treat people more humanely, but I had always relied on data to back me up. Having realized the powerful human stories here, my desire to be a voice for change led me to realize I could never rationally explain or doctorally exhort nearly as impactfully as I can share their many voices with the world.

Additionally, it has dawned on me on a whole new level just how much more important our relationships are than anything we can put on a resume. My career, an academic dream of teaching, making knowledge, and changing policy had just begun when my unexpected incarceration ended it. Forever. I'd worked so often through the night, past dawn, and up to the moment it was time to teach or be dad just to get there. Don't get it twisted, I always set aside work for parent time completely and maintained many strong friendships, but to do so and still advance my career meant doing it all. That meant never turning off.

I was a real go-getter. Then I got gotten myself. By this system. And as the dust settled, I found out that the hard stop on my vitae stings occasionally, but it's easy to move past. Mostly I don't even think about it. I have found other ways to teach and study and make a difference. More limited in scope, but they are often more profound in the personal impact. Mostly I don't even think anymore about my lost career.

What hurts every day, even on the best, is not being next to and helping out those I love, especially D, Gin, and Mom, all of whom have expressed how they need me. The worst part of prison by far is not avoiding gangs, lacking autonomy, living in a cement and steal bathroom, or eating meat rock and beans constantly. It is not the lost income or prestige or professional opportunity. By far, the worst is being kept away from those I love.

Ever the family man, "It's all about the people!" I constantly preached since college. It was my catch phrase, my go-to ultimate priority, but I had no idea until I had no people around me just how much those bonds matter. It wasn't until D and Gin asked me to commit when I get out to just being with them before worrying about changing the world, that I realized how much better doing anything with those who matter most is than doing exactly what I want alone. It wasn't until letters and calls with my son, parents, siblings, true friends, and Gin stopped me from killing myself after a year in solitary without hugs, sunlight, or hope that I realized how much connections truly matter most. Thus, when I get out, being with all of them is where you can find me.

I learned, too, the endless power of purpose. Viktor Frankl, psychologist and Holocaust survivor, spoke of resilience this way first. His book brought me to examine that idea among those thriving around me despite this deprivation, and those men taught me lessons. Not the least of them was that any positive purpose empowers the person engaged in its pursuit. Examining it was a step back into purpose for me, after staying connected with D. Now, my purpose has become being the spotlight and amplifier for so many meaningful human beings behind bars and to write this book for my boy—because I can still be the best Dad I can be, even here.

This book, then, is a microphone for the voices of real people. This book is better than research or diatribes because it will show humanity and build those bonds for everyone. This book is because it's for D and compiled with Gin. This book is because I learned just how powerful people are and just how much they truly matter.

As parents, one of our most important jobs is to provide our children with the tools they need to thrive. While they may or may not listen at first and on the surface, the lessons we prioritize are the foundations of their values and understandings.

This does not end when we are stuck behind bars. The irresistible urge to not just pass on genes but also the lessons of life continues for all the parents behind bars. And as long as we stay connected, our kids still revere what we say.

Given where we find ourselves, sheepishness seems likely. Avoiding hypocrisy appears tough. Yet the desire to help our kids live their best lives trumps all that and we tend to want even more to ensure they receive the crucial messages we pass on when we cannot be there every day to show them in person.

This probably also sounds scary on the surface, parental wisdom passed on from "convicts" and "felons." What could be valuable about the values of such lowlifes?!

Well, as these letters show, many people in this situation felt compelled to include their greatest lessons in this one-time letter to their children. These lessons were priority content, and they did not shy away from hard truths. Some were learned within these confines, others are more worldly. They reflect a variety of viewpoints, philosophies, and priorities, too. The one commonality, though, is that they are brave and honest and spoken boldly without avoiding this prison context but precisely because it exists.

Many were lessons learned the hard way, while others reflect specific concerns arising at home where we cannot be. Regardless, they are honest and heartfelt, reflecting an innate desire to give our progeny the chances and wisdom we lacked. Above all else, these lessons speak to the fundamental desire for parents everywhere to do their best for their kids.

The wording and tone may differ from mine, and they may not be the same as I would say first. Still, not one of these lessons would be anything I would not want D to hear. These are the revelations of parents just like those in suburbs, on farms, and atop high rises across the country. They had to be said, as evident in my own letter and the others in this section. Perhaps they're even a bit stronger than everyday. Unlike much in today's world that is catchy shallow shorthand for life, these are the lessons taught when only one shot is available. These are the lessons filtered through pain, loneliness, and a muzzled voice. These are the lessons that show how familiar and relatable parenting is behind bars.

Letters on Lessons

"...if you take your time, apply yourself, and work hard you can achieve anything. Never be afraid to fail either. Not everything you attempt in life, no matter how hard you try, no matter how patient you are, is going to be a success. Don't let the fact that you failed stop you from trying again either. Learn from your failures and let them motivate you. Sometimes our greatest achievements rise from the ashes of our failures."

♥

Timmothy Rummage

Emma and Lily,

I love you. I've said it to many people over the years but never have those three words meant so much than when I say them to you. You're my everything. I think of you always. Anytime I do something I feel is worthwhile I find myself wishing that I could share it with you. Every basket made or shot blocked on the basketball court, every clever fix I come up with when fixing someone's electronics or every incredibly bad joke or ridiculous pun I come up with throughout my day. There's nothing I want more than to share every little part of my day with you and to be your dad and help you grow up into beautiful, strong women. However, I made my choices and now I'm paying for them by watching you grow up through pictures and stories told by other people. That's the greatest punishment in the world.

    I get through every day by telling myself that even if there is just a slight chance that I could make up for lost time and be a father to you again then I have to keep moving forward. I have a little over 5 years left and by the time I get out you'll be adults and you'll think you have the whole world figured out. You probably already think that. I know I did at your age. I was so stubborn and no one could tell me anything that I didn't already know. Someone would tell me not to do something and no matter what it was I would do it anyway. "Son, that stove is hot, don't touch it." Five minutes later mom is wrapping up my finger because I didn't want to listen to her. I don't know if it was rebelliousness, or arrogance, or just flat-out stubbornness but whatever the reason I had to learn things for myself, usually the hard way. That being said you probably won't listen to anything I'm about to say but here goes.

Don't ever be in a rush to do something no matter what it is. Take your time. I've screwed more things up in my lifetime by being impatient. One of my favorite sayings is actually from my favorite book *Swan Song*. It goes, "One step at a time and the next one gets you where you're going." No matter what the task, be it a math test or a science project, learning to play the piano or being in a relationship, if you take your time, apply yourself, and work hard, you can achieve anything. Never be afraid to fail either. Not everything you attempt in life, no matter how hard you try, no matter how patient you are, is going to be a success. Don't let the fact that you failed stop you from trying again either. Learn from your failures and let them motivate you. Sometimes our greatest achievements rise from the ashes of our failures.

Always be yourself. Never compromise who you are for anyone. I spent so many years of my life being who I thought everyone around me wanted me to be. I wanted so badly to be accepted by the "cool kids" that I began to lose sight of who I am because I was always trying to be someone I wasn't. I used to get picked on and bullied because I was tall and lanky and I dressed like a metal head skater. I eventually started dressing and acting like one of the preps in an attempt to be accepted but I never was truly happy. It took me years before I was comfortable in my own skin and happy just being me. Nowadays I am unapologetically goofy and playful and like to laugh all the time. I make bad jokes and poke fun at myself. I'm 6'6", I have big ears, big feet, and a nose you can ski on but you know what? My friends love me in spite of all that. You'll always have haters. People who think you should conform to their standards. Those people aren't your friends. Your friends are the ones who love and accept you for exactly who you are.

Finally, tomorrow isn't guaranteed. I put off so many things in my life because I thought I had all the time in the world. Now I'm filled with regret over things I'll never have the chance to do. So many times you would ask me to go to the park or go ride bikes and I would be tired from work and I would say, "maybe tomorrow." Now I would give anything to ride bikes with you or go get ice cream or whatever it is you want to do. Don't take anything for granted like I have. There is nothing worse than looking back on life and having your regrets outweigh your triumphs. That being said, my greatest triumph was meeting your mother and being given the two of you. My greatest regret is not being the husband your mother deserved and the father you needed.

I don't know what's going to happen when I get out. You may ultimately decide you're better off without me. I know I'll never stop trying though. There will never be a time that I won't be there for you. Right or wrong I'll always support you in any way you need. We could go years without talking and the second you need something from me I'll be there. Why? Because you're my daughters and I love you more than anything else in the world. There's nothing that you or anyone else can say that would change that. You can do no wrong in my eyes.

With every fiber of my being, I love you both and miss you terribly. I'm sorry I'm not there but one day soon I will be, if you want me to. Take care of each other, love and care for each other, and always look out for each other. I'm always here for you and I always will be.

* * *

Love always,
Dad

"Rather than ridicule or mistreat in some cases you should applaud or give them a simple smile to let them know that you recognize their bravery for not being afraid to be who they are. Now don't get me wrong, there are some evil people out there but it's very rare that a warm smile can't disarm them. I am not saying to walk up to everyone who looks different to you but rather than stare in puzzlement you should smile in support."

♥

Gregory Brown

To truly understand the relationship between an incarcerated parent and their children all it really takes is for a person to put their feet in the shoes of someone incarcerated. Imagine what it feels like to be away from your child and not be able to partake in their everyday life. This is truly a form of torture. It makes you feel like the scum of the earth at times. How could you abandon your child? That's the question that most people would want to know the answer to when dealing with circumstances like this. Although, I talk to my 4-year-old (5 tomorrow) and he visits every 6 weeks I still miss the father/son bond that we should have. Of course I love my child and he loves his father but not being there hurts. In addition to writing a letter I am submitting a back-and-forth conversation that occurred between my 4-year-old and I:

Father: Good morning Juelz.
Son: Good morning daddy.
Father: Did you sleep good?
Son: Yes, I'm watching T.V.
Father: Oh, did I interrupt you?
Son: No. Daddy?
Father: Yes, son.
Son: Why do we look so much alike?

Father: 'Cause I made you son.
Son: And God made me too?
Father: Yah he helped. But I did all the work.
Son: Oh. But daddy how did you make me?
Father: Magic, Juelz.
Son: Like a magic wand?
Father: Exactly like that son.
Son: Can I see it?
Father: No son. One day you'll have your own magic wand but you can't cast your spell on everyone.

Kids are so inquisitive. They are growing up every single day and being away from them we are missing the little things. Just because I am incarcerated doesn't mean I am heartless or love my child any less than someone who wakes up with their child every morning. I miss the sickness and the laughs and the growing pains and experience he gains daily. I am fortunate enough to be in a rare situation for incarcerated parents. Most of the individuals who have children have little to no contact with their kids. That is torture. Not knowing if they are ok or just what's going on with them in general is a stressful situation in itself. The main question I ask my child is how was school today? Isn't that what everyday parents should do? So what is the difference between you and me?

Dear Son,

I may not be there in person now, but above all else I want you to always know that I love you. If you don't feel as though you can learn something from someone in my current situation, it makes what I am about to tell you even more important. Never judge. Simple, two words with so much power behind them. Some of the people you think look the oddest or different looking people in this world are some of the sweetest, most honest and genuine people on earth. Don't mistreat people that aren't afraid to express who they are whether it be through baggy pants, blue hair, gold teeth, overweight, black makeup, glasses, or anything that is a symbol of who they are, or it may just be something they like. Don't condemn someone for the choices that they have made without first attempting to educate yourself on their reasons. Rather than ridicule or mistreat, in some cases you should applaud or give them a simple smile to let them know that you recognize their bravery for not being afraid to be who they are. Now don't get me wrong, there are some evil people out there but it's very rare that a warm smile can't disarm them. I am not saying to walk up to everyone who looks different to you but rather than stare in puzzlement you should smile in support. I love you.

Love,
Daddy

> "Successful people fight for what they believe in, for what they know and want in life. What makes a loser is not what place you come in, but the effort you put in!"

♥

James P. Woody

I may not be there in person now, but above all else I want you to always know...

    I love you and think about you every day! I can't wait to come home and experience life with you, to shower you with love and make up for every day we've lost! I want to make you proud to call me Dad.
    I want you to know it was the absolute worst mistake of my life to make the choices that led to me leaving you! It hurts every day! I am truly, truly sorry!
    I am going to make it up to you, I will make it up to you! So that these days will be forgotten, the memory swallowed up by tons of fun times and good memories, that we will laugh and talk about with family and friends, when we are both old and grey.
    I want you to be happy and successful. So, always be aware of how your actions affect your life and others. Take life slow and plan, don't live the fast life, life is chess not checkers. Sometimes people make mistakes, and life isn't always fair. But no matter what happens in your life, you have to fight to not let anger, sadness, and other negative thoughts and feeling stake hold in your heart. Because then you will make decisions based on these thoughts and feelings and just like a poison or disease they will spread through your life. They will rob you of love, peace, happiness, and freedom—all the good things!
    I want you to always know everyone has problems, some just hide it better, so don't get caught up in comparisons. Successful people fight for what they believe

in, for what they know and want in life. What makes a loser is not what place you come in, but the effort you put in! You are somebody and all things are possible, and your father loves you with all his heart!

Love,
Dad

> "Know who you are as a young man, your strengths, as well as your weaknesses. Never be afraid to fail at anything because failing or losing gives you more room to grow, to learn where or how you went wrong. And in this you become a better and stronger you."

❤

D.L. White

To my son Davaren (AKA D.J),

I just wanted to take some time to talk to you about a few things. First, I love you and always will. Second, I want you to know nothing in this world should come before family. And to be the best at anything takes hard work and dedication on your part. What I'm telling you will determine who you become in this world.

Being that I'm in here, I now have a better understanding on what this means, and how distracting and noisy the world can be. I'm asking you to have confidence in yourself to accomplish any goals you set. I'm always going to want the best for you, son. Know who you are as a young man, your strengths, as well as your weaknesses. Never be afraid to fail at anything because failing or losing gives you more room to grow, to learn where or how you went wrong. And in this you become a better and stronger you. Try not to make excuses for anything you may do but take responsibility and learn from each and every experience. This, later in life, will make you harder to knock down and a dominant force in this world. DJ, whatever you want in life can be yours. But I want you to understand something: nothing is given to you in life. Focus, drive, and your determination are what reward you your dreams. Study hard in school, listen to your mother even if you don't understand why. Just trust she has your best interest at heart.

I wish I could be there to watch you grow up. It tears my heart apart that I can't. Know that it's not your fault but mine. If you take nothing else from me, take that in your life your actions always have consequences. Always try to do the right thing even when everyone else is doing the wrong thing. You set the example. Don't be like your ol' man. Be better than me.
I love you son to the moon and back,

Your Dad: Derek L. White

"Regardless of what your view may be, time has the ability to teach or torment. And it is how you approach either one, that will determine exactly who you are."

♥

Alfonso Skyles

I may not be there in person now, but above all else I want you to always know...

In the beginning, I never thought that I could do this much time. Knowing that I had no choice in freely coming and going, having no idea of what to expect weighed so heavily on my heart. There was no way to prepare for a place that I had never been, no way to imagine the impact it would have on my life. I don't think that I've ever reached the worst of it. But I've definitely witnessed its effects on the sickened bodies and in the broken spirits of imprisoned men.

As the earth continued to spin on its axis, I began to only see time as a looming shadow, instead of a clock face and swinging pendulum. I was at the mercy of a sentence that felt more like a paragraph, livelihood, and the elements of circumstance. Having to come to terms with the fact that I would lose all of the important people in my life, left me plagued with moments of depressing thoughts, thoughts that if spoken aloud would only lend weight to the very questioning of my own sanity. Sanity—there were times that I even questioned my own. I fought against the most primal urges to hurt others as a result of the pain I was feeling, never completely sure that prison life was even worth me living. It seemed just easier to die.

Having to accept the freedom I lost was easy, but I had become terrified of the things that I still stood to lose. We are only three or four generations removed from it being illegal to read, write, or even name your child after yourself. But yet, I had squandered every opportunity and sacrifices that had been made for me to avoid such suffering. All I could think about was a fortunate turn around that would provide some kind of early release, or at least the chance to earn my freedom. It was as simple as putting on the headphones and closing my eyes. I daydreamed of everything a young man in their early twenties would be experiencing, or at least what I thought they would be doing. Life was as illustrious as an awakening twilight.

See, what I was never told was that there were no rewards for actually changing, no benefits gained for really becoming a better person than you were when you came in. No, I'm not perfect. I'm not an individual who had the answers to questions I should've never been asked. For my actions, I deserved what those actions had earned. Craving a miracle should've been my name. They all watched as I sat. My posture was straight, my eyes attentive, and I had once again become my mother's son, for it is only her who proves to stand firm in spite of it all. Street credibility served no purpose on that day. Who I was known to be in the eyes of my peers had succumb to wounds of truth and authenticity, Dwindling ideas of nothing worth mentioning sat alone as I shed the mask I had been wearing.

I used to really believe that I was "bout that life", figuring that I had time to check and correct myself when I was done being reckless. Sometimes I wonder if I was just displeased with who I was as an individual, and that's why I strove to be accepted by those I thought were relevant and cool. To me, the skin that I was in was alright, but it wasn't what everyone else's was, and it didn't get me the attention I was looking for. There were times that I was so embarrassed, I would skip school to avoid the jokes that would come my way—sharp whispers that slashed at an already apprehensive ego. We're just now starting to shed light on bullying, but I can tell you from experience, it has always been a factor in shaping the temperament, behavior, and identities of children.

My mother once told me that I needed to forgive myself or else I'd never fully heal and have a life that I could enjoy. And as I tried, I realized that the dead will forever be linked to the living, and being able to move forward means to do so without living in regret. I will never forget his name. I will never forget the eyes of his mother or the quiet strength I witnessed in his father as he informed the courtroom about his son. While there was a crowded space, it felt like only he and I remained. I was becoming acquainted with every memory and dream he had, every moment shared, and every lesson taught. Everyone lost something that day—branded images that would remain without request.

The last meaningful conversation I had as a free man was with my mother. With tears in her eyes, it was as if she had read me from cover to cover. I can describe that entire conversation, the way she looked, and the point of clarity made on a statement, "Skip, the devil's got a hold of you." At the time, no one knew what kind of trouble I was in. That statement broke through every single barrier established to protect myself, laying low shoulders that were not equipped to handle such situations. She would forever be my champion, but this was something that I would have to endure on my own, and this was something that she knew. People will come and go, but I will remain is what she told me. They will fake a stay is what she meant.

Twenty plus years—equivalent to 7665 days—almost a quarter of a century has passed since I've known what it is to be physically free. I've gone from having no beard, to being able to grow one. And the very beard I've been able to grow, has now grown grey. There's a stark reminder with every glance in the mirror of just how long it's been. Where there use to be an irresponsible and unaccountable young man, now stands the very opposite of him. I'm more than they thought I would become, more than something basic and recognizable. I longingly want my freedom. We will set our goals and won't let anyone else set them for us. But I'm afraid that the movie I'm watching may end prematurely, that the storyline doesn't match the script.

Maybe there will always be pain on my doorstep, a common void upon my windowpane. What is typical has been made natural, the usual as clear to see so usually. It is such an absence, such a debilitating waste.

I may not be there in person right now, but above all else, I want you to always know...

Criticism? In our neighborhoods, if you drove a nice car, do you know what they said about it? That you didn't pay for it. If you wore your clothes a certain way, then they questioned your sexuality. If you were smart in school, then you were a nerd or fell into second class citizenship. If you had a disability, they highlighted it, and made sure you were reminded of every limitation. There's no praise, not even if you've earned it, only criticism and the need to scrutinize what's misunderstood or different.

They tried to bury us, but had no idea that we were seeds–beauty sprouting from what was thought to be a deathly resting place. I am untitled, I am my ancestors, I am the bluesy sound of heavy rain, I am more, I am life and light, so on and so forth. I am exactly what they wanted me to be, rehabbed from my own deficiencies, cleaned up, eyes wide open, and completely aware of who I am and who I use to be. They fear me. As a matter of fact, they fear us! Not for the threat of our fists or feet, but our ability to think, rationalize, and speak eloquently with truth and conviction in tones that sound off so melodically. I am everything they said I could never be, that which they thought long died in the breast of my predecessors. More than the brand of "Brand News", we are far greater than the brands that branded us.

Our lives hold many lessons. And in between the tests, there comes a knowing, a quiet awareness of what's required to move to the next phase, the next level, the place where the blessings start to flow. I am inspired by the fire of a fighter, the desire of a dreamer, and the tenacity of an artist. Clarified is the world outside my window. I move differently, I think differently, and I speak differently. I realize that I am living for so much more. Perspective and patience guide the ambitious, challenge and triumph cultivate the individual. Individually, we war for the ability to be recognized. In solidarity, we strive for the right to be accepted, as we are, indivisibly. Socially, we search for an identity that is harvested from memories coveted, and some forgotten. The record of events says that I'm not supposed to know any better. The Eugenicist made sure they stepped up their efforts on policies to separate the races. By pushing pseudoscientific IQ tests, they try to argue that I'm intellectually inferior to whites. But I, and those who've proceeded me, made liars out of their deceptively wagging tongues. In knowing what they know not, or choose to ignore, we will always be asked to do the most with the least.

The biggest myth is that the poor quality of our situations exists because we don't want better. The myth that we are satisfied with the limited opportunities we're given, has long been a tool that has been used to discourage efforts of venturing out into something else. Government, education, business, technology, and agriculture, are all sectors that we have begun to tiptoe in, rather than stomping our way through. We readily step over those dollars in order to pick up leftover dimes, settling for the invite, instead of taking our rightful seat at the table. What's sad is that, most of these pervasive myths are held by peoples of color—the self-shackling their own feet.

But it is in that space between fear and exploration that the seeds of our mutual empowerment and liberation are planted. We no longer live in a time where adults or wise elders are, or need to be, the keepers of all knowledge. So to push a culture, there must be an acceptance of generational change and adaptability. For instance, when a child is over-helped it can lead to a path of false expectations. The obstacles that are cleared out of their way by a parent or elder, can ultimately become a harm for them. Getting rid of those bumps of life, robs the child of the necessary experience of learning and failing, overcoming and conceding. As we rush to fix every little blemish in our child's life or try to influence their way to success, we cause more irreparable damage than we know.

Matters will most certainly determine their consequences, intentions will determine the value of ones reward. Insurrection? Civil disobedience? You can't organize on behalf of the people, if the people you're organizing for aren't a part of the organization. Yes, it's hard to be heard, and it's even more difficult to be listened to. But there has to be a place where complacency ends, and the passion for change begins. So what do you do? I guess if you can't do the impossible, then you do the honorable. Should it be foul that the Sun rises and sets, or that the flowers grow from soil made fertile from buried body and bone? Regardless of what your view may be, time has the ability to teach or torment. And it is how you approach either one, that will determine exactly who you are.

"One thing about this place is that it cannot take away my memories—such as when you guys would make forts in the living room, going on trips, chasing you boys around the yard with clippers and an extension cord. You three have truly made my life worth living."

❤

Kevin L.

Z, J & L,

Remember—no matter what—I'll always love you.

Z,

I hear from your mother that you are starting to slide down a slippery slope. My advice is to stop while you are still ahead. Times have changed a lot since I was your age. Don't throw away your future due to someone else's actions. So you may ask, "Dad, that's great advice but how do you go about that?" The trick is to focus on your long-term goal and think to yourself before you make a decision: "will this possibly ruin my ability to attain my goal?" I know you have a lot of talent and ability to focus though your choice of professional football team screams glutton for punishment.

J,

I know you don't care for school, but you still have to go. Think of it as in life, half of it is just showing up. You'll do fine in life, you just need to make it through school. Like I told you on the phone—I don't care if you get A's, B's, or C's, just avoid the D's and E/F's and get that diploma! You have always been excellent at teaching yourself new skills and that is truly awesome. Keep marching to the sound of your own drum—or guitar riff. You are going to do well.

L,

Keep working on your reading and writing. You have an excellent work ethic and that will take you far—very, very far. Also, keep working with your hands and stay active. You have always made friends easily and that is an excellent attribute. Pursue your dreams and enjoy what you do if you are going to spend a lot of time doing it. Remember to always be you!

Z, J, & L,

I have missed a lot of y'all's lives due to the wars and deployments and work. Combat was dangerous yet exciting and there was an overall purpose to it. However, this experience has taught me that someone's lies and accusations are far more dangerous and destructive. One thing about this place is that it cannot take away my memories—such as when you guys would make forts in the living room, going on trips, chasing you boys around the yard with clippers and an extension cord. You three have truly made my life worth living and as I said before, I will always love you.

> "It's also important to know your past does not define your future but it is what you learn from."

❤

Christine White

Dear Matthew, Luke, & Sofia,

I may not be there in person now but above all else I want you to know that I love you more than words can begin to express. My poor choices had nothing to do with you but everything to do with how broken I was back then. I take full responsibility for my actions and lay the blame nowhere but upon my own shoulders. In life it is important not to shirk responsibility or point our fingers at others when we are to blame. It's also important to know your past does not define your future but it is what you learn from. I heard this quote and thought it fitting for this journey: "not all storms come just to disrupt your life. Some come to clear your path." And I know without a doubt this is true. God used this situation not only for my ultimate good but possibly for yours too. No longer am I broken. So much healing has occurred behind these brick walls and bars. Depression, anxiety, anger, and unforgiveness—all gone. Alcoholism—gone. This benefits you because not only can the three of you learn from my mistakes, but you will have a mom who is healthy, happy, and whole. God cleaned the debris from my mind, heart, and soul. He filled my spirit with joy, humility, and gratitude. No longer will I take life or you three precious kiddos for granted. Please forgive me, because I know it came at such a high cost to you and to your childhood. You should have had a mom to comfort, teach, and play with you these last seven years. I am sure it has been hard on you and for that I am so very sorry.

    Know that I love you dearly, pray for you daily, and

Parent, Trapped

miss you like crazy.

XOXO
All my love,
Mom

"And that secret is that I never knew how to be a father. And I'm willing to learn if you will help me. I don't want you to allow these walls to come between us. Just because I'm in prison I might be locked up, but I'm not locked out."

❤

Born Mathematics Allah

Dear child of mine,

I know that I'm probably the last person that you want to hear from. Then again, I could be selfish. And you have been waiting for a long time for this day, this letter, a chance to connect and finally start and have a relationship with me, "Your Father."

 I know by me not being there in your life, it has caused quite a few circumstances to arise, not only in your mental state, but also in how you act and express yourself. I know that you have heard a lot of things about me. And by me being in prison it may seem like a "dirty glass" on a table. I'm not telling you to put or throw away the "dirty glass." I'm just asking you to allow me to place a clean one up beside it. Yes, I would be a liar if I told you some of the things that you've heard weren't true. But the truth of that is that I love you–never stopped loving you–and I want a chance to show and express that love to you.

 First things first, I want to tell you about a secret that I had balled up in me for so long. And that secret is that I never knew how to be a father. But I'm willing to learn if you will help me. I don't want you to allow these walls to come between us. Just because I'm in prison I might be locked up, but I'm not locked out. It's sad to say that it had to take coming and being in prison to learn how to recognize and take responsibilities for my own actions. Society tends to shine or have a negative outlook on prison. Don't get it twisted, because there is a lot wrong and bad circumstances. But again, don't be one of those who are on the outside looking in. Listen to me, child of mine, prison is like fire. And a two-edged sword. If you are in harmony with it, it will shape and mold you. If not, it will burn you. Me, I saw what prison can do to those who chose the latter. So I chose to be in harmony with the fire. I got my G.E.D., college crews, picked up a couple of trades–electrical, custodial maintenance–learned Spanish as a second language, earned an associates in Business Ethics and got certified in Serv Safe for the food industry. I've accomplished a lot. But what I want to really accomplish is to have a relationship with you. To be the father the Creator intended for me to be. I know you're like, "that's prison talk." Yeah, you're right, it is. Because if I would have stayed in the streets you would have never had the chance to read these words. The road that I was going down, I would have died. I know that it's hard for a child to tell their friends that their mother or father is in prison. Look at the bright side, you said prison not the grave. Remember, child of mine, a wounded Lion is better than a dead dog anyway. (Smile.)

    I leave this letter saying these words to you, child of mine, and to other children who have parents in prison: My love is like a cold glass of water. Set it on a table, you can see it. It's transparent. You can see through it but you can't see the power in it. I love you child of mine. Love, hell or right. If you love someone you will go through hell with them until they come out right. I know that some of us parents confuse the words love and responsibilities. And I learned the reason why children are so rebellious is because we didn't know we were attacking your personal desires. I want to write more but I'm getting emotional. What if these were my last words and you would read it?

Your Father,
Quincy E. Glen
A.K.A. Born Mathematics Allah

> "I want you all to know that genuine change demands nothing less than an abiding faith that you can become the person you want to be, that you can do whatever you put your mind to, and you can have whatever you want in life..."

♥

Keith Emmander Harris

Being a father behind bars has been both painful and challenging for me. Though I've had limited communication and physical contact with you all I truly want you to know that I love you with all my heart and soul and you all are the source of my motivation to live, learn, and grow as a better father and man.

Every award, certification, and program I complete is solely to increase the contents of my character, so that when I am released from prison I can be a productive member of society and in my own community. I want you all to know that genuine change demands nothing less than an abiding faith that you can become the person you want to be, that you can do whatever you put your mind to, and you can have whatever you want in life, just as Dad is doing now. I want you all to know that in the lonely hours of reflecting on my life I was able to see how conflicted and confused I was about my role in life. Dad was a mess. However, I have long since acknowledged that I needed to get my act together for the sake of myself, my children and my grandchildren.

Today, my four beautiful children and grandchildren, I am free of the guilt and pain of my crimes, and I am moving forward in my new way of life. Life has new meaning to me now. I want to do more than just get out of prison. Dad is going to stay out! Please, all of you, build yourselves up in faith and knowledge and make yourselves worthy of better surroundings and wider opportunities.

Before I close, I will be grateful to say these words to my children and grandchildren, and all those who may have the opportunity to read this: use your innate ability to recognize the strength and goodness in others, be sincere in your purpose, humble in your heart, and have full recognition of the truth that you nor any man or woman knows everything. Also remember to be of service to others, be grateful to God above all things, and my most humbling advice to you all would be to embark upon the journey to recover and restore the God nature and Christ conscious within yourself, a journey that I am still upon.

"If circumstances had the power to bless or harm, they would bless and harm all people alike, but the fact that the same circumstances will be alike good and bad to different people proves that good or bad is not in the circumstance, but only in the minds of those who encounter it."
- From the book: *As A Man Thinketh, So Is He*

This quote inspired me beyond words. It helped me to realize that I am bigger than my circumstances. In my final words to each of my children individually, may each of you be inspired by this. Jamal Long my oldest, remember, "I love you son and I'm proud of you." To you Jasheka Pryor, "You can do it if you believe you can, baby girl." To Taaj Macklin, "A single failure does not mean a permanent failure." And last, but not least, my youngest, our little princess, Kecharn Harris, "Self-management of your mind is the key to all your success, little one." I pray you all continue to be blessed and know that I will love you from wherever I am because you four are my reason to live.

Love,
Dad

"Sure, there's also pain and sadness in life, but how would we know happiness if we couldn't compare it to sadness? Everything would just be bland if there weren't ups and downs. There would be no reason to get out of bed if we couldn't make the day a bit better."

♥

John F. Ballentine

To Gina Marie, on Your Wedding Day (10-8-11)

My baby girl, I wasn't there when you came into this world. Nor was I there to hold your hand when you took your first steps, or when you got on the school bus for the first time. I am not able to walk you down the aisle to give you away to a far better man who will take care of you.

And yet, you have grown into a beautiful and smart woman in spite of my bad influence. I am so very proud of you.

Today is your wedding, a day of great happiness and joy. It is a day of new beginnings. You and Larry are now forever entwined. Two have become one. You are now a team.

I have no present, but I hope to give you a thought that may stay with you.

It is easy to think that the grass is greener on the other side, but it isn't. The reason for this is because you view grass with your eyes. It is still your personal perception. Everything looks the same if you are depressed. Everything looks the same because it is you who is doing the looking. The only way the view changes is if your outlook changes.

I'll give you an example of what I'm trying to say. It is easy for you to blame your mom for a lot of things, but that is wrong. Your mom gave you life when nobody else would, including me. So when you think about it, your ability to get mad at your mom is a present from her!

Parent, Trapped

She gave you life, and everything else is secondary from that fact. Everything else builds upon that foundation. You couldn't be happy right now if you weren't alive. The pure and simple fact is that you couldn't experience Larry's love, the fun, the sorrows of life, if you weren't living, right? Everything depends upon giving life. It is a God-like action, this giving of life. And your mom did that for you.

So the grass upon which you stand is the greenest.

And the life you now enter upon is a gift that you may give to others. Gina, you and Larry can now procreate, cooperate with God in His divine action of giving divine life to others, so that they, too, can experience some of the happiness and joys life brings that you were given.

Sure, there's also pain and sadness in life, but how would we know happiness if we couldn't compare it to sadness? Everything would just be bland if there weren't ups and downs. There would be no reason to get out of bed if we couldn't make the day a bit better.

How would you know that you love Larry if you didn't know that other guys act like jerks?

Giving happiness to others brings happiness to the giver, doesn't it? You feel good when you do something for Larry, don't you? Think about how happy you will feel when you give the ultimate gift of life! And down the road, just as your life brought joy to Larry and me and others, your children will bring joy to you and others. I know that we joke about being barefoot and pregnant. But you cannot save up to afford a baby. You'll never save enough because life is priceless. You can never afford it because it is a gift! You were given life free of charge. And there is not much you can do when life leaves you. When the Big Guy says it is time to go, you gotta go.

So all that gobble-de-goofy-speak about saving up to afford a baby doesn't make sense. Life is lived one day at a time, so you just pay on the installment plan! You bought your car on payment plans, right? And a car has a price tag, life doesn't. You could total your car and just be thankful that you lived through the wreck. Life is much more important than a car. You'll never ever be ready to be a parent. How many times did you giggle because you freaked your mom out over something you did as a child? She wasn't ready for half the stuff you did! Again, you take life on as a daily thing.

We love to make plans, as if we really have control. But we aren't promised tomorrow, are we? It is now your turn, Gina, to give others a life just like your mom did for you. Look at how happy you have made people with your life. You and Larry love one another in truth, and love isn't always pretty or flattering, as you have found out. You two remain truthful, abide in truth and love, and you will prevail.

A dude named Pascal said it much better than I can, but I can relate it to your life better than that rascal: we run carelessly to the precipice only after placing something before our eyes. We conceal the present from our sight because it troubles us...we try to sustain it for the future and try to arrange matters...but it is not in our power. There is no certainty in our reaching the future...but all of our thoughts are occupied with it. The present is never our end, so we never really live. We always plan to be happy and are never so.

Be happy today, Gina. Plan for your future happiness. Live in the present. Bring life. God will provide.

That is my present to you.

I love you, now in the present and always!

Daddy
Ave Maria

Originally published by John F. Ballentine, in *Thunder in the Cell: Catholic Apologetics for Convicts and Prisoners of Doubt*; 2018, 40-43.

"When I get y'all in my arms, just remember it's a new sign of life, a new beginning, and a story that ends with true happiness for us as a family."

❤

Robert Crawford-Bey

(I shall share...)
"I may not be there in person now, but above all else I want you to always know"
I shall share a Note expressed by an Oath, And
sealed with a kiss.
From a father who Really cares, About his
Children he Really Miss
For 2 be A King, A Father of a child
A Nobel Husband of A Wife, A foundation has been Found
Words of the Lost,
Run through My Mind at Night.
Why did it Have 2 come this Far, For Me Have 2 Fight
Fight for a Wish, Maybe A Little Hope.
Fight for Understanding, Even Such Freedom
2 Come 2 Light.
A Dream that shall come true, Without a Father
Fight.
Well Rooted, Beyond Any Bond,
Not even a Judge can take away,
A father Aspects of Life is ParentHood.
It's for him 2 LOVE and STAY.
I shall share a Note expressed by an Oath, And
Sealed with a kiss
From Your Father who Really cares, About his
Children, That he Truly do Miss...
(We shall Teach....)
We shall teach our Children Obedience,
So They can conquer their Lower-Self.
We shall teach them Modesty, and

they shall not be Ashamed.
WE shall teach them Gratitude, and
they shall receive Grace.
WE shall teach them Charity, and
they shall gain Love.
We shall teach them Patience, and
they shall gain Knowledge, In Time, They
Will become Wise.
We shall teach our Children Justice.
(In all Degree's)
So They shall be honored by the world.
We shall teach them Sincerity, and
Their own Heart shall not Reproach them.
We shall teach them Benevolence, and
their Minds shall be Exalted.
We shall Present True Science, and
their Life shall be useful.
We shall teach them Religion, and
they shall Understand, The Divine Love within...

"Daddy may not be there in person now, But above all else,
I want y'all to Always know"
    I Love Y'all more than Life it's Self,
Knowing our Journey has been Long and Hard
But now it Must come to a End.
When I get y'all in my Arms, Just Remember
It's a New Sign of Life, A New Beginning,
And, A Story that End with True
    Happiness For Us As A Family.
Daddy Loves, An Miss' you More
Lil DK, Sahrea, A'Mollian,
See You Soon. :)

DAD

> "...I wanted you to know of how proud I am of how you turned out. No father could wish for better daughters."

♥

Siddiq M. Salam

May 2020

My mother asked me once after she overheard me advising you about boys, why do I speak to you in such a tone which has always been straightforward and to the point? And I'm writing this letter to you because you may now, as grown women with children of your own, be wondering the same thing now that you are looking back on our conversations when you were younger. The truth is I was scared for you both because I was in prison, and I knew I would be unable to protect you from life's pit falls and hardships like all fathers live to do so I never blind folded you to the reality of this cold world. I know it has to be even colder for little girls without their fathers around to kiss their knees when they fall down, or attend your basketball games, or a modeling shoot, or make you a big breakfast in the morning before you go out to take your SAT tests, or to simply hold you in my arms and wipe your tears and tell you that everything will be okay no matter who or what it was that had upset you!

I'm also writing this letter to you both because I wanted you to know how proud I am of how you turned out. No father could wish for better daughters. I would like to believe that my straight talk with you both, that some believed was too authoritarian for little girls, helped mold you into the women you have become today!

I have missed your adolescent years and the joy and pain of being a father to you both, but once I'm released, I'm hoping you will allow me to be your friend!

Love Always,

Dad

February 2019

"Get Rich or Die Trying." The saying is old now, but it is still applied and actively practiced throughout the streets of America. Men are so focused on acquiring wealth, large homes, expensive cars, and beautiful women that once these goals are accomplished, then they must spend the rest of their lives trying to safeguard and protect them from loss. In reality, there is nothing wrong with having the finer things in life, except for when we make these things the purpose and drive behind our living and dying.

In contrast to the "Get Rich or Die Trying" philosophy practiced by the misguided masses, the Muslim say, "certainly, my prayer, my sacrifice, my living, and my dying are all for Allah the lord of everything that exists," so how can we consider ourselves intelligent beings when we are willing to die and make sacrifices for created things such as money, jewelry, cars, homes, and the "Hood," but we're not willing to sacrifice, pray, live, and die for the one who created all of those perishable things? Just look at all the wealthy men who committed suicide by injecting the same narcotics that once made them money making legends around the way?

You see wealth and success without knowledge and guidance only leads the way to misery, and it's a fact that what is valued and highly desirable today in the material world, will soon be worthless.

So I propose a slogan for the new millennium and beyond, "Get Right or Live Trying!" Being incarcerated we waste so many minutes and so many days of our lives involved in things that will not benefit us in here, on the streets, or in the Hereafter. Activities such as gambling, getting high, gang banging, or just larceny in general. Many of us have children, wives, or girlfriends that we are unable to teach anything beneficial, because we gather all of our knowledge and vernacular from the latest rap CD of the latest XXL, King, or Don Diva magazines. The majority of us have mentalities and vocabularies shaped by the media and music industries, and we as a prison community allow ourselves to sit dormant, pacified like babies with the comforts of a commissary system that helps them fund and finance our incarceration. In other words, we're paying them to keep us locked up. BET leads us to believe that all minorities do with their lives is sing, dance, joke, and spend their money on intoxicants and fashion. It's time for us incarcerated men "To Get Right!"

Recently a female friend wrote me explaining the conversation and mind state of the majority of men out there, she said, "the only conversing they do is to ask when and where can we have sex!" We as men have to elevate our minds past the level of only sexual and animalistic thoughts and speech. Basically, it's time we start functioning at the highest capacity of human thought and action available to us. Our children need fathers that do more than just put fly sneakers on their feet and designer clothes on their backs. They need fathers that can teach them their purpose in life, without finding pleasure in exposing them to the street life. No, in order to teach them what the purpose of life is, we must know and understand it ourselves, and those answers can only be found in the authentic teachings of Al-Islam! See, many of us live in our own realities and we claim that we are upon the truth, so I challenge you to put your reality, your way of life, your religion, and your personal philosophy to the test, and if it holds up in debate, then I will be forced to consider your way of life as the undisputed truth. But on the flip side, if your personal philosophy, reality, way of life, or religion takes a beating and exits the ring bruised, battered, or knocked out, then I encourage you to study and look into the perfection of Al-Islam for the answer to the question: "What is the purpose of life?"

Just something to think about,

***

Siddiq M. Salam

> "When I gave someone permission to make me feel inferior, I learned later on it was my response that gave it to them. Getting defensive, giving the response they were anticipating. Caring about what they and everybody else thought. When I stopped responding, giving them what they wanted, that was when I took back the power they took from me."

♥

Robert L. Guillory

Dear Alie,

I may not be there in person now, but above all else I want you to know this: no one can make you feel inferior without your permission. Allowing someone to make you second-guess yourself—whether it be your thoughts or actions—you are giving them dominion over you. In the ten plus years I've been away, I have both grown and regressed as a person. There were times I have felt inferior to someone because I allowed them to make me feel that way. That is the worst possible feeling one can have. It feels like your soul has surrendered to a force that is greater than you. That is the regression that I have experienced.

No, as I put these words on paper, I have taken that power back and will never relinquish it again. Behind these walls are men who want to be a better person in the eyes of those in here and men who want to be a better person for those who are waiting for them outside these walls. There will be times when those who want to look better to their fellow "inmates" at the expense of another, giving them that inferiority complex they were seeking. I once heard someone say that, "life is ten percent what happens to you and ninety percent how you respond." When I gave someone permission to make me feel inferior, I learned later on it was my response that gave it to them. Getting defensive, giving the response they were anticipating. Caring about what they and everybody else thought. When I stopped responding, giving them what they wanted, that was when I took back the power they took from me. That was when I started to grow, to become the person I want to be when I walk out from behind these walls to you.

My life may not have turned out the way I planned it. I have clearly made mistakes that I regret. But you are the greatest accomplishment I have given to this world. You can achieve any goal you seek. Don't let anyone tell you different, thereby giving them the power they desire.

Your Father,
Robert L. Guillory J.R.

"Life is about choices, even the most meaningless decisions can impact your life in ways you will not understand until years later. When you have an important choice in life to make, don't follow your heart, it carries the weight of the world. Don't listen to your head, our heads carry the recent chatter of the day and can be ego driven. Go with your gut instinct. It has the high ground and cannot be influenced by you or anyone. It carries your moral compass and is never wrong."

♥

Brian

Dear Zach, Anna, & Emory,

I love and miss you all. I may not be there in person now, but above all else I want you to always know my time away from you has not diminished my love for you. A lot of times I just sit and think of y'all, what might be going on in your lives, what paths you may be taking. I miss the silly little conversations we used to have, playing Sonic the Hedgehog, having meals together. All those little things mean so much to me. They are the golden moments of my days now.

 I used to get so angry at my dad all the time. I spent a lot of time thinking negative things about him for not doing this or messing up that. I just considered him a failure. At that time, it was me who failed to realize that at least he was there, and he was trying. He may have messed up here and there and done some things wrong, but he was there and at least he was trying.

 Now that time has gone by, I realize how wrong I was about my father and how my life and absence of my life has affected yours, more than likely in a negative manner. I'm not there for you now. I'm not helping, not giving encouragement. I'm not even there so you can call me a sorry piece of shit. I don't even get to make the category of a failure. I feel like a nothing, like a sperm donor. It's something that gives me a heavy heart and something I will have no choice but to deal with.

I am so sorry I let you down and please don't waste your time being angry at me. Life is too short. If anything, look at my life as an example of what not to do. Life is about choices, even the most meaningless decisions can impact your life in ways you will not understand until years later. When you have an important choice in life to make, don't follow your heart, it carries the weight of the world. Don't listen to your head, our heads carry the recent chatter of the day and can be ego driven. Go with your gut instinct. It has the high ground and cannot be influenced by you or anyone. It carries your moral compass and is never wrong. I didn't listen and now I'm paying the price.

I think that when we die, we go meet our maker. This being will not judge us or condemn us. It will give us the knowledge and understanding of everything. Everything. And after you soak in all this knowledge and understanding, our maker will ask us, "are you here now with clean hands and clear eyes?"

When I am released, I want to right my wrongs, cleanse myself. I am trying now and I hope one day you can find it within yourself to forgive me and I think you will. Can I forgive myself? No, I don't think I can. I don't feel worthy. I don't think I can.

I love y'all,
Dad

"Every day I'm here is a day closer to me coming home to physically see the fruits of your labor. Live your life to the fullest. Don't hold back and really enjoy every day. Make those memories and share them with the people who are important to you. You can never lose those memories. Please keep sharing them with me."

❤

Mark S.

Dear kids,

I hope you guys know how much I love you all. I also hope that during our time together you have felt the love from me and know the love you've brought me. Being incarcerated has made me appreciate all of the little things in life. I also get reminders of things we shared in our past that usually aren't top of mind. Images of sporting events, cheering, school orientations, holidays, car rides, etc. constantly pop up in my head. Good times and bad times, laughs and tears show up. Throughout all of these events and times the only constant is my love for you.

    I know me being here means I miss most big events like graduations, college admissions, children, new career paths and many more. I know this is not what anyone wants, and I'm sorry for that. Even though I may not be there to celebrate these milestones in your life, don't think for one minute that I don't feel the joy and happiness from your achievements. I beam with pride thinking about these things and I know you have a lot to offer this world. Do not let anyone tell you different or let them bring you down.

    Every day I'm here is a day closer to me coming home to physically see the fruits of your labor. Live your life to the fullest. Don't hold back and really enjoy every day. Make those memories and share them with the people who are important to you. You can never lose those memories.

Please keep sharing them with me. I know it's not the same as me being there, but hearing the happiness in your voice brings me some as well.

    I love you guys so much and I think about you every day. I've made mistakes and I own those mistakes, but I will never not love you and I will never forsake you. You are my children and the ultimate loves of my life. Stay true to yourself, be there for one another, and always show love and respect for each other and the people around you. This is one way you will always make a difference. Stay safe out there in that crazy world we have, and just know I miss you and I love you.

Love,
Dad

"...we are born into this world for each other to love, live, and encourage one another through our individual journeys, not to bring hurt, harm, or destruction. People and the relationship we have are the most precious items on earth next to the earth itself for neither can be replaced. We should live our lives to love all and encourage others to do the same. Love is the only thing that will transcend space, time, and loss to keep our loved ones close."

❤

Carlos Raymond Robinson

Dear Carlos,

I may not be there in person now, but above all else I want you to know that in spite of my prolonged physical absence, you are always loved, always in my thoughts, and always in my prayers. I have been gone since you were three-years-old and it still amazes me how much you remember from those times: our home, the cookouts in the parks, the fishing and crabbing. I always wanted more for you than I had but I failed miserably in that respect because my father was there for me. You are 31-years-old now with a life you built that I can take no credit for. Since 1991 I've always thought that I would somehow make it all up to you one day, but I know the reality is I can never make up for the times you needed me to learn how to be a strong, loving, honorable man. I was not there. The times when you had to explain away my absence when your friends or teachers never saw your father. The times when life at home was hurtful or when you needed to seek refuge and reassurance at my side. I was not there. My heart spills over with grief for living a reckless, selfish life when I should have been stronger and self-less for you and our family.

 Son, I can admit to you that I devalued my own life by making the choices that ultimately ended in a lengthy incarceration and tore up two families. That is my cross to bear. Through it all and against all odds you took a stand and have never seen the inside of a jail cell. I am so proud of you and thankful to God and your grandmothers for raising you in my absence with love and compassion, celebrating your success and encouraging you through your mistakes. For you growing through the trials of youth and being strong enough to choose a better life for yourself.

I watched you grow up in the visitation room from a baby until you were 21. Since then, even though you are physically free and living your best life, it feels like you are locked up too not having seen you in ten years. I pray that one day we can sit down and talk about it all without the interruption of a Global-Tel operator alerting us that we have one minute remaining on the only communication we have.

In closing son, I want to share with you the most important lesson I have learned throughout my life, that we are born into this world for each other to love, live, and encourage one another through our individual journeys, not to bring hurt, harm, or destruction. People and the relationships we have are the most precious items on earth next to the earth itself, for neither can be replaced. We should live our lives to love all and encourage others to do the same. Love is the only thing that will transcend space, time, and loss to keep our loved ones close. I'm so very proud of your life son. Continue to live, learn, love, and always be thankful to God.

Love you son,
your Dad

Other Family

Another powerful lesson that's fallen from this darkness and knocked me on the head is: love cannot be silenced.

A voice is a fundamental part of our humanity, and to express our emotions is to act, to be human. Other creatures do so, too, sure, but it is the ability to share emotional bonds and the languages we've developed to share them that make us human and first allowed us to evolve these big, rational parts of our brains that differentiate us.

Yet this system silences people. Intentionally. They are not officially allowed to stop us from writing letters, but those letters are subject to censorship and each stamp costs more than an hour's pay. The phones, the email, they exist but are prohibitively expensive and only reach those we already know. Anything we want to say is filtered through authority and the stigma of a big, red stamp on the envelope that says it's prison-born. When it arrives, most of what we say is ignored or assumed useless or untrue. It took me, with all my degrees and experience, years and countless failures to even get a poem or essay published obscurely. That is why we began The Humanization Project.

Coming from a platform with a megaphone, muzzled silence was a very difficult transition for me. In compiling this book, though, I have realized that it is even worse for those who have never had a chance to speak, yet have so much to say. When given the chance, people of character need speak their truths. Even when not permitted freely, people of character will speak of love.

My eyes were opened to this when this project first began. I was invited to speak about it at the weekly meeting for Nation of Gods & Earths, a religious program focused on building understanding and knowledge and strong families and communities—basically the perfect place to seek dedicated writers and fathers. I knew most of the guys to be thoughtful people and a few had helped with other humanization efforts. Still, I was blown away by the response.

Not only did every single parent there eagerly volunteer to participate, they extended the project inadvertently. Swill looked over at me after my explanation, and said, "That sounds awesome and I really want to write something, but I don't have kids. Can I write one to my mom? She's my rock."

On the spot, looking at his face, hearing his desire to do something positive and have it be for his beloved mother, I gladly invited him. I decided I'd figure out how to make the segue in the future. The point of the book, after all, is a chance to shout our human voices about the love between a parent and child.

Then, as I continued to invite guys I knew to be parents, their enthusiasm continued to saturate this compound. Repeatedly, guys without kids but with powerful voices and strong family bonds wanted to be part of our mission.

This final section is that unsolicited but enthusiastically included collection of voices from children who have grown up behind bars to the parents who helped them survive these circumstances. These are people condemned to live a nightmare before adulthood. That's why they have no progeny. It is obviously good that no kids were also left lonely when they fell. It is also terribly sad because these are the exemplary guys who would make some of the best parents and most of them likely lost that chance with sentences of many decades doled out to them when they made childish errors. These are the voices of men who have grown from boyhood in the worst circumstances and have managed to come out thoughtful leaders anyway. These are their voices, speaking to the parents who taught them and supported them anyway.

Just as there is an inherent beauty in the bonds maintained between parents behind bars and their children, there is a strength, understanding, and protectiveness in these letters. Those of us who learn during these decades of deprivation recognize most strongly the value of family of all types.

I know that I would not have made it through my initial unexpected introduction to incarceration, dropped into extended solitary, without the unconditional love and miraculous strength of my parents. They made countless calls to get me better treatment, even when it didn't work. They let me call them anywhere they traveled and answered during any meeting. They spent thousands and came thousands of miles, over and again and again, being there for every terrible hearing and to see me on a video phone for half an hour once a week. My mom even got ordained online to get a couple extra clergy visits and spread a positive, spiritual message. They even managed to cooperate and work as a family, despite drastically disparate lives since a divorce thirty years earlier. Most of all, they made sure to stay connected with D and make sure I have the chance to do so, too. Seven years in, and they still do all this. They did everything despite the crappy situation my being here made for them. As Tupac said, "I reminisce on the stress I caused. It was hell, huggin' on my Mama from a jail cell." So for guys who lost their freedom younger and have been down longer, I completely understand the need to say something powerful about amazing parents.

I had not originally written a letter for this section myself. Yet I had, numerous times, I realized. I have shared admiration and gratitude with KJ and Howie so often it's become a joke in the family. I have always had great parents and knew it, but there's nothing like prison to make me want to tell them every day. See, my folks are getting to numbers larger than fits my image of their invincibility. Since I got locked up, one of my biggest fears has been them having health problems while I'm stuck here. Likewise, that they might have a negative sense about me or even take my being here as a reflection on them.

Plus, Mom has battled some leg and back issues and a sense of lost purpose. Most of all, this terrible situation motivated me to spend every chance I could talking with them. We are now closer than we've ever been, I'm glad to say, and it's made me determined to do all I can to lift them up and make them proud. It's the only thing I can really do for these amazing folks of mine.

Included here are poems I wrote to honor each of them. It is from the darkest places that we can best see the glow of the brightest stars. These were birthday gifts, all I could do for those who gave me life and kept me going long past when I wish I needed them. But maybe that's a gift of this nightmare—the chance to recognize the importance of the relationships so easily taken for granted.

My actual letters to my parents are not here, though, because they do not hold a candle to the powerful expressions of these guys I proudly call friends. They are only a few, the voices of those without their own children, but they speak so clearly and poignantly. They tell of all that we have already discussed, but aimed in the other direction. Deeply devoted love, promises of endless support that could never repay what has been provided, lessons learned, and loss felt to the core. They drip with tears unable to be shed from fear of vulnerability and opening a gate that cannot be closed. They pulse with a desire to be seen by those that matter most with pride, despite the youthful mistake that defined life. They bleed crimson gratitude and loneliness.

Imagine being locked up as a teenager, facing two or three times as many years as you've known without anyone to watch out for you in arm's reach. You've seen all the TV shows and maybe even met some callused personalities who've done time. Imagine how important the voice and acceptance of your Mom is now, when you can't hug her or get fussed at. Imagine how much you would want to make Dad proud after he kept humbling himself to visit on his weekends after work. Imagine what you would say to them

to show them all you feel, all you care, and how much
you've grown and learned.

"When I was low, you was there for me
Never left me alone 'cuz you cared for me
Don't ya know that I love you, sweet lady,
Dear Mama
Place no one above you, sweet lady,
Dear Mama"
-- Tupac Shakur

Mother Warrior
Born in natural splendor
amidst a cloud of trees
raised every moment after
in the glow of fundamental truths
by my mother warrior
defending values fiercely

Saving whales and elephants
my first care beyond myself
stopping at the Greenpeace tent
my first D.C. memory
"no artificial," period
decades before Panera did it
organic, local without fanfare
my mother, eco warrior

Granddaughters in tow
pink-hatted lioness queen
roaring at the newest fallacy
generations of male feminists
committed to your example
Trump calls you shrill, bitch
compliments you wear as jewels
my mother, vagina warrior

* * *

We may have yelled a little
we're a passionate brood
but "use your words"
"turn the other cheek"
our bread and butter staples
you've raised the only prison pacifist
my mother, communication warrior

Poppa's 70th

I still recall your 40th
last time anyone surprised you
or have we really ever?
and you've always deserved
more celebration
but never our words felt worthy

Back then, not like other dads
more curls, less belly
far less bluster
didn't know much about you
not hiding it, we later learned,
just you refuse to ever brag
I wished I knew you better
wished I could make you proud
never sure exactly how

Now I'm 40, too
your slow motion mirror I see
and so much more clearly
do I perceive you then and now
lessons painted between all the lines
principled without pressure
playful and sincere
this guy's hero still
and now confidant too
my favorite gift from you

* * *

Those truths shining bright upon
now more than ever
the image of the man I strive to be
and the human we all should
embodiment of fatherhood
gentle intelligent masculinity
too proud to ever fail
but not to hug your son in prison

A true teacher
ever learning still
a true warrior
ever sacrificing
truly invincible
'cuz you believe you are
so you skip your check ups still,
Poppa Doc
and do your best with today
mindfulness without yoga

Now at 70, I see you best
fewer curls
but still no belly
all grinning heart
and rosy cheeks
never asking
only offering

Letters to Other Family

"Thank you for remaining in my corner. You may think it's just your duty as my mother but it's much more than that.
Terms like mother, father, family, and friends are just words, they're just nouns. However, it's the action a person displays while upholding these titles that give them power and meaning. You have given so much power and meaning to my idea of mother."

Harry (Justice) Traynham

Dear Mama

You and I have been through a lot and I have to shamefully admit that I didn't make our journey easier. But I hope somewhere in between then and now that you've come to not blame my heart. Please know that when it comes to you, my heart always beats pure and true, and it's from that purity and sureness that I write this to you.

I write to say that I'm grateful for you. My life has been difficult to say the least but the unconditional love and support that you have always given to me have made my struggles a lot easier.

As my mother you've loved me regardless of all the hardships that I've put on you. You loved me through all the disappointment that I've caused, and you loved me enough to constantly push me to be a better person. The man I've become is grateful for that and for you not allowing me to settle and succumb to the negative epitaphs of my circumstances.

Thank you for remaining in my corner. You may think it's just your duty as my mother but it's much more than that. Terms like mother, father, family, and friends are just words, they're just nouns. However, it's the action a person displays while upholding these titles that give them power and meaning. You have given so much power and meaning to my idea of mother. Many a family and friends stopped cheering for me a long time ago but every time I looked into my cheering section, you have always been there rooting me on. I, with all my heart and soul, thank you for that. I am thankful because when no one would accept my calls, no one visited me, wrote to me, thought about me, missed me, loved me, and refused to believe me, you were always there and it was through each one of these mediums that you encouraged me to keep going and to stand for something.

When the waves of hardship constantly crashed into this ship I call my life and the darkness would not let me sail to safer waters, you stood as the brightest lighthouse to guide me to safety. I know in order to be that lighthouse you had to sacrifice a lot. I recognize your sacrifice for me and Tee-Tee. Please know that your sacrifice is not unknown or unfelt. I recognize it and Tee recognizes it. It's because of that recognition of your sacrifice that Tee and I have the bond we have. Your sacrifice taught us the meaning of family.

Before I close this letter, I must extend to you my deepest apology. I disappointed you. I've caused you a lot of heartache and hardships. Mama, I am so sorry for letting you down. If I could change a lot of my mistakes, I would, but that's not possible. So to make amends I make this promise to you:

Mama, I promise not to be the sum of my mistakes. I promise that I will continue to be a good man and a great human being. I promise that no matter the circumstances of what is left of my life I will do the right thing and always stand for the right thing. I promise that what life I have left it will be in sacrifice to a higher ideal.

In closing I just want you to know that all that is written in this letter is to express my gratitude, thankfulness, and love for you. What often gets lost behind these prison walls is our humanity. The bond between mother and son is a

strong principle of humanity, at least in my opinion, and it is in large part that bond that caused me to grow into the man I am. Simply put, your love and support means the world to me, and it is a force I will pay forward.
With unconditional love,

Your Son
Antwan a.k.a. Justice

> "Deep down, I want you to always know that I appreciate you both for the times of understanding me even when I didn't understand myself. For being there for me when my world felt empty."

♥

Malik Hobbs

Dear Mom and Dad,

I may not be there in person, but I am by thought 'cause that's where it all means most and where our messages of love are delivered by the heart. Feeling something inside that you think you know for sure is right there. Truth and living are what the underlying source or motive is saying to you. The hugs are felt from a sympathetic mother every moment of feeling down and out. Handshakes from a strong father that salutes me even at the hardest of times. Remember that you both asked me in unison: "Malik, do you know what you're doing?" My thoughts scrambled and my heart raced, following slowly, I answered: "I'll find out and then I'll answer the question." Not realizing the impact, ability, and confidence that you two instilled in me.

    Not in person is my presence, but by circumstance. The beautiful sky that you'll see when reading this, just know that I'm gazing at the same sun, in the same world as you. Not there as in the flesh, but through connection. The laughs we shared may be let out as a cry of some sort now, but just know that I'm still that same laughing and joking Malik that made the day.

    I want you to know that I've surrounded myself with more positive individuals now, and that I think before I react knowing that I control myself and my actions. Deep down, I want you to always know that I appreciate you both for the times of understanding me even when I didn't understand myself. For being there for me when my world felt empty. I want you to know that I've embraced the name that you've given me, which has a definition of "king!"

Peace & Love,
your son,
Malik

> "As I look back, it pains me because my sentencing was a sentence for you also."

♥

Alejandro Ruiz

Dear Mom,

I want to apologize to you for what you have had to endure because of me. I regret a lot of choices I've made in my life. I regret that no matter how many times you've tried, how many sleepless nights I've caused, how many times you tried to help guide me, show me, and teach me, I just didn't listen. As I look back, it pains me because my sentencing was a sentence for you also. It eats me up inside because it seems like all the sacrifices you've made were for nothing.

You tell me every time we speak that you are proud of the man I've become. Even though I recognize the change in myself, more often than not, I feel ashamed of what it took to get me where I am today. If I had just listened and paid attention to what you and all my loved ones were only trying to help me understand, I could have been everything you wanted me to be and more.

Mom, I'm writing you this letter because I want you to know that I finally get it. Everything you've told me, everything you've said that will come to pass. I understand now that your words come from experience, and it was my inexperience that made me doubt you. Every day is a struggle for me to do better, to be better. And being where I am will not make the struggle any easier. But now is my time to endure just as you have. A parent's love for their child is amazing. Some people don't know how to express it, and some don't know how to receive it, but at that point where it's truly felt and reciprocated it can make the weak mighty.

Through self-reflection, I've learned where I was weak

and honestly strong. I've learned humility and patience. In those most troubling moments, I sometimes hear your voice telling me the same things I was too immature to heed when I was younger. That voice reminds me of my value and significance. Your love and optimism for me and my future planted the seeds of love and optimism I have for myself, that have grown into an unwavering faith in my potential. It reminds me that I can do anything regardless of my circumstance. All I have to do is maintain that faith in myself and my god, be conscious in all my actions and always consider others.

Sincerely,
Alejandro Ruiz

"My worst attribute is also my best. It's taken a lot of pain and mistakes to put it all into perspective. This has been one giant pendulum swing, oscillating from one extreme to the next, and I'm finally at a standstill with you. You've forced me to face myself and own my wrongs. Thank you for being my teacher and helping me find my path."

♥

Dominique Benjamin

"A fool knows the price of everything and the value of nothing." My mother gave me that gem at a time when I thought I had everything. Imagine the humor in discovering at the lowest point of my life that I had nothing then and everything now. Substance was something I never grasped the concept of until losing everything of "importance" in my life.

What do you do when your foundation has been built on materialism, superficiality, and trivial things, and life comes and hits you hard? All facades are temporary and eventually reveal their true selves.

I was living as recklessly as possible so these epiphanies weren't that hard to see. It's a sad truth, but "the truth hurts and the truth shall set you free." Those are a couple more gems from your grandmother. She's given me so many, but they've never had any value or resonated. Jewels I've so carelessly tossed aside are all coming back to haunt me.

However, my most precious jewel, my biggest ghost, has always been you. You've been such an enigmatic force in my incarceration of thoughts and reflection. My greatest achievement and failure, never to see the light of day. Would you believe the reason you weren't born was born from my unwillingness to compromise? I refused to change, to grow the hell up. Stubbornness is a wicked trait. Between your mother and I, I imagine you would've been the epitome of the word.

I wonder if you would've had my widow's peak? My grandfather gave me mine. He also gave me gems to forever cherish, like understanding my heritage and how it would take me far. As a boy in Trinidad, kids teased me for my widow's peak and for having a white grandfather. In our culture these are both signs of the devil. He taught me that the devil was once an angel. He was God's favorite and was cast out because he was rebellious and stubborn by choice. He became the devil by choice! He then taught me that my first two names, Dominique Dion, are French. In French customs a widow's peak can be a double entendré, something with a double meaning. It can indicate that someone is stubborn, but it can also be interpreted as being immovable or having a strong will. My worst attribute is also my best.

It's taken a lot of pain and mistakes to put it all into perspective. This has been one giant pendulum swing, oscillating from one extreme to the next, and I'm finally at a standstill with you. You've forced me to face myself and own my wrongs. Thank you for being my teacher and helping me find my path. I now know what's important and I won't lose sight of all the gems I already possess. I hope you're proud of me. Above all else, I need you to know I always wonder about you and will always love you. "Hoch soll er leben, Hoch soll er leben, dreimal hoch!" ("Long may he live.") That precious gem is from my dad. God, I wish you could've met him. I miss you much kiddo. "The greatest measure of a man is not determined in times of comfort and peace, but in trials and adversity." - Dr. Martin Luther King, Jr.

Dominique Benjamin

PART 2
Policy Suggestions

How Can We Encourage the Bond Between Parents in Prison and Their Children On the Outside?

Perhaps the biggest lesson I've learned in my time behind bars is about the scope and normal range of humanity. So many wonderful people, so many decent ones, maybe a few jerks, just like the rest of society. I knew about the arbitrary punishments and demographic inequities before, in theory, in evidence, and with a couple friends locked up briefly but I did not know it with such conviction until I got to live in a steel and concrete box next to the boxes of all these other guys nothing like me but just like me, too. We have had to stand in line together interminably for meat rock, beans, stale bread, and wormy apples. We have had to take turns on two washers and dryers among 78 people, each with only three sets of underwear. We have spent sweaty weeks locked down when the cells were over 100 degrees even at night. We have had to figure out how to be decent in complete degradation and deprivation, making three or phones work for almost 80 people on Christmas and Thanksgiving.

So many regular people, and for nearly everyone, family—especially our kids—matters more than just about anything else. That is abundantly evident in the words of the people in the previous section. Nothing demonstrates our humanity like when we speak to our children and our parents. Those are the most sincere words. That is where our differences disappear within the broader, diverse singularity of simply being human.

Given all that clear and evident love, given all those completely reasonable voices, given all we know as a society about the importance of family bonds and regular interactions, of course the Department of Corrections (DOC) must go out of its way to promote all the positive interactions possible, right? If nothing else, they must be as helpful and kind to the kids and their other parents, for their sake, right?! Nope. Quite the contrary.

Despite ample evidence that strong connections make everyone safer and despite the clear benefit for all children of strong bonds with their parents, wherever they are, this is not promoted. Programs that help parents connect with children while behind bars are so rare as to be newsworthy, like the random father-daughter dance in Michigan. Or else any such program is a one-off experiment, limited to the vision of an overworked and underfunded person or small organization and never institutionalized and often discontinued as soon as possible behind vague claims of "security."

Our children do better when they know us and feel supported by us. Their other parent needs our help and can raise them better with stronger relationships and social support. We do better here and upon release when we have those bonds to focus and rely upon. Everyone is safer and healthier and better prepared for the world when they get to have strong family bonds. Who would ever hear these voices of parenthood and want to deny that love to the children involved? The children of incarcerated parents—and the parents of incarcerated children—deserve to not be punished, too.

Yet even as every ounce of logic and decency tells anyone with a heart and a brain to build and encourage these bonds, to bend over backwards to help kids stay connected to parents and grow up fully supported, especially when they have the fundamental disadvantage of a parent behind bars, DOC in this state and nearly all others is blind to this. So are broader criminal justice systems and social services for the most part. Rather than take a therapeutic approach that decades of research has demonstrated better for individuals and community, rather than simply prioritizing traditional family values even, the system takes an entirely retributive mindset. Punishment is the goal, making things as difficult as possible, based upon the foundational presumption that everyone here is worthless and therefore must be distrusted and must suffer. Little consideration is given to rehabilitation except lip service and none is provided to the collateral consequences–the real, innocent people who therefore suffer along with us. Certainly exceptions exist and reform is the actual goal in some progressive places, but even in New York, California, Hawai'i, Vermont, Massachusetts, Washington, and Oregon, states proudly waving progressive banners with well-meaning leaders, corrections–and often still prosecutors and police and probation/parole officers–operate from a punitive mentality in very insular and opaque conditions that make true progress difficult.

For this reason, we now switch gears from the human voices of parenthood behind bars to examine some specific problems, from localized policy on a human scale to broad systemic (lack of) support systems. For each problem noted, we provide brief ideas about effective solutions guided by a nearly unique combination of social science background and lived experience. After all, critical thinking is not just criticizing. It is only in suggestions for change can we make progress, and it is us who know best the importance and fragility of these bonds who must speak to how to maintain them.

We wish to stay brief and human in our tone, as well, so we deliberately avoid bogging the reader down with citations and social science speak. The trends referenced are well established and logical.

Even if the correctional system had legitimate excuses for not investing heavily in proactive family building programs–it doesn't!–it would seem fundamentally obvious that we ought to at least make it as easy as possible to share in-person visits, where hugs and smiles and presence are so profound, even in small doses. I know for me, one or two good hugs with my son would be heaven and they are life savers with my fiancée and parents and siblings and friends. Yet, even just letting people sit, sit together, watched over by people and cameras in an otherwise empty room, is made as difficult as possible.

Remember the "grosser than gross" jokes of childhood? Quickly, what's gross? Wearing used underwear, ever. What's grosser than gross? Wearing communal tighty-whities–they're called "slingshots" here; not sure why–in prison. That is a highlight of what we've been recently subjected to in order to maintain our opportunities to spend time with family and friends.

Without a doubt, the best part of my existence in prison is visitation time. In a world of hyper-masculinity, where affection is prohibited and displays of joy perceived as weakness, that weekly connection with loved ones is like oxygen to a suffocating man.

We are allowed but one hug and kiss on the way in and one leaving, but they are electric and the comfort lingers for days. Unlimited, each smile beams like the first dawn.

I am very fortunate in that my support system is so incredible that I almost never miss a weekend, coasting through the beginning of most weeks on the winds of companionship. This may sound ephemeral, but there really is no way to fully express the power of connecting with those you love when living a life of designed isolation and deprivation.

Hence, it is not surprising that Virginia's DOC claims commitment to maintaining strong ties between people behind bars–they reduce us to "offenders," of course–and their families. Operating Procedure 851.1.IV.A.3 states, "visitation provides offenders with opportunities for involvement with family and participation in community activities before final release."

In this era or purported reform, it is surprising that they recently instituted pointless statewide changes that directly attack those bonds and discourage visitation. Recently policies we–families and residents–have had to endure put lipstick on the lip service they offer about promoting familial bonds.

Until mid-2017, we were able to wear our "blues" to visits. Those are the institutional uniforms, and they were bad enough—elastic waisted male maternity jeans and rough chambray shirts. On the way in and on the way out, we underwent full searches examining literally every inch of us, as did our visitors—not fully nude for them, though. This process could not have been any more secure already. Visitors even had to go through multiple scanners, more than airports.

However, they have now arbitrarily added the most demeaning possible attire to the process arbitrarily. We still have to submit to the full search on the way in and the way out, so the actual security procedure has not changed. Now, though, we must put on socks, t-shirts, and underwear from a communal supply. Yes, here, in prison.

My friends who work in the laundry area have assured me that, while they do get washed after every use, they find drawers with streaks, spots, and stains. The administration cannot let it be communal boxers like the boxers they have us wear at all other times. They choose this one time to force us to don the undies that get most personal. With the search, the switching of underwear is entirely redundant and only meant to inconvenience and dissuade.

Furthermore, during our visits, we are now forced to wear backwards onesie jumpsuits, shapeless, enormous, and beige, like a cross between a straightjacket, oversized infant attire, and a burlap sack. They are highly uncomfortable and unflattering, but more than that, they are degrading. We are grown men being forced without cause to clothe ourselves to see the people that matter most in something that requires us to ask for help zipping and unzipping. We are deliberately made to look and feel ridiculous—visual shaming and marking.

In addition, the recent rule changes also included a loss of eating privileges in the visitation room. If we are lucky enough to have a visit that lasts more than an hour or two, we likely miss an official meal—of what they claim as food.

Previously, the impact of this was mitigated by the opportunity to purchase overpriced gas station sandwiches and chips from vending machines. In fact, while far from Panera or Chipotle, those microwaveable snacks were the best thing we ever got here. More than that, they gave us and our visitors a chance to eat; nourishment being essential, and all. Now the new visitation rules include a ban on all food except the least nutritious and filling. Yup, now all we can have at visits are candy bars.

On what grounds did they make these changes? The official claim here is security, but that is simply not a legitimate justification. It's a matter of making an easy scapegoat of those already behind bars and therefore allowed to be presumed guilty of everything.

Certainly, the opportunity to eat potato chips and sandwiches instead of candy did not create a greater risk of contraband. When the DOC was questioned about this, they claimed it was necessary to stem the tide of drugs coming in through visits. Yes, that does rarely happen, but the numbers they quoted were minuscule, amounting to hundredths of a percent of the visits that occur, less than a couple dozen times a year throughout the whole state with nearly 40,000 people behind bars.

Everyone here will tell you that, yes, drugs are available. They will also tell you that the availability did not change at all with the new visitation rules because, frankly, the vast majority of drugs enter with employees, not residents. Having considerable secondhand knowledge of the process, I would estimate 85-90% is coming in via guards and contract workers. Most of what arrives simply cannot make it in through visitation. The authorities know this and simply prefer to scapegoat us because it is an easier way to claim they are doing something when an incident occurs. It requires much more introspection and admission of a systemic problem to deal with the real sources of most contraband.

When the biggest contraband bust happened last year at the largest state penitentiary on the East Coast, thousands in cash, pounds of tobacco, nearly a pound of weed, and a dozen cell phones in boxes were found. Where? In the guards break room ceiling, where we have no access, ever. They even arrested a contract employee in the process.

Certainly, none of that could fit inside any body cavities during a visit! Seems fundamentally obvious that boxed phones or pounds of anything did not come in via the private parts railroad. Ouch! Yet they responded by locking us down for two weeks and canceling visits for a month, even with the outfits. Such is the extent of the scapegoat mentality.

What these changes really amount to is a public shaming of both us and our loved ones. It visually marks us and serves to remind them of the judgement against us and the presumption of guilt against them by association. This is also entirely out of line with the claimed philosophical foundations of contemporary corrections. Furthermore, it is entirely out of line with the rubric of evidence-based practice. It is well established that shaming is a poor way to teach lessons of any sort. Instead, it creates trauma and emotional scars that lead to isolation from society and feelings of disengagement. It encourages future insecurities and secretive behavior.

The shaming of our loved ones extends beyond the visits too, serving as an ongoing reminder that we are deemed "untrustworthy" and "criminal." It is hard enough on them to brave long drives, unpleasant guards, pat downs, and razor wire for limited time at a plastic table. Now all memories and our only photo ops look like a medieval Missy Elliott video.

Sadly, these dehumanizing rituals discouraging visitation are counterproductive for all. People behind bars do much better, both here and after release, the stronger their links with external support networks. My own experience here is emblematic. Without outside bonds when I began, I would have succumbed to depression following an unjust and unexpected incarceration. I would have either committed suicide or committed to chasing highs. Instead, the desire to maintain my standards for the sake of my son, my incredible fiancée, my parents, and my friends motivated me past those darkest days. The interactions we shared pushed me to find hope and purpose in my existence here, leading to reinvigoration and self-motivation. Every hug and laugh during a visit helped save me.

I am not alone in this, either. One of the purposes I have found here has involved utilizing my unique intersection of sociologist and prisoner roles to conduct ethnographic research. My unprecedented access allowed me to learn a lot about the guys here doing the best despite the circumstances. One thing that stood out was how the positive leaders in these environs almost unanimously described family relationships as a primary motivating factor. Visitors are a common theme among the rare few who conquer context to be authors, organizers, and teachers while being actively dehumanized.

This is a very focused window into a broader pattern, too. Discouraging visits is a terrible idea for broader society because strong relationships with loved ones make up one of the two most clearly beneficial things for people behind bars—education being the other one. Those locked up are almost all going to be part of society again in the future, and all of us here are still living now, even if it doesn't always feel that way. The people that have strong bonds while here avoid trouble best, feel the least discarded by society, and are most likely to remain positive members of their families—remember the millions of kids with incarcerated parents. They are also most likely to have the necessary hope, confidence, and support to succeed in a tough world full of stigma once released. That is safer and cheaper for everyone, along with being aligned with the stated rehabilitation and public safety mission of the DOC.

My partner, my family, and I continue to find all the joy possible from our visits. We will not allow administrative buffoonery to steal that from us. Plus, I have a pretty high gross tolerance when it comes to seeing that gorgeous woman. Many guys do not though. For many, these changes have made visits too much to bear. For others, it is too much to acquiesce to such mistreatment.

I have battled internally about this issue myself, and I'd like to join in if there were collective action against this. However, that is unlikely because there is actually a policy where if we organize any group movement, no matter how peaceful or small, it is considered "inciting a riot" and we will be sent to the hole, losing our meager 45¢/hour jobs and meager good time that this parole-less state allows us to earn.

In the meantime, I suffer the literal and figurative shit stains of this situation in order to share those precious moments of connections. Be it known, though, that they occur despite rather than because of the policies here.

Problem 1: Not enough chances to visit in person with loved ones.

Simply put, the primary obstacle to closer relationships between people behind bars and their families is the application of onerous limits and conditions by DOC. Many years ago, Virginia's DOC formally dedicated itself to rehabilitation rather than punishment in recognition of public safety as the primary goal. Since 95% of those incarcerated will get out, the best thing for everyone-- economically, socially, psychologically, etc. -- is to help those behind bars improve themselves, their opportunities, and their relationships. Rather than actually make it a priority, it is made as cumbersome as possible. Every state has different policies, and some are likely better–and worse–than Virginia, but the collective approach is to set limits and hurdles that discourage visits. Not only is visitation not a priority, it often seems to be actively de-prioritized.

While those in ultimate power may know that it is useful, the mentality in correctional departments is actually still quite punitive on the ground and all the way up through most decision makers. Rather than try to correct and rehabilitate, the mindset presumes us all deserving of punishment that many feel inclined to mete out themselves. More than that, the presumption is that we are inherently untrustworthy. New officers are literally trained to presume we are lying and attempting shady behavior. This mentality is then applied to visitation, and it is treated like something they are obligated to officially provide but would like to limit in the name of the vague but powerful notion of "security." Thus, by making it as much of a pain as possible to do, visits become less common.

Just in my time behind bars, I have watched them force upon us the aforementioned adult onesies and eliminate potato chips and sandwiches from the vending machines that are the only food permitted when we "choose" to pass up our provided meals and see our families. In the name of security, of course, but really just being burdensome. The same mentality pervades the entire process of a visit, as my partner regularly experienced at Greensville.

She was one of the lucky ones, too. Gin "only" had to drive about 90 minutes each way during most of my time there. Because most prisons are deliberately located in isolated areas, most visitors come many hours. The rest of my family has to drive between states, leaving before dawn, and some must even fly and get hotel rooms. This is common. Yet once people arrive, the experience is deliberately complicated and slow.

Being from relatively close by, Gin would have to commit a full day just to see me for about an hour and a half. She had to leave around 8 AM in order to get there around 9:30 AM, at the tail end of the initial rush. It would then take her a full hour or even 90 minutes to be greeted, checked in the computer, searched, scanned, searched again, loaded on a bus to my area of this large prison, searched again, and finally let in. Then, our brief peck and hug hello, followed by an edge of the seat time talking that was perpetually in the shadow of ending unexpectedly. Even with the waves of arrivals well known to us, the best timing in the world usually only got us about an hour and a half, two at the most—except in rare instances of terrible or wonderful weather or unobserved holidays keeping most people away. Thereafter, we would be pushed out suddenly because the room had filled and more people were arriving. This made each visit feel stressful, even with our dedicated efforts at mindfulness and staying in the moment. For all the joy these visits offered, our twisted fairytale love story notwithstanding, we knew we had to squeeze every bit of happy from just a very limited time. That meant we were inevitably periodically distracted by each new arrival, chipping away at our precious time together.

DOC policy only allows us one day per week to visit together, either the even or odd day—depending on my state number—of the weekend. That day is only 830 a.m. to 3 p.m. Once there, they only guaranteed us one hour, and once we were even kicked out at 58 minutes, and often the end came just after the hour passed. Then, Gin had to spend half an hour or more getting lined up, transported, and let back out—over 30 minutes, just to get out! Then, of course, the drive back home.

All that could have been avoided, too. They put visitation not in the gym, but in a separate, much smaller room. Originally it had been both, plus the fenced in outside area with picnic tables, with the option of opening an attached secondary room. All this meant everyone could fit and stay as long as they wished, even having some space. In fact, years before my arrival, Virginia had regular family days and weekends, where everyone basically had cookouts on the rec yard and mingled and could play and fully enjoy time together. By my time, though, they had eliminated the gym as a place to seat people. They had stopped allowing anyone to sit outside. They no longer opened up the addition portion of the visitation room. Even just during my time there, we watched as they gradually removed tables in that last remaining room, going from 32 to 24 slowly, without announcing it. This meant that the 1,032 people sharing that visitation room had only 24 seats to rotate. The cumulative effect was to drastically, deliberately reduce the number of available spaces, making it inevitable that visits would be ended for space reasons soon after they began. For many people, between the long drives, understaffed and unpleasant "greeting" procedure, and short time together, it became simply not worth it.

On top of all this, DOC continues to try to claim that security needs are forcing them to reduce access to visitation, even after the state passed legislation attempting to ensure it in light of the clearly therapeutic effects. In 2019, DOC announced a new rule that reduced access to visitation for many residents and, subsequently, hindered the chances loved ones have to connect with us. Each person behind bars is now limited to ten people approved to come visit them during any six-month period. Uncommon foresight is now also required, as the list must be submitted months in advance. If it is not, we are not able to see anyone during that half a year.

In this era of criminal justice reform, this change is directly contradictory to the stated rehabilitative mission and all scientific evidence. Strong bonds with positive community members are essential to staying out of trouble now and in the future. All related research demonstrates that such bonds are crucial to reducing recidivism for us and, more importantly, mitigating the negative impacts of our absence for our families and communities. Additionally, evidence also demonstrates that in-person visits that are being limited with this policy are the most valuable way to improve reentry outcomes. On a simple human level, what sense does it make to reduce anyone's chances to hug and laugh with their parents, kids, and partners?

This change is not just detrimental in principle; it is terrible for my family. I have nine siblings, four parents, a fiancée, and a number of close friends and extended family members who are currently approved to visit. I have never been in any trouble during nearly eight years behind bars, having only taught, volunteered, and helped my peers, while continuing to parent and partner daily and helping found multiple advocacy groups. Yet none of that would have happened without the hugs, smiles, encouraging deep talks, and surprise visits from so many wonderful people. I was despondent, nearly suicidally depressed after finding myself unexpectedly locked up before I rose up while looking forward to those precious moments of freedom and hope found in those visits.

I had to cull nearly half of my approved visitors, including my stepmother, stepfather, and at least six siblings. How am I supposed to explain that? "Sorry, you have been too busy living life and working in another state to come every month, so now you can't come visit when you finally have a chance. No offense." Or is this perhaps intended to allow me to make some money with a bidding war for the chance to get invasively searched and eat vending machine food? Of course not.

    According to the brief article on the subject that I saw, they were supposed to allow those of us with larger immediate families to apply for exceptions. Unfortunately, they have announced no such thing to us in here. No one I have asked can provide me with the paperwork to do so or even to whom I should apply. That option appears to possibly be a PR effort as part of the release they sent to local papers. Even if it exists, it is not a solution. Just allowing me the extra spots for my immediate family would mean excluding many close friends and extended family who are closest with me. And what of those people whose entire social network does not officially qualify as "immediate family?"

    The issue here is that the entire policy is a hindrance without purpose. The stated rationale is security, a desire to reduce contraband coming in via visitors. However, security is not at all addressed by this change. Every single visitor already has to undergo an extensive background check before getting approval. Once approved, every visitor must go through scanners and pat downs before entering. We are zealously watched during visits. Those of us living here already get full "squat, spread 'em, and cough" strip searches coming in and going out, and while we're there must wear a giant onesie that zips in the back. Only three people max can come in at any time, too. Limiting the total approvals adds nothing to this. Neither my family nor I have done anything to warrant this suspicion, either.

    Really, security is not the true motivation here. In reality, the added media attention to scant drug overdoses in the system have encouraged DOC to handily scapegoat us and our families. The reality is that, yes, drugs are available to a certain extent in some facilities, but overdoses are less common than in the average neighborhood. They have just gotten more attention lately in the press.

In fact, they would simply rather blame us and make visits more difficult than actually tackle contraband effectively. Given the low wages here and high rewards, it is well known that 80-90% of contraband enters with staff, who have more trust and less suspicion. If they really wanted to stop drugs getting in, they could simply put a dog outside each gate every weekend. Searches wouldn't even be needed unless they smelled something. They limit and scapegoat us instead, though, because that would take away their handy pincushion and force them to examine much bigger issues.

Additionally, this recent change is likely motivated by private financial interests. No coincidence that just a month prior to this mandatory limited list of visitors, JPay, a for profit company that already charges absurd fees for our emails or the privilege of sending us money for food, began offering video visits. These conveniently do not require loved ones be on our list made months prior. They also conveniently charge our loved ones large sums for twenty minute Skype sessions where they still must drive to a secure location.

Ultimately, between the limited slots and extremely slow and cumbersome greeting and search process and the ever increasing list of reasons to stop people from visiting, the pattern is clear: DOC is actively pursuing a situation where visits are as difficult as possible on everyone. This serves to reduce family connections, to stand between parents and children. It can be easily remedied, too.

Policy Suggestion 1A: Make visitation opportunities an official priority within every institution.

The evidence is abundantly clear: visitation is beneficial on many levels, for everyone. From our own research, we know people behind bars gain resiliency and it helps them focus on positive behavior. We also reoffend less often and reintegrate more effectively after prison when we have strong external relationships, and visitation supports those bonds better than anything else. Strong bonds with parents behind bars help children do better in school and avoid trouble. All this makes communities more prosperous and safer. Visits are fundamentally aligned with the notion of rehabilitation that every DOC now claims as its primary mission. Yet they are limiting and reducing such access.

Instead, they should make visits as widely available as possible, not just one morning a week on weekends. Make it a priority to offer these invaluable bonding opportunities so that everyone can partake. Include weekdays and weekends, even evenings, as it is often those stuck in unpredictable shift work whose loved ones are behind bars.

Likewise, dedicate staff to making the time coming in and out as streamlined and pleasant as possible. Ensure they understand and internalize the fact that the people coming to visit are not being punished and should be treated kindly. Dedicate as much space as is necessary to accommodate the maximum load for a given day, based on past results, the simple predictive planning used by restaurants when ordering ingredients and staffing. Reduce the time and stress burden in every way for those coming to visit. Importantly, enshrine this all in actual policy, including an edict that the maintenance of in-person, contact visits should be a rehabilitative priority not to be superseded by security concerns unless an active situation is occurring, and then only those involved should have their visitation privileges reduced or eliminated.

Policy Suggestion 1B: Offer visitors a lengthy mandatory minimum they can stay, commensurate with all-day travel.

* * *

Promoting this prioritization of visitation opportunities should specifically include a policy that indicates that visitors be permitted to stay at least four hours, if they so choose. No one should ever have to drive long distances to see their loved ones behind bars, endure the searches and stigma, then be asked to leave after only an hour or two. For many, these visits can only work logistically or financially very infrequently, so they should be encouraged to enjoy the time fully, without the distraction of impending termination every time someone new enters the room. This is especially true for those who bring children to see their parents behind bars, where the time should be entirely unlimited to maximize that bond and eliminate all possible stress.

Administrators may claim space issues will prevent this, but those can be alleviated with the initial commitment to adequate space and more days to visit. The current logjam is simply a result of shrinking spaces and policies that channel everyone to only a small window of hours.

Policy Suggestion 1C: Offer fully subsidized travel to all visitation days.

No one should be unable to afford to visit their parents or children behind bars, yet that is often the case. Many of us are from families with the most limited resources already, sometimes lacking adequate transportation and other times even gas money. Even the fifteen dollars for the once-a-month bus from an urban center can be prohibitive, as can the singular location.

Instead, a relatively small sum can be invested to subsidize entirely free rides to each and every prison from all urban centers, at least twice a month. Even better would be a more personalized dedicated van service, available to all who qualify financially, that could be reserved periodically.

Families not in urban centers should not be excluded

for being isolated. Additionally, a rideshare coop website or even app should be developed and administered by the state. Fuel costs could then be split or, ideally, readily reimbursed for anyone under a financial threshold.

Policy Suggestion 1D: Guarantee that all family members and close friends are automatically approved to visit unless they have specifically been caught bringing contraband.

Currently, states and local jails have a patchwork of cumbersome, disjointed rules and processes to approve visitors. They often change without notice to those already approved, and approvals expire without notice. More than once I have had people show up from out of state, previously approved, only to be told, effectively, "Tough shit about the hundreds of miles you came and dollars you spent, not to mention your feelings. Your approval is no longer any good," for whatever arbitrary reason. From paper to digital forms and back to a combination of both, it is hard for me to even keep track of, and I live it. Filling out forms and even getting computer access and proper identifications can also challenge many of the loved ones here.

 Even when someone wants to get approved, they often cannot, either because they are on someone else's visitor list or they had a conviction themselves at some point. This is a manifestation of the system's presumption of improper conduct being applied to our loves ones, too, hurting everyone. What if a coparent cannot get approved? How will the kids come?

 In order to further maximize the visitation opportunities and the bonds they foster, a single approval process should be good right from the start. This means creating a uniform application, easily accessed, that applies to the jails where people go before convictions and state prisons. It should be nearly automatic approval, hindering only those people who have been found to have brought contraband into prisons or actively breached security in some other way. Past unrelated convictions should play no part. Most of all, once approved, this should be acceptable indefinitely, except with cause.

Policy Suggestion 1E: Eliminate maximum approved visitor thresholds, and allow multiple visits in a day and larger group visits.

In just the same way, no one should ever be denied too many visits or visitors, given the value of those bonds for everyone involved. Right now, in Virginia, policy dictates that only three people at a time can visit, four with special pre-approval twice a year. If we have already had a visitor arrive, they may not be joined by anyone coming later, even if extra seats are open. If we have already had a visitor come and go that day, we may not return to the visitation room anew.

I personally have had multiple visits lost to these rules. When a friend tried to surprise me early in my bid, driving from four hours away, leaving before dawn to bring light to a depressed friend, he ended up being told he had to just turn around and go home because he did not know my mom was already planning that same weekend and arrived sooner. Likewise, I have watched friends have some of their family come from hours away and be too many and have one person be forced to drive away and wait off property while everyone else visited.

And now they have added these arbitrary limits to the number of approved visitors, too. Already these existing limits have no bearing on security, serving only to discourage and hinder bonding. How could the number of people approved matter to whether one of those people brings something in when everyone is already being watched and searched multiple ways?

All of these arbitrary boundaries should simply be

eliminated. The more visitors and visits people receive, the better they will feel and the stronger will be the ties to family that aide everyone.

Policy Suggestion 1F: Guarantee in-person, contact visits be made available at all jails and prisons to maximize therapeutic impact.

In the name of that ever present, ever malleable ghost named "Security", many prisons have been reducing traditional visits where we all get to briefly touch and share physical space. Really, this is just a continuation of the punitive mentality, a control mechanism, and not coincidentally timed with the recent advent of costly video visits. Many jails, where most people arrested go first and stay for short sentences, have entirely eliminated in-person visits. The New River Valley Regional Jail where I was held only permitted video visits, and my family had to drive and fly all the way to that remote outpost to get on the video phone in their waiting room, too. That meant all the inconvenience and cost, yet all we got was about thirty minutes of a misaligned webcam and an old school pay phone receiver for sound, each located in crowded rooms, once every other week. No actual hugs or even real eye contact, and the context certainly reduced the freedom of dialogue and smiles. Don't get me twisted; even those visits felt precious, like air to a flailing, drowning man. But that was relative, in comparison with solitary confinement for over a year. When I got to have actual visits that included even brief affection and actual presence, I understood the true value of an embrace. Much research corroborates the importance of human contact, especially between a parent and their child. It makes tangible the connection and creates physical and emotional well-being.

Therefore, all visits should be enshrined by state law and correctional policy to be in-person and include contact, unless the visitors decide otherwise, or an actual contraband violation has been confirmed to occur. This should also be extended to jails, with the video visits for profit being relegated to an option for those unable or unwilling to travel in person.

Policy Suggestion 1G: Make the conditions and breadth of visitation opportunity a mandatory part of ACA accreditation.

There is an organization, technically a private nonprofit, called the American Correctional Academy. This ACA sets standards and independently monitors the adherence of prisons across the country. This is the confirmation the federal government uses to decide that state systems are eligible for millions in grant money to support programming, like reentry. Thus, the leverage of this accreditation could be leveraged to enhance visitation opportunities. The goal of the ACA is to ensure that correctional facilities meet basic standards of humanity to house people such that they and the public will be safe, and rehabilitation will be maximized. Thus, the access and prioritization of family contact, as well as other policies set forth hereafter, should be added to their requirements for accreditation. Given the existing strain on state budgets stemming from mass incarceration, the federal funding dependent upon ACA approval would drastically improve the promotion of family connections. In turn, this would support public safety, the well-being of children and other loved ones, and advance the ACA and official state correctional missions.

Problem 2: Invasive, degrading treatment during search procedures discourages, traumatizes family, especially kids.

The quickest way to discourage positive bonds is to make the visitation experience traumatic. The best way to discourage parental bonds through the bars is to make it traumatic for children. Already these visits must overcome the stereotypes in most people's minds created by too much HBO and evening news. If co-parents are traumatized during these visits or, worse, their children, the visits will end and a bad taste will be left in visitors' memory banks. The easiest route to such trauma is through degrading, invasive searches of visitors, especially kids.

Yet DOC facilities are widely notorious for extreme mistreatment of visitors. Again, this seems part and parcel to the punitive mentality and the tendency to discourage visitation, period. Of course there are rare instances of drugs coming in through visitation rooms, but DOC's own numbers indicate this is far less than 1% of the time. Our internal experience shows us that most drugs come in via employees, for they are barely searched at all. Point being, nearly everyone who comes to visit is law abiding, having passed a background check. We understand a pat down and even scan or sniff may be necessary, but there is really no justification for cruel and terrifying use of strips searches without actual cause. Our loved ones have not broken laws just because we are here, so they should never be treated like they have.

The New York Times recently ran an investigative examination that uncovered a rash of unwarranted strip and cavity searches at Rikers Island, often involving people of color. Earlier this year, Virginia's DOC. announced a new rule where female visitors would be disallowed from wearing tampons and would, if they did, be subject to a cavity search. In the latter situation, public outcry prevailed and someone higher up nixed the rule, but the mindset is evident. Around the country, prisons have made habit of such unnecessarily degrading ways of treating visitors trying to see their families.

A recent event here in Virginia elucidates the human experience and the mechanisms of power and coercion involved. First Born—and his son and mother—is a visitation regular, and their family is very, very close. They go to reform-oriented meetings and talk with Gin there, so we know the strength of their character and bond. First Born was one of the first people to volunteer for and complete his letter to his son for this book for exactly that reason. He fell right around the time of his boy's birth, yet you should see the fluid and caring dynamic between them. His son is 14 now, a man-sized but baby-faced, amiable and respectful guy. When we're seated near each other I regularly hear First Born and his mother sharing lessons about priorities and honesty, interspersed with three generations doubled over in laughter at some silliness all together. In the epitome of bad circumstances, they share an ideal family dynamic.

And this moral and ethical strength is no hypocrisy, either. First Born was one of the founding members of our for-us-by-us educational and community engagement organization, POINT (Positive Offenders Implementing New Thinking). There and around, I have seen him use his street cred and his imposing figure to allow him to call out self-defeating and dishonest tendencies among peers. At the same time, he's an avid reader of history and social science books and a sponge learning new things. Soft spoken but influential within these walls, he brooks no bullshit. Knowing the whole clan, I was shocked when he sought me out at dinner that evening and explained the day his family had.

They had submitted calmly to the search everyone faced that day—full searches of each car coming onto the property. They were unconcerned due to innocence. Nothing was found in their car, of course, nor did the drug dogs signal it. Suddenly, though, the canine unit sat down next to his son who acted calmly but was terrified. Why would this happen? The only thing he had on him was the 20 dollar bill from his allowance, which he was planning on leaving in the car before going in.

What followed was a parent's and grandparent's nightmare. Naturally, they searched his pockets and socks and everything after that indicator, but nothing was found. It quickly became clear that the issue was the bill, not him, as the dog no longer indicated drugs once that was gone. No other evidence of any issue and this clearly could have come from any of thousands of hands touching the bill previously. It has been estimated that between 75 and 90% of circulating bills have cocaine residue on them, after all.

Yet the officers would not leave it there. Next, they felt the need to do an invasive search on First Born's mother, too. Then they told them they could not visit unless his son underwent a strip search. Yup, strip search of a minor at the most awkward age who just wanted to visit his father. Just like he does without incident almost every weekend.

When the boy's grandmother hesitated to allow the strip search, they amplified the threat. Now the officers said that if the boy did not get a fully invasive, fully nude search and pat down, he would never be permitted to come visit his father again. In a system that is insular and legally shielded, after 14 years of seeing petty retaliation against First Born for standing up for his rights, the family caved. Visits were what kept their family close, after all. Sacrosanct.

Remember, there was no way to ask First Born or receive legal advice. This had to be decided in the moment, under duress, under the gaze of intimidating guards.

When the timid, tearing youth finally agreed, the officers ramped it up again. They attempted to take First Born's young son into a private search room alone, without his grandmother. At this she had to object. After some initial debate, the officers permitted her to accompany her grandson as they made him strip naked for no reason. Better than alone, but still in front of his grandma at 14!

Worst of all, accepting this treatment got them nowhere. After his son went through this entire ordeal, tears running down his cheeks, nothing found on him but fear, he was still not permitted in to visit. Without up front warning, they were told the dog's sitting (most drug dogs sit to indicate they have found drugs) about the 20 dollar bill disqualified them from an in-person visit this day anyway, regardless of the degradation ceremony and proof of innocence. In fact, they were further told that First Born's son would have to submit to the same treatment at every future visit, too.

Just as First Born's efforts to find justice began, this place up and shipped him to another institution, further from his family, without any infraction or request to move. Now we cannot strategize and verbalize collectively anymore, but this needs a louder voice than anyone here can muster. Hopefully his mother has had good fortune getting the attention of the American Civil Liberties Union (ACLU) in this case. Something so egregious cannot be ignored for so many reasons. (Please note, that Virginia legislature has passed legislation prohibiting the strip search of minors since this incident took place.)

Morally, ethically, such treatment of families and especially a minor is indefensible, obviously. It runs so much deeper, though. First off, talk about encouraging a young person to distrust authority and feel unnecessary trauma. Certainly the new stress added to visits and pressure to stop them this creates is detrimental to the family dynamic, too. That makes it counterproductive to the entire correctional goal of this institution, as much research has demonstrated that strong familial bonds drastically reduce recidivism and promote positive lives after release.

This entire situation is fundamentally contrary to law and policy. About a decade ago, the US Supreme Court ruled unequivocally in Edmond vs. The City of Indianapolis that it is unconstitutional for police to have random checkpoints where they seize and search every vehicle without any individual indicator of probable cause. The entire forced search for everyone should never have occurred for any of our families' vehicles.

Furthermore, the singularly terrible treatment First Born's family received was the opposite of legal and completely contradictory to DOC's own promises. Yes, they have policy that a drug dog finding a scent can trigger a further search, but not when it was knowingly localized only to legal tender. Courts have repeatedly ruled that to be public domain and any residue there not the responsibility of those holding it as stand-alone evidence. Instead of applying that and some basic human reason, their overreaction was then a clear violation of their own visitation rules. The operating policy on visitation clearly states in its purpose (851.1.I), "The DOC encourages visiting by family, friends, clergy, and other community representatives when such visits do not pose a threat to others or violate any state or federal law." It adds that (851.1.IV.F(1)(b)) "Staff selected for visitation assignments should be carefully screened for their customer service skills..." and that (851.1.IV.F(2)) "[a]ll visitors shall be treated courteously and assisted promptly."

Does a coerced strip search of an innocent 14-year-old boy with his grandmother under threat of not seeing his father anymore meet those standards? What about the demand of nudity and degrading pat downs by strange uniformed figures with every future visit? Does this meet even our society's lowest standards of humane treatment of a minor? Do we call this family values?

How would any of us feel if this was our child? How does this young man feel now? Besides the fear, trauma, and strain on familial bonds, how does he likely feel about the system and authority figures afterward? This makes no one safer, only hurting families without any benefit. It also reeks of racism and power tripping.

Policy Suggestion 2A: Produce universal, simple conduct rules for visits that only bar visitors when actively caught smuggling contraband or involved in other actual security threats.

The desire to see loved ones is strong, and the authority of officers is currently quite absolute in search situations. Part of the reason that such egregious abuses of power are possible is because of the vague hodgepodge of visitation rules. They essentially allow officer discretion to terminate visits permanently, even without full evidence of wrongdoing.

Thus, to help eradicate this behavior, a clear set of standards is essential. They should eliminate subjectivity and require actual evidence and a full hearing before anyone be banned. They should also be oriented towards maintaining visits in all but extreme circumstances, in line with family and therapeutic goals.

Policy Suggestion 2B: Eliminate strip and body cavity searches except in instances when drug dogs or scanners indicate actual contraband on the person repeatedly.

In the above case, once the bill was removed from the young boy's pocket, the dog no longer indicated any contraband. Thus, there was no ongoing evidence to warrant this treatment. Yet the officers involved insisted anyway. In most such counterproductive situations, it is officer discretion gone awry that produces the problem.

To further ensure that such traumatic and unnecessary situations are curtailed, the goal should be to not strip search people unless absolutely necessary. The only time this should ever be necessary is when there is actual evidence of an attempt to smuggle. Policy should indicate this conclusively, and explicitly deny individual officers the right to decide. Abuse of this authority should elicit major sanctions, starting with immediate removal from the post while investigating any legitimate complaint. If actual evidence of security breaches is believed to warrant a strip search, it should require administrative approval and full documentation before being conducted. The public should be treated as they are, innocent of any wrongdoing, and their due process rights given priority.

Realistically, there is no longer a need for forced searches at all, except under the most extreme conditions. Even a simple pat down search is not needed except as a backup when today's technology indicates the need. Instead, facilities should each invest in the same scanners available at airports and place a drug dog at the entrance. If either indicates a problem, policy could allow for visitors to submit to a clothed search and then additional scan. If that still does not solve the problem, a strip search can be voluntary, or the visitor can just leave. These machines and the dogs do create false positives, but they reliably do not miss anything. If the whole goal is to keep out the contraband, their use and presence will ensure that nothing gets in, even as no one is forced into traumatic or degrading searches.

Policy Suggestion 2C: Eliminate entirely the possibility of minors being strip searched.

Under no circumstances should a child have to be strip searched by an adult in a uniform just to see their parent. DOC policy should be universally rewritten to ensure this never happens for numerous reasons, even beyond the effect on parental bonds. Not being strip searched should also never be grounds for a child to lose permanent access to their parent. Such searches and threats are only a reflection of stereotypes and abuses of authority, not actual security risks.

While I cannot say it has never happened, I have spent almost a decade behind bars at facilities full of contraband. Not once have I ever even heard of a kid being used to smuggle drugs into a visitation room. Given the love, devotion, and positive values evident in this large sample of parents presented here, this is simply not where the risk lies. In combination with the use of non-invasive scans and dogs and the requirement for multiple positive screenings and pat downs, nearly all risk can be eliminated without any trauma to our children.

Policy Suggestion 2D: Develop an independent agency to monitor the use of searches empowered to independently investigate complaints and regulate any misconduct.

This kind of abuse of authority also stems from a lack of oversight and recourse. While there is officially a complaint department located in central DOC. offices to deal with visitation issues, they are slow to respond and only available after the fact. The benefit of the doubt is often given to the officers who remain on that same post and can enact retribution at future visits, refuse to allow them entirely, and harass loved ones behind bars in the interim. This is partially why this young man's grandmother did not intervene more forcefully. These visits are so precious, and the authority is absolute by the administering officers.

The way around this is to create an outside agency unbeholden to DOC's insular culture that is well documented to cover up for its people and seek revenge. That agency must have teeth in their authority, and they should be available—at least by phone—in the moment. They should be able to inspect at any time and intervene as necessary with a civilian perspective. Ideally, they should be somehow integrated with the ACLU, as they have been repeatedly involved in defending people's rights regarding such searches and prison officer abuses. They know the law, their perspective is committed, and their voice has clout.

Problem 3: Officers are often impolite, disrespectful, and demeaning during visits, hindering connections and demotivating visitors.

Even when it is not so extreme as a strip search of an innocent child, unpleasant interactions with visitation officers can matter deeply. Within such a one-sided power dynamic and where a history of abuse of authority and retribution exists, visitors and people behind bars are forced to simply accept however we're treated. There is no independent oversight, and the presumptions are against us. Even things as simple as attitude and demeanor hold enormous emotional sway because of the inherent threat of losing this opportunity. This is even more pronounced for our loved ones, especially kids, who are not accustomed to unreasonably unpleasant treatment and power dynamics. As a result, the therapeutic and bonding value for everyone is highly dependent upon the approach of the officers.

Certainly, there are kind officers who welcome visitors like family, such as Mr. Newburn here who refuses to use the word "inmate" and welcomes all new visitors with a non-confrontational upfront rules explanation. Unfortunately though, more commonly the visitation shift is treated as an opportunity to express frustration upon the powerless.

In fact, my amazing partner, Gin, has been traumatized by being watched over by two committedly unpleasant officers. One, Mr. Fern, only sporadically gets posted in visitation, so we can move on, but the other, Ms. Wilson, has been in charge of our entire interaction half of the weekends for the past year or so.

She was curt towards us from the start, but we were not initially worried. We visit every weekend; this is the highlight of our existence. Both of us bend over backwards to be polite and respectful on principle and especially in this context. Gin is extremely charismatic and we had already built good rapport with nearly everyone else here.

We figured it was just overcoming a universal tendency towards distrust. Until it seemed to be focused mostly on us.

First, she would choose to end our visits early even if the room was empty, saying we had had more than the minimum. Then we noticed that she seemed to be disproportionately often requiring we sit at a table immediately in front of her while the room was still mostly empty, where we were unable to have a conversation she could not hear. It even seemed she allowed many others to choose their seats, or at least mixed it up. Then, at 3 p.m., as everyone gets forced out and shares the one goodbye kiss we get, it seemed like she was almost immediately singling us out in a harsh voice, calling out my name and saying "That's enough, Mahon-Haft," even as we never pushed it, were often the first to stop, and others kept kissing after that for quite a while without comment. When we tried to politely ask about this, we were rebuffed with attitude and a claim of complete authority. When we asked one day politely for a supervisor, the sergeant came in and told us she could do whatever she wanted and we had to listen because, "Visitation is a privilege and it can be taken away." The same thing was told to Gin about four times, with emphasis, when she called the assistant warden to report it during the week. This was clearly an indirect threat to us not to complain, the weight of our precious time together held over our head.

Then, talking to a friend, we found out it was even worse than we thought. We were not being sensitive; we were genuinely being singled out exactly because we were sharing joy regularly.

This is what Mr. S recounted:

"I bet her back hurts when she leaves," Ms. Wilson mumbled. "Yeah, I'm sure her back hurts after that."

No response. Mr. S wasn't paying attention as he continued to fiddle with the digital camera (circa 2004) and paperwork to document residents' only way to create family photos. Each weekend he had to come down once, twice at the most, for like fifteen minutes to the visiting room and snap these pics. Today, while he was between "customers," jotting details so the images would find their way to the right people when printed a month from now, Ms. Wilson was talking at him apparently. Not with him, but at him, as he was simply the closest person to her as she spent the whole day watching people chat across beige plastic tables three feet from each other. She was the guard with the resting grumpy face and default irritated tone, so he didn't know why she was suddenly talking to him. Thus, he didn't respond at first.

Even more saltily, she continued anyway, "Yeah, I hope she gets a bad back. She should be in pain after leaving here."

At this point, Mr. S was curious. None of the half dozen or so tables had been engaging Ms. Wilson at all. They were the regulars, too. On this small compound, he knew each of them, and the reason they all got weekly visits was not coincidentally because they were all the most friendly people you could meet behind bars. They had all even introduced him to their families and partners and kids when he was in to take photos, so he even knew the visitors to be ubiquitously polite and kind. "What did you say, Ms. Wilson?" he queried.

"That blue haired girl over there. I hope her back hurts. They're leaning in so close to each other all the time, staring and talking."

Mr. S sought to express his chagrin with this attitude—as he knew and liked the couple well—without antagonizing an officer. "Why do you say that? Seems like they aren't doing anything wrong."

"Hmmph! I just don't think anyone should come up here to see him every time. That's why I kick them out as soon as they hit four hours and stop them from kissing quickly when they're leaving. I just don't like it," she ranted caustically.

Mr. S did not know what to say, so he tried to extricate himself while pointing out the issue. "Okay, but it doesn't seem like they're bothering anything. I'm going to go back now, Ms. Wilson."

"Well, I don't care. I just don't think they deserve it. I'll see you later."

I am not Mr. S. I am the guy blessed with the most amazing, gorgeous partner ever. She does have blue hair and she does bring that and a smile to visit me almost every day we have a visit. It's the best part of both our weeks, that time in uncomfortable Walmart lawn furniture in a cramped, windowless, institutional beige room being watched. We're really that in love, and we really do lean in to share heart deep stares and sweet words most of the time we're there. It's a way to make a love bubble that allows us to exist above the circumstances.

I found out about this conversation recently, in great detail, because Mr. S is a good man and a good friend of mine. We're very different demographically, but we are both men of principle. Plus, we used to play volleyball together at another spot. He brought this to me out of deep concern for us being singled out.

It confirmed an attitude of undue hostility we'd sensed and mentioned but could not prove.

They stick the same guards in that room pretty much every time that shift is on for the weekend. My partner and I go out of our way to be kind and polite to everyone, both by principle and personality. Gin, my love, warms everyone everywhere she goes.

We had been really perplexed about it, too. Accustomed to getting along with everyone and being ever polite, we couldn't figure out why it seemed Ms. Wilson had been singling us out when she was in the visitation room. We had joked and reveled in the conclusion that she must just be jealous of how much we loved each other. Turns out we were right.

But who does that?! Why would two people's happiness

together in those brief moments of life while suffering years stuck apart while one is behind bars so irritate someone who herself gets to go home every night? More to the point, what kind of existence is it when we are subject to the whims of this woman–and others like minded–at the one time we can bask in joy.

It's not just the briefer kisses or the reduced privacy and comfort or even the one-sided negativity. Sharing a relationship here requires making the most of what we've got. The awareness of being deliberately harassed without cause casts shadows upon the mood of anyone. It takes away from the entire experience to be bullied out of sheer spite and have no recourse.

Now we knew for sure we were being mistreated, and we also knew there was nothing that we could do. We continued to try to kill her with kindness, to strive to make friends and avoid conflict. Nothing helped, now it was in our heads, and it actually got worse. One day recently she went so far as to verbally threaten, "Oh, I guess it's time for me to start suspending your visits," at the end of a visit after barking at us to stop our kiss. It had been about ten seconds of our only embrace, and we had not been told to stop nor argued. It was a loving kiss and hug, and nothing but PG. Everyone else was still kissing, but we were being threatened with the loss of our everything even when we followed the rules because of her personal disdain for our happiness.

We still visit; it's too important not to do so. But we have been traumatized by the constant nastiness where we hold no rights. Our dialogue is muted, sitting there right in front of her. As soon as we see it's her walking in, we both get anxious, stealing the carefree we typically share and replacing it with foreboding and a sense of persecution. Rather than an embrace tight enough to warm this cold concrete existence all week, Gin actually flinches, sometimes when Wilson is there, pulling away from kisses that are all we get but on these days are drained of their typical passion. On a number of occasions Gin has been reduced to tears of frustration. Other times I have cried over the reduced sense of connection and tension created in our words. The visits are considerably less meaningful, sometimes downright stressful even, directly because of her treatment. And this is what has happened for two people who are educated, emotionally intelligent, and resilient with more resources than most. Imagine how it impacts others.

Admittedly, this trauma is between partners, not parents and children, but the effect projects. In fact, my mother, after nearly 2,000 miles of travel, had much of one visit left vapid and tense because she got scolded for sitting the wrong way and became anxious thereafter. One of my brothers came once and then apologized, saying he could never go through the stigmatizing process again. I know dozens who've forbade their parents and children from coming specifically because of the negative attitudes that bring tears. Bonds fractured.

Policy Suggestion 3A: Staff visitation areas only with people trained and certified in customer service and conflict resolution.

Communication skills are not required to work here and are not typically taught. Fortunately, plenty of evidence shows that effective treatment of others by authority can be learned. Thus, the very first step to improving the bonds forged during visitation experiences is to demand that visitors be treated as stakeholders—as essential customers. It should then be made a requirement that anyone working in visitation be certified as having passed training that stresses the importance of these interactions and has them practice understanding how to make the experience positive and avoid conflict when enforcing the rules. Ideally, certification would be periodically updated with refresher courses.

Policy Suggestion 3B: Provide independently-run comment card-type feedback that determines future staffing of visitation areas.

Currently, there is no recourse for nastiness and the oversight of visitation officers is done by their co-workers inherently on their side. Retaliation is ever a risk, even for minor complaints. To ensure that positive interactions are maintained, a system for offering feedback that can be optionally anonymous should be installed, as well as independent arbiters available in any particular moment. Oversight should be regular and unscheduled, with constructive feedback to promote improved performance, just like any other customer service job.

Policy Suggestion 3C: Incentivize working the visitation area.

Attitude really is everything, and those that see customer service work as desirable perform the best. If we want officers to treat visitors kindly and maximize the therapeutic value of visits, they should be happy about having this shift. Really, that should not be difficult because it is people at their best and happiest, and the shift requires virtually nothing. Yet currently it is often seen and treated as a punishment, with officers placed there who hate being there, starting from a point of animosity.

Thus, the first step is to make it an ideal shift people will want, perhaps by allowing it to be shorter or offering higher pay for having the aforementioned certification. Only those choosing to be there should be asked to work visitation. Then, there should be real rewards for those who receive the most positive comments from people visiting. Behavior is, after all, most effectively modified with attainable positive reinforcement. This would match the therapeutic mission of the institutions, too, as every great visit helps strengthen family and community bonds that benefit everyone.

Policy Suggestion 3D: Eliminate authority of visitation officers to unilaterally terminate visits without documented evidence of wrongdoing and due process.

No one acts or feels their best when feeling threatened and powerless. Thus, a simple way to improve the quality of visits would be to ensure that officers simply cannot arbitrarily end the visits. Doing so should require evidence of meaningful wrongdoing beyond a delineated threshold and multiple people's approval, including a supervisor also trained in conflict resolution and the importance of visits. Any officer who demonstrates personal disdain that impacts visitors should be suspended from these desirable shifts.

Problem 4: Crowded, harried, institutionalized visitation settings make many visitors uncomfortable and degrade bonding experiences.

"Because I can't handle seeing you in there. I mean, I know it would be awesome to see you, but I'll cry if I have to see you like that."

So said D, my remarkably-communicative-for-a-14-year-old son, and with it broke my heart with my full understanding. I've never known a father and son closer, ever since he was born, and that has continued to this day, even after seven years locked up. Forget spankings, I've never even had to yell at him. Not once. We speak lovingly and openly about everything.

Yet he told me this a few months back to explain why he does not at this moment think he can come visit me. His mom had said for years it would make him too sad, and she's been great so I didn't agree but certainly agreed to respect it. Now older, he has echoed that sentiment. He desperately wants the hug and the in-person time together, but from what he imagines and has heard, the setting is more than he can handle. So we talk all the time on the phone, write letters, and I understand but we are both missing out. In nearly seven years, I have not seen the son that is the center of my universe. Worse, nor he his dad. Because of this setting.

The initial hurdle is that media images have painted a picture of prison garb and ever-present danger or maybe talking through glass partitions on modified pay phone receivers. With intimidating images in mind, getting loved ones to visit is tough enough. While the reality is not typically as bad as seen on TV, it really is not pleasant even when it is not quite so barbaric. We get used to it in here, but all the locks, uniforms, fences, and cold industrial spaces are jarring to most sensibilities.

Rather than create spaces that facilitate enjoyable visits, DOC sets aside multi-use areas for visitation on the weekends. They are afterthoughts, cramped and mindless. Perhaps they have a single, ancient mural, but they are otherwise devoid of decoration. The seating is on uncomfortable plastic lawn furniture in an empty institutional sea of tile and concrete. Cameras and officers are everywhere, and nowhere is comfortable. The tables are so low we must hunch over them, and the chairs are all terribly rigid. Often no windows exist, but if they do they only frame concertina wire and guard towers. There is no food except candy bars from vending machines. Bathrooms are outside the room and require us to obtain accompaniment, leave, get strip searched again. For our loved ones, even, the restrooms require leaving and another search. We have to wear the shaming outfits described previously. Once seated, we are not permitted to touch at all or even get up and stretch or take a step. I was once scolded and threatened to lose my visit for showing an irregular mole on my foot to Gin. She was threatened the same for taking a stray hair off my face. All the while, we are seated so close to other visitors in this undivided space that we could touch them, if so permitted, but never avoid overlapping conversations. Collectively, the spaces are designed to be as physically uncomfortable as possible.

And it has an effect. It keeps many people away, like my D, hindering those relationships. Even for those who do come, the structure of the experience can create serious stress.

For instance, earlier this year I was witness to an incredible mother/son reunion steeped in joy. Then, I was also witness to its unravelling into tears and trauma through a terribly designed situation.

I confess that I did not know Hooch at all before this event, and I still only know him through a few harried conversations. Prison is funny that way. I know a decent amount about his character because he spends his entire life within 100 yards of me and I see him nearly daily interacting with people I know well at the "chow hall" and on the rec yard. Yet we live on different floors of a "controlled movement" building, so we are not officially allowed to interact the vast majority of the time.

Still, I have seen enough to share that he's a young man who is often laughing and smiling, leading others around him to do the same. He hangs primarily with guys from his hometown, some of whom are friends of mine. He's a pretty good baller—I'm slightly envious because he's my height and can dunk—and does not start arguments. By all accounts, he's a genial guy, fairly new to the system, and his youthful impulsiveness is probably behind his trouble.

When we finally met after his cousin, Matt, found out I wanted to help him out, I know he was extremely polite and appreciative. With a firm handshake, contrary to prison fist bump standards, and his actual name, defying penitentiary norms, he introduced himself. To my principled outrage at his situation was added liking him, too, so my determination was to do all I could to help. Hence, I found myself writing about the tragic visit he had. I was there and saw it personally.

Mother's Day, and I could see he was stoked when he walked into the visitation room. It's small and there are regulars, but he and she were both new. Beaming smiles.

Turns out it this was his first visit ever, that special day, first time they've seen each other since he was locked up, the first real hug the man'd had in years. Their joy was evident. They were laughing continuously.

Then "count time" was announced. He was unaccustomed, so he didn't know we could not leave the room during that stretch. As soon as he realized this, he told them he had to pee. He told Officer Miller first, around 11:40 a.m. He'd been sipping soda, a special treat, and had to go soon. Miller told him he had to wait, but did nothing else. In fact, Hooch told him again before he left, and Officer Robeson entered to take over visitation duties. It was then around 1 o'clock, and he'd been holding it a long, long time.

When Officer Robeson took over, Hooch explained to her that the situation had grown urgent. She called on the radio to ask for someone to come let him out, finally, but did so without urgency. She also failed to use the key on her belt that opened the bathroom inside the visitation room. Technically off limits for absurd "security" reasons—even though we get into giant onesies to go in and receive fully intrusive searches leaving visitation—there had been a bathroom within the same room this whole time.

Once it hit nearly 1:30 p.m., nearly two hours after telling people that he needed to use the restroom, Hooch could take it no longer.

Suddenly, we all heard the distinct sound of a lot of change being dumped out. I looked up and he had poured out the quarters his Mom brought for the soda machines and was standing, doing that infamous dance. His Mom stood, alarmed, and unzipped the ridiculous suit in a hurry. He had the bag in his hand.

"I can't hold it any more. I'm sorry," he explained to the officer. She said she called but that she couldn't let him out, even though she could have fixed the situation numerous ways. Instead, she laughed a little and walked to the other side of the room—seemingly for either privacy or plausible deniability. She was fully aware of the whole situation.

Hooch positioned himself as deep in the corner of this rectangular, open room as possible, behind the large support beam. He had no choice except to pee in his pants in front of anyone, we could all tell. So he went in that bag, as privately as possible, not exposing himself at all. He then waited and they finally came to let him officially go, and he took the bag with him and returned. Robeson made no effort to stop him or warn him it would be a problem.

No one was offended or bothered. We all felt badly for the poor guy. But we returned quickly to our own visits.

About an hour later, a ranking officer showed up and unceremoniously kicked his Mom out, ending early their joyous time with further embarrassment. For both of them. Worse, they took this young man straight to "The Hole" and placed him under investigation. He had to sit in solitary confinement for five days and they gave him an institutional charge that came with the loss of future visits for months.

Because he had to go and couldn't hold it any longer after nearly two hours.

He wrote a complaint about the incident quickly, before I connected up with him, but they conveniently lost it and he has not gotten a receipt or response.

Then, weeks later, when he went to defend himself against the charge, rather than a fair trial, they suddenly upped the infraction. Hooch was informed that it was now a 100-series charge—indecent exposure—that stood to take his visits away even longer. Worse, he would not be able to get a job and he would lose about a month and half or two of good time—meaning, yes, he'd have to stay in prison months longer because they didn't let him go for hours when he had to pee.

He's fighting this, of course, but given that they already lost a complaint and upped the charge, it is an uphill battle. Defying logic and justice, rubber stamps tend to find these situations around here.

More broadly, this is a basic human decency issue, illustrative of how dehumanizing the mindset is amongst the administration. No one should ever be disallowed the chance to use the restroom for hours. No one should ever have to pee in a corner after their Mom had to help them out of a suit zipped in the back. No one should ever have a Mother's Day end like that.

Punishment and degradation should never be a risk during an innocent family reunion. If we want to truly encourage the relationships that are so important to self improvement and pro-social behavior, if we want to help families connect at every possible turn, we must make it so that visits are as inviting as possible.

* * *

Policy Suggestion 4A: Invest in creating visitation spaces that provide space, comfort, and amenities necessary to minimize stress on visitors while facilitating positive experiences.

Plenty of research has demonstrated that the design of physical space affects our moods. Colors impact moods. Comfortable seating impacts the quality and tone of interactions in a room. The ability to access or even see nature prompts calmness and speeds healing. On every level, a well designed space can improve the experience of people behind bars and their families visiting. Meanwhile, poor design has the opposite effect, with cramped, drab, physically uncomfortable spaces discouraging folks from staying and opening up.

Therefore, visitation spaces should be dedicated to that purpose, or at least designed specifically to encourage it. Seating should be nice enough to not be uncomfortable after a full day, and it should allow for the old and the young, as well as the large and infirm, to feel welcome. I recall last spring witnessing an ever-smiling, kind, full woman, the partner of a friend, not fit in one of these tiny, cheap deck chairs and end up crying and not wanting to return for weeks. Love, interrupted. The spaces should be large enough to accommodate as many people as come to visit in a way that doesn't have people crammed together. After all, this is the one chance for private, personal conversation necessary for bonds to be strengthened, with emails, letters, and calls all monitored. Even perfectly legitimate dialogue isn't comfortably shared with others when about sensitive topics. We all feel more comfortable with our personal space, especially sharing tender moments with family. Obviously seating can't be partitioned off for security reasons, but it can at least be spread out and the space shaped to reduce echoes.

Likewise, design the spaces to fulfill all basic human needs. Visitation should not require hunger or entrapment in gloomy tombs. Real food should be readily accessible, even if it involves a cost, and that should be subsidized to encourage even less fortunate families to visit as long as they want. Natural lighting and pleasant scenery should be actively incorporated, as both are known to improve moods. Outdoor seating should be optional in decent weather.

Of course, there should always be plenty of accessible bathrooms for everyone. If residents must go slightly away so they can be patted down again, fine, but the opportunity should not be limited for anyone. Visitors who have already passed a search should be able to use restrooms at their leisure. Embarrassment and bladders should not hinder family bonding. And no one should ever have to pee in the corner to avoid doing so in their pants, it should have gone without saying.

Policy Suggestion 4B: Make the visitation space personalized and pleasant by paying artists behind bars to decorate regularly.

Where people see art and color, we feel better. Similarly, when we get to express ourselves, we feel better. No one likes being in hospitals or warehouses, with impersonal decor. Instead, turn all visitation rooms into ever-rotating canvasses. For moderate compensation, allow confined artists and decorators to make them pleasant. Make it a contest or incentive even, providing both purpose and pride to show off to loved ones. Perhaps even incorporate a competition between facilities, with small but tangible rewards for the spaces that get the most positive feedback from visitors via the aforementioned review system.

Problem 5: Visitation settings are ill-suited for good family time, especially with young children.

Like baby birds imprinting, the most important time for children to build lifetime trust with parents is during their formative years via physical contact. The benefits of strong early bonds last a lifetime, benefitting children's education, emotional health, and behavior. For children of incarcerated parents, staying strongly connected at any age improves outcomes.

The benefits of these bonds can transcend even later challenges with proper dedication, in my experience. D and I managed to form a powerful connection in his first seven plus years. Thanks to that, his resiliency, and his strong mother, he has managed to thrive despite his circumstances. Statistical odds suggest he was likely to get in trouble, struggle in school, and have social problems after my unexpected incarceration, but he manages to make the honor roll, avoid all serious troubles, excel athletically, and act as a positive leader among peers, even reaching out to other young people with troubling parental situations. He is not saintly, certainly, but he is in no danger of any of the big pitfalls and stands out in many good ways. When I have asked him about this, he always explains that he is really sad I'm gone, but he still feels really close with me because I constantly reach out and because he knows how much he means to me, and he had so many good memories already. Even as a male teen, he reflects positively on our hugs, snuggles, games and play.

Unfortunately, not everyone has this foundation, or even the chance to build it. Many young fathers are incarcerated just before or after their kids are born, often due to feelings of economic pressure. So many of my peers here were caught hustling drugs to try to pay infant bills, so too many very young ones have to forge these bonds through prison constraints.

Therefore, the best thing for families, communities, and

especially the kids would be for visitation to be made as friendly as possible for families, especially with young children. The opposite tends to be the case, though.

Families, even with small children, are seated in the same chaotic, cramped area on the same uncomfortable lawn furniture. Lucky is the facility with kid size lawn chairs. Nothing soft or made for cuddling, ever. Actually, kids are expected to stay seated, regardless of age, and there is nothing to occupy them but perhaps a handful of ancient board games with missing pieces or some religious books. I have repeatedly seen parents scolded and even threatened with having their visits terminated for picking their kids up too playfully, trying to tussle even slightly, and even just when the little ones did not sit still well enough or playfully engaged neighboring tables. Three-, four-, and five-year-olds wander and move. It's necessary to maintain attention, but not permitted. One friend, KY, had to end his visit with his baby girl early because his mother was not physically able to chase her around and she kept meandering about after the officers told her not to. She was six, and he only got to see her once a year and could not usually afford to call.

There is also nothing to sustain children's nutritional needs. Vending machines are the only option, and they only contain soda and highly processed junk food, no juice or water or anything even marginally nutritious. Multiple times, I have had friends tell me their kids left early because they needed to eat. Other times, I have seen disastrous tantrums end previously warm visits after hungry kids had been told they could not have any more candy or soda.

Perhaps most telling, though, is the lack of necessary amenities. Traveling with little ones requires acting as a pack mule, as any parent knows. Diaper bags, strollers, and changes of clothes. While it is marginally understandable–though unnecessary with technology–to disallow big bags in with parents, making the space accessible requires some concessions for young children. Yet parents are not even allowed to bring in diapers, wipes, or empty sippy cups, and there are none provided by the institution, either. Moreover, if a change or bathroom break is required, it involves exiting at others' behest and an additional search.

Just a few weeks ago, Dan had his precious time with both sons, two and six, after his mother-in-law brought them over two hours each way. This is only about twice a year. After only an hour or so, though, they suddenly left, despite the enthusiastic smiles and giggles I'd plainly seen. When I returned to the pod and asked him, his youngest had had an accident because he couldn't get out on time and had no way to get changed right there. Then, on the way out, he tripped on the steps and sliced his head open beside his eye. No huge fault, but yet the officers failed to even tell Dan and only offered paper towels to the young boy. They smiled but shooed him away quickly, and they ended up having to change a dirty diaper in the car while the boy bled everywhere. His older brother had to keep replacing towels the whole drive back before he got the stitches he needed.

Policy Suggestion 5A: Create separate family visitation areas with appropriate space, seating, and family-friendly staff.

The vast majority of people behind bars are parents, mostly to young kids. There is plenty of need, so part of the prioritization of visitation should include the creation of dedicated areas for family visits. Include more comfortable seating and even free play areas in that space. Provide more room so no one feels cramped, even sanitized places for babies to be placed if necessary. Offer bathroom and changing areas in the same space, at least for visitors. Allow basics like diapers, wipes, and cups to be brought in after being scanned. Sell or provide healthy, substantial food and beverages in line with USDA guidelines for all ages. Stock this area with toys and books and even art supplies that promote cognitive development. Make it separate from the main visitation area to some degree to provide an ideal tone and reduce feelings of having to leave to avoid upsetting other visitors.

In short, require the creation of a family-friendly realm encouraging appropriate family interactions and affections, including minor movement and regular contact. All sorts of airports, hospitals, and other institutions have such areas that can provide models. Design them so no one will ever have to end a visit just to deal with basic child needs. Doing this will extend the visits that have some of the greatest positive impacts for everyone.

Policy Suggestion 5B: Develop and institute optional family activities in the family visitation area.

Beyond simply creating these family visitation areas, they should proactively foster beneficial interactions. Start by staffing them with either incentivized officers or outside volunteers or staff trained in childhood development. Allow—but do not force—participation in both fun and educational group activities during visits, perhaps using a pre-posted schedule so parents could plan for or around them. This will provide both familial bonding opportunities and a chance for children and parents to learn things sometimes otherwise inaccessible. Offer rewards to individuals and institutions who receive the best feedback from families about their staffing and activities.

Policy Suggestion 5C: Institute regular family days providing an incentivized opportunity for freer movement and field day-type activities.

As kids, we tend to be most impacted by and remember most thoroughly the big events full of many joyous activities that we anticipate before they happen. Things like basketball games, carnivals, and amusement parks are built up beforehand and cemented in our minds as a result. To make family visits most impactful for kids, institutions should regularly schedule—and not cancel except in dire emergencies—similar special days just for families. Field days when it is warm and school carnival style events indoors when it is not are some possibilities, as are small concerts or plays put on by residents. Most people here cherish chances for special times with their kids and fiercely protect such opportunities. By instituting fun, free-roaming family only events that last a while and allow parents and children to just be together and have fun, bonds and memories will be formed in ways that overcome the prison context and last forever. This can be highly incentivized and closely watched, but the focus on limited freedom within is crucial. Missing the best moments with mom or dad strongly contributes to the challenges faced by kids growing up with parents behind bars.

Problem 6: Not enough contact for kids who can't visit often or ever.

Unfortunately, not everyone can visit their loved ones in prison and build bonds that way. Limited time frames challenge working parents. Institutions are often in isolated rural areas, hours away from where our families tend to live. Travel is expensive and stressful, especially with young kids. Many coparents are not willing to make the trip due to strained relationships. My family is as supportive as can be, yet I only see my parents about four total times a year because they live full lives in distant states. D is 2700 miles away, with his mom who does wonderfully but remains my ex-wife. And I'm fortunate that they have resources and desire to make it work. The fact is that the majority of people behind bars never get visits at all due to these limitations, and I estimate that less than half with minor children get to see them in person even once a year.

In person is not the only way to connect, thank goodness. Studies show that regular interactions with parents strengthen children's futures everywhere. This is especially true when parents are absent from physical daily contact. Other types of engagement help avoid the worst outcomes for children with parents behind bars, and they help parents cope. Thus, clear logic and basic civic priorities dictate that correctional institutes and state governments maximize every possible way to connect children with parents.

Sadly, no such commitment is made. In fact, exactly zero resources are provided to this as a standardized approach here in Virginia. If we do not get visits from them, they will deduct child support from paychecks of pennies but otherwise we here are on our own. I have known guys who had bad relationships with kids' mothers and therefore have not been able to see or engage with their children for decades even though everyone sought it.

Commonly guys are forced to go months between interactions. There is not a single parenting-oriented program available at my current facility. When I wrote everyone at my last one about trying to find or start such, I got almost no responses. A single one did come back: "We do not currently support such programs. We do not know if we will." No direction or encouragement. Thus, it remains: no visits, no bond, and the kids must suffer the most.

Policy Suggestion 6A: Develop and incentivize programs directly engaging parents and children across distances.

We see things on TV, online, and in papers about innovative programs that connect kids with parents who are locked up. Heartwarming accounts, these lend the impression such opportunities abound. And such programs do exist, but they are rare and local, usually the product of individual vision, and leadership. They are almost never widely scaled or funded, typically relying on innovative actors constantly struggling for volunteers and grant money. They are out there and getting attention and results. They just are not available here. Yet. That needs to change for the sake of the kids, the families, the communities.

Such programs could be singular one-off social events that get time between parents and kids outside traditional visitation settings. Create and fund events that allow kids to get here with volunteers, social workers, even schools, taking the burden off parents. An example of this already being effective is through father/daughter or just parent/child dances held in the gyms, with DJs, refreshments, and a chance to experience social settings together as kids age. These have happened at individual facilities in Connecticut and even one Virginia jail. This could also be done with sports or theatre or whatever else. The key is that it be funded and logistically supported by the state.

Even better would be the widespread implementation of programs that allow for fundamental activities central to childhood development. Doing things together even while apart allows the formation of normal skills and essential bonds crucial for future success.

One such valuable idea worth expanding involves parents getting to read with/for their kids. When I first entered the system, I saw a local PBS special about how some researchers were allowing parents behind bars to make videos of themselves reading to their kids, then sending those to the kids as DVDs so they could watch them repeatedly. How wonderful, I thought, but no one at Greensville admitted knowing anything about it. With outside search assistance, I learned that it was no longer being done but that the results had shown improved reading interest, emotional benefits, and–I believe– improved parental bonds. Why did they have to run out of funding? Why not expand this? Why not take it a step further and make it a regular program that is free and utilizes the existing live video feed technology that for-profit companies are otherwise charging our families exorbitant fees to use? This would be an ideal investment of state resources that would repay itself down the road manyfold. More importantly, it would foster bonding activities crucial to young people's development academically and emotionally.

It is well established now that parents reading to kids, starting very young and continuing, creates emotional ties and confidence, improves language and executive reasoning skills, and helps children read well and actually enjoy doing it. Even beyond prisons, we need this desperately, as 2018 saw yet another nationwide drop in reading scores for 4th and 8th graders. Many other factors are also involved, but it would certainly help if the millions of people who have children and spend time behind bars in any given year were actively engaged, even incentivized, to read with their kids. Storytelling, artistic projects, or even collective work on writing children's books could work, too.

My own experience is instructive here. D and I used to read every day a little and every night for an hour. It was our thing. I did voices, and we covered every Seuss and every single Dahl book multiple times. Thus, it was very tough on him when this ended abruptly.

Having heard about this reading program and then getting no help in trying to create something similar, my wise Aunt Joan, herself a librarian, suggested we do it ourselves on the phone. She sent us both copies of each book, and we would take turns on the phone as often as possible. Those moments were precious, and he has since explained that he treasures the memories of us reading— but mostly the stuff before prison. The limitation was that doing it that way was less personal and disjointed. He let it fade away after one book took us about six months to press through. Even as someone with resources and given relatively high amounts of respect, the prison phone cost too much and I could not get on at a particular time with any regularity. Often phones behind bars are "run" by cliques or gangs that only allow certain people to use them, especially at key times. This DIY version was far better than nothing and helped us traverse early years of being apart, but it is not an accessible approach for most and not the same as video would be.

Therefore, state and local institutions should be required to seek out the best programs to connect parents with kids who cannot visit. Find initiatives with evidence of emotional and intellectual benefits, and commit meaningful resources to expanding them. In the end, it would benefit everyone, especially the children, if it was mandated that access to programs that forge parental bonds be available without charge to every parent behind bars at every facility, and for children of every age. In this realm, there is no one that should not be able to opt in.

Policy Suggestion 6B: Institute educational

programs connecting parents behind bars with children directly and separate from visitation.

Education is where the most concentrated benefit can be found in this regard. That is where having a parent locked up has a dramatic negative impact on outcomes typically, but also where parental involvement is shown to improve outcomes tremendously. Investment in education is the most cost effective way to improve outcomes and reduce crime.

Currently, it is almost impossible for parents behind bars to help our kids in school. I have decades of professional teaching experience, and I was actively instructing people in middle and high school work as a tutor, perfectly aligned to help D. He does quite well in school, but it is due to his developed work ethic and effort. At various times, he has had struggles with topics I am adept at explaining. He has always told me what was going on in school, and I tried so hard to help in every moment possible. I stayed up till 4 a.m. writing out detailed lessons and practice problems for multiplying and adding fractions, just to get it in the very next mail pick up after he told me about it challenging him. It got there after his test. The next year, it was exponents just the same. This month he has been stressing the electron ring patterns related to the periodic table in his advanced science class he loves. I offered to help, but he said, "Thanks, Dad, but I got it. You can't see the problems and it will be due before you can get stuff here." We tried discussing stuff on the phone, but have you ever attempted to explain math or science without visual aides or seeing the questions in a 20-minute window in a gym full of men yelling and laughing?

Thus, administrators should give dual learning situations for students of all ages and levels to work in conjunction with parents behind bars. Ideally, this would involve a web seminar or live video feed. Provide corresponding materials. Enlist instructors to offer assistance if desired. With many people behind bars still finishing their own diplomas, some students and parents would get to work together on matching materials, forging bonds and overcoming doubts together. When parents are able to instruct themselves, it will improve bonds and interest in school while elevating our value in the eyes of our kids. It will also boost up some parents' sense of purpose and meaning, just as Keith Harris described earlier the moment he got his GED and could help his daughter with her math homework. Progress and engagement in this realm could even be incentivized at schools and in prisons, ceremonies perhaps even held. No matter the abilities involved, students will work better and feel better with the active support and attention from their parents. All it takes is a little organizing and today's everyday technology.

Policy Suggestion 6C: Automatically include parents behind bars in all school communiqué.

Even if parents behind bars cannot directly help our children with their schoolwork, we absolutely must be fully informed about it. For a number of years, I wrote every teacher and principal D had, with Colleen's support, asking for copies of his grades and assessments and a chance to correspond directly. Introduced myself, explained my teaching background, and talked extensively about how important it was to support him in every way. Not a word back, ever, even when they promised his mother they would. Not every coparent is connected to parents behind bars, and not every coparent has the time or opportunity to be so effectively engaged as his mother is. Kids with parents behind bars have much greater odds of falling behind in school. Meanwhile, just having parental engagement with what is happening in school has been shown to improve student achievement.

For these reasons, the kids with parents behind bars

most need us to be part of their scholastic progress. Mandatory copies of all official communication should be sent to us here, plus quarterly dialogue with teachers.

Problem 7: Exorbitant costs of staying in touch outside visits limit family bonding opportunities.

Most of the people locked up here come from situations where budgeting was required constantly. Not necessarily poverty, but the families of most of us are working their tails off to make ends meet once our incomes are gone. I know that was the case for Colleen, D's mother, who required social assistance once I could no longer provide health insurance. Through skill and hard work, she has built more resources now, but she still doesn't have money to spend keeping me in touch with him. Luckily, my family has more resources than most of my peers and can help me out, and I can give my whole meager paycheck to pay his cellphone bill each month so I can reach him. That doesn't even include the costs of actual calls, emails, and letters either, let alone the new video visits they charge so much for. I am quite fortunate that between my loved ones, we can keep money available for that so I never have to tell him I cannot call or write because of costs. That freedom has allowed us to remain close all this time.

    However, that freedom is incredibly expensive for exactly this population with the least resources. Unfortunately, most parents behind bars cannot afford, nor can their families, to pay all the bills and still keep us daily connected with our kids like they want, need, and deserve. Even in my situation, staying in touch had costs and required some sacrifice to pay for it. Most here can't even afford that choice. Worth it, of course, but should it ever be that way for parents and kids to maintain even basic contact?

    I may be the most fortunate man behind bars, I believe. I have a son with whom I speak almost daily–even as a teen!–thriving despite his circumstances. I have found the best relationship I've ever dreamed of at 40, equality and mutuality with a beautiful scientist spiritualist healer who was already my best friend. I have a broad, loving family. I already was educated and I have maintained a purpose teaching and writing while here. This also makes me the poster boy for low risk of recidivism and a strong future. Unfortunately, it comes at a financial cost that most here cannot pay. Even more privileged than most, I must make some very tough choices to maintain these relationships thanks to a cascade of exploitative privatization efforts.

This starts with a lack of income. I have the highest pay rate in an institutional job, 45 cents per hour, 30 hours a week. That amounts to $54 per month, a 98.6% pay cut from my former work, doing the same thing–teaching–ultimately for the same employer–a state school in Virginia. In order to help with my son's bills at least a little and make sure he has a phone I can call even when his mom is at work, I send the entire thing to her monthly. Most people lack this "luxury," but it's about principle and I make a small amount with science writing on the side still, an additional $200/month. This qualifies me as "prison rich," but it doesn't go far at all in this gantlet of privatized services.

On a logical level, connecting us with external loved ones is both humane and humanizing, building bonds and maintaining families while reducing prison's impact and trauma. All the research also confirms that strong external connections and much communication are one of the two clearly evident routes (education is the other) to improving public safety, aiding rehabilitation, and avoiding recidivism. If we are loved and valued, connected with others, we have purpose and drive and hope. Yet rather than invest heavily in encouraging and providing access, the opposite has happened. This state, like many others, has accepted bids from private companies that pay the state a small percentage kickback for the right to charge a literally captive audience to maintain family bonds. And, boy, do they charge us every chance they get!

Even after the crackdown on runaway prison phone pricing (which did nothing for most jails), we still pay about a dollar per twenty-minute call. Maintaining strong ties and building a strong bond with a child and fiancée without personal contact necessitates much communication. I spend the maximum I can on calls, $100/month, but even that is only about three calls a day, split between too many people. My fiancée adds more on her end, but we try to limit that because she is building a new business now. Still, she pays nearly another hundred herself each month, and we only get to talk about an hour and a half per day. Not a lot when it's all we have, but that's highly fortunate here and we have managed to make it into the best relationship ever—despite the situation and at such a cost! Likewise with my son and family: nine siblings, four parents, and a couple dozen others I am staying in touch with.

It is still not enough to maintain those other bonds that way, and we have a limit of approved numbers we can call. Thus, I also rely heavily on email. This is run by another group of profiteers making tens of millions off the misery of others. The cheapest rate we can pay, buying bulk, is a quarter per email "stamp." Length limits and per attachment costs make many emails cost multiple stamps. Who pays per email?! Ever?! We do, those making the least, typically from the least privileged areas. So staying in touch costs another 20 or 25 bucks a month for me on email. That's even as I consciously limit myself in the process.

Still, some people require physical letters on top of that, particularly my growing son and any reform organizations. These must be purchased from yet another private company providing commissary: stamps, paper, pens, but also snacks and hygiene.

The commissary service is essentially a return to sharecropper life, as we are forced to buy basic necessities from the "company store" at prices that are impossible to afford on our paychecks. Many do not even have jobs at these cents per hour rates, and many jobs are only 27 or 35 cents an hour for only 18 hours a week. Most guys earn paychecks between 20 and 40 dollars a month. Yet the private commissary company raises prices reliably every year, charging at or above retail despite income limits. The cheapest deodorant is nearly three bucks, a day or two worth of work. When it's all said and done, I must spend 50 bucks a month on just necessities with them. About 10 for hygiene products and about 40 for stamps and stationery products to send letters to loved ones and share my activist voice. Ramen noodles are staples, the most affordable thing here, yet still somehow they cost more than "on the street" at a store with rent and advertising and employees to pay.

Thus, I am typically left with less than a dollar a day to eat commissary food. This would be fine if it was only supplemental, but the privatization cascade continues and food service has become for profit. This incentivizes spending less by the company hired, and a recent budget change means the state is paying them $1.40 per day–NOT per meal!–per resident. And they are profiting. With bonuses for supervisors for getting lower costs. As a result, the quality is nearly inedible, and the portions are miniscule. Dishwater-colored cabbage, unseasoned industrial beans, and over boiled squash are staples. Whatever protein is listed on the menu, be it "chicken," "hamburger," "steak," etc., 90% of the time is made from what we unaffectionately refer to as "meat rock." It is a more processed, lower quality part of the turkey world, all beaks, intestines, and buttholes. It comes in tubes of pinkish gelatinous mush and is squeezed onto pans and cooked, ultimately resembling a grey, shapeless stone. It is even marked "Institutional Use Only. Not for Retail Sale."

On top of that, I reside at the oldest prison in the state, Shawshank style, and anything prepared in the kitchen is potentially hazardous. No exaggeration, the tables and prep areas sit below exposed ancient sewage pipes that often drip a unique combination of rust and excrement. The roaches are countless, bold, and enormous, literally falling from the ceiling as they scatter about in daylight, two inches or longer. I have been part of documenting this and sending it to both OSHA, on behalf of a kitchen worker, and the Health Department. The former claimed institutions are not required to have safe conditions, the latter never responded. Grievances here have been summarily denied.

Hence, I cannot get enough edible food of a decent quality to fill myself ever, especially not when trying to stay healthy via regular aerobic exercise. Even if they served more and better fare, my fiancée made me agree not to eat food made here because of a distinct cholera risk. You know, like the slums of Bangladesh have.

Consequently, my dollar a day must stretch far. When it comes down to it, I often have to choose to not eat healthy or fully in order to be able to afford to stay connected with loved ones. And I'm one of the fortunate ones here! Most must do with even less contact, not eat, eat risky food, or have often impoverished families subsidize the state for keeping them locked up. Morality, families, communities all suffer the costs of this privatization cascade while a select few mint money.

Policy Suggestion 7A: Provide minimum subsidized communications of all formats for immediate family each month.

In this world, not every family can afford to go visit expensive restaurants, attend prestigious events, or travel on fancy vacations. Every family can afford to talk, though. The one thing that's still free, and it's how we bond best. Luckily, new research shows the more we simply talk with—not at—and listen to our kids, the healthier and happier they grow up.

I can personally attest to these benefits, current situation notwithstanding. I grew up in deep dialogue with my family, everybody but especially Momma, even during times of food stamps, Thanksgiving ingredients from food banks, and Christmas gifts donated by strangers. The whole time, I felt loved and confident, doing well in school and making a career eventually exactly because of that eternal communication. D now says the same, telling me (contrary to teenage standards!) how glad he is that we talk openly and that I always spoke maturely with him, even as he is likely still unaware that when he was young and I was in grad school, we were paycheck hopping and using subsidized healthcare. He thrives now with skills and emotional confidence built from dialogue with both his parents.

Talk is cheap, but talk is also incredibly valuable when it comes to families, both kids and adults. Therefore, no one should ever be unable to afford to talk with their family just because a parent is behind bars.

The current system has enormous corporations, like Global Tel Link and JPay, making tens of millions in profit annually off of our captive audience status. They capitalize on our need to stay connected to loved ones. Those opportunities are dependent on state approval, though, so all states should simply mandate that these contracts include language requiring regular freebies for families.

Specifically, I propose that every person behind bars receive one free email and one free call to each parent, sibling, and child each week. The state can also pay postage for one snail mail letter per month.

Costs here would be minimal. The emails and calls would use existing infrastructure that is typically free to everyone else already. No one on the outside pays for individual calls or emails. Given those more direct contact chances, the traditional postage costs would stay low as most people would use it only as a backup plan. So, while little outlay would be necessary, the impact would be priceless. Our children would gain esteem, love, and communication skills, improving their lives moving forward. Relationships would be strengthened for all, setting up us and our families to find greater success after we are released, thereby benefiting communities, too. Well-loved people with effective communication skills are the foundation of strong societies.

Policy Suggestion 7B: In conjunction with guaranteed communication access, require all parents behind bars with children under five to be trained in the importance of dialogue for child development.

Many people were themselves raised to talk at or around very young children with whom we cannot have fully adult conversations. Spring boarding off of evidence of the importance of language development built from early parental dialogue, a few programs have recently begun to spread this gospel. The more we talk with our children, starting even in infancy, the better they do, and these new programs have shown success in improving the quantity and quality of how already loving parents engage their children.

A simple extension of the previous policy could then involve requiring parents of young children to take these quick classes themselves. Alternatively, they could test out of it by having the coaches and researchers observe and verify they already say enough words directly, at eye level, using complex concepts, asking questions, and waiting for answers. Like talking with an adult. If this is valuable for all parents, it would be especially useful for our kids.

Policy Suggestion 7C: Provide two free video calls with children each month.

People today, especially our kids, expect more of communication than just emails and phone calls. Saying it on InstaFace is the only way it's real, right?! I even had D refer to emails as "old school." No awareness that they were only available mainstream when I went to college. He apparently thought that was multiple generations ago, I guess. Hilarious, but also telling.

Everyone, everywhere has access to video tech free now, or nearly so. The added eye contact, visual stimulus, and body language add depth to such exchanges, too. Of course, people prefer that, and video does a better job of capturing attention and eliciting comfort today, culturally speaking, too.

The technology is nearly ubiquitous within the criminal justice system now also. Between visits and distance court hearings, pretty much every jail and prison has live feed capabilities. Most are using this to offer video visitation from homes now, ostensibly to extend access. It does, too, for people without travel funds great distances away but it's not the same and the providers are also lobbying to use it as an excuse to reduce priceless in-person visits and charge exorbitant rates for the opportunity. Here, it is something like $15 for just 30 minutes, creating plenty of profit from thin air. Thus, if these companies—or, preferably, public institutions themselves—can provide this "service," there is no reason they cannot also provide actual service to families and communities. Two free video calls per month per child should be guaranteed. In order to spread the demand and ensure accessibility for all families, it could be installed at schools, public libraries, and community centers.

Policy Suggestion 7D: Eliminate private communication contracts, replacing them with non-profit state-run services providing at cost communication. Require those services to be scaled to allow ample contact with family using only prison employment wages.

There is a fundamental philosophical disconnect between profit and prisons. Multibillion dollar private prison companies have armies of powerful lobbyists spending millions to maximize income, while people behind bars are nearly voiceless. The result has been that many states with private prisons have passed laws guaranteeing that those beds will be full. The same has happened with private local jails even in states without private prisons. The cumulative effect is that laws and financial pressure now ensure that families will be broken up, regardless of the public safety needs or crime rates at historic lows.

Even states with correctional systems without private prisons officially still contribute to this by privatizing nearly all services. Virginia has public prisons but our food, our medical care, and nearly all our communication with loved ones is provided by companies pursuing maximum profit. Profit from monopolies guaranteed by exclusive contracts acting as gatekeepers to know our parents and children. Would anyone anywhere else be okay with companies charging them as much as possible for the only way to tell their kids they love them or ask about school? The longterm solution here is really for state and/or federal legislators to outlaw profit relying on the caging of people and separating of families. Take over the existing infrastructure with one time payments and then operate them at cost that would allow for free or nearly free contact between parents and children.

Problem 8: Difficulties maintaining bonds with stressed coparents of our kids.

When Pane got here and I got to know him, I was entirely stoked about having him be part of this project. Everyone invited was excellent, but his youth and spirit and adoration of his kids I witnessed made me especially eager to include his voice. He was enthusiastic, too. Yet, he's not included. He hit a roadblock and never finished.

"I want to, man, but I just don't know what to say to my oldest son. I haven't been able to talk with him in years and I know his mom is saying bad things," he finally explained to me a few weeks ago. My heart dropped, as I know how much his kids mean to him and I can only imagine what it must feel like to not even know where to start after this situation created such a rift. Even more heart wrenching, what must his son be thinking at this point, a new teen, becoming a man, and not a word from dad permitted by mom even though he was your best buddy?!

I first met Pane at the library, where I work. He came in religiously every chance possible as soon as he arrived here. He was reserved and chill, but he immediately showed me an intelligent and thoughtful character by seeking meaningful reading and enjoying dialogue analyzing what he read. He gradually grew comfortable with our regular library crew, and he offered great quips but ever careful to not judge or offend. So I asked him if he had kids and if he wanted to participate. Three sons, and total enthusiasm over the mission and his chance to write.

Shortly thereafter, I saw him at visitation with two sons for the first time. His mother brought them, and they gave him those running, leaping, full embraces that only good parents ever earn. Anyone who saw his smile at that moment would know his heart is kind. And nothing but gentle love was evident every time he got to see them there. One of our favorite opportunities during visits is to watch the happy reunion moments. There is no greater joy than the greetings of good people separated by prison bars.

When Pane then moved to my floor, I liked him more the better I got to know him. A sneaky but careful sense of humor, he'd pull me aside to joke about officers' idiotic moments and such, but ever careful not to offend. We enjoyed sharing stories of our boys, as he has three. I inquired then as to his progress on the letter for this book, and he was thrilled about what he'd done. "I'm doing one for each of them. I only have one more to do," he happily exclaimed.

That was four months ago. I don't pressure, but it became time to get it finalized, so I had to ask again. What a tragic thing to find, that he could not write the letter from his deepest heart to his son because he can't seem to stay positive with the boy's mother. One of the most positive, loving fathers I've met here, unable to connect with his eldest at all. And he is not the only one. Many of the letters here subtly reflect similar obstacles, and I know dozens of kindhearted providers who cannot fill their parental roles as a result of animosity with the other parent. The kids suffer most.

In contrast, D and I are still so close, and much credit is due his mother, Colleen, for constantly encouraging the bond. Not once has she refused to let him talk, even when she was initially quite mad at me for being here and being extra stressed financially. My family has worked with her to arrange visits to his extended family, helping him feel more connected. Even when he's been rarely grounded or lost phone privileges after a nasty comment or stupid preteen trick, talking with me has been the exception. She and I even talk on the phone regularly to share strategies and news and goals. Throughout this, I have bent over backwards to communicate kindly and gratefully and calmly, and it has paid off. She has never hindered our bond, even encouraging it, and he is better for it as we remain so close.

If we want great relationships with our kids, we must be

able to sustain productive coparenting interactions with their other parent. The skills to do so are too rare across society, as so many harsh divorce proceedings demonstrate. Often this is not due to poor character but just the stressful nature of being apart with kids. As the profound portrayal in "Marriage Story" recently showed, those endearing intimacies and quirks that bring us together so easily become potentially despicable mistakes when framed by separation, even for people who try to split as friends.

Now, imaging how much more difficult that becomes with the added stress of full physical separation involved in a parent being locked up. Even the best parents and people, even when still continuing relationships, will be challenged. And most of us who are here, even when good people, came here while struggling with something. Drugs, finances, anger, whatever it was, many parents here left with existing challenges for coparenting interactions. And, quite frankly, many people behind bars and many of our partners have not been taught the best relationship skills and habits. Or the best emotional communication skills. These are learned social behaviors that not everyone is taught. Many people all over the world struggle with this, but it is probably even more pronounced and common here. Not universal, but it is often very decent and good folks never taught great abilities at working together who end up here inherently. Often that is the root of the conflicts behind the charges against us.

Thus, the best way to help our kids is to make sure that all parents behind bars and all their coparenting partners forge strong bonds. The skills involved in doing so will carry over and help our relationships with all loved ones, too.

Policy Suggestion 8A: Offer free conflict resolution and couples counseling to parents in community centers.

* * *

An ounce of prevention being worth a pound of cure, we should help parents improve their interactions before they become estranged. Certainly, it is easier to maintain a good rapport during a prison term if the issues are worked through before that stressful separation occurs. Maybe some coparents can even remain couples who would otherwise break up, likely helping parents maintain bonds with kids further. Even for people who do not end up going to prison, the chance to strengthen ties with coparents is valuable. All kids want their parents to get along, tending to do better when they do. Such services, though, can be particularly concentrated in areas with elevated incarceration rates. There are many places where most people were never taught to be good partners and work together but would love to do so. Not everyone, but many of the guys here take very quickly to counseling and emotional skills training.

Policy Suggestion 8B: Turn to a summons for counseling all domestic complaints and temporary restraining orders between parents.

So many arrests and interrupted lives result from domestic conflict. Often this is due to the escalating nature of disputes that do not get solved initially. By intervening immediately so that parents in low level domestic disagreements automatically receive professional help resolving the root conflicts and improving conflict resolution skills, more dangerous situations can be reduced and families kept intact. This would provide a cool down period under observation and an incentive to resolve rather than seek revenge. Currently, when domestic disputes instead lead one person immediately behind bars, stewing and often financially dependent upon the person with whom they have been in conflict, they are often more inclined to act out more severely upon release, disturbing families further.

Policy Suggestion 8C: Offer free, on-site couples and family counseling at prisons and jails with incentives for completion.

We do not know what we haven't learned, and many behind bars have never been taught great skills in relationships. Likewise, many have never had the chance to experience professional counseling. Many of my friends here have expressed the desire, but DOC. only counsels those in acute emergency situations, not preemptively. Even the healthiest relationships can benefit from the outside professional perspective, as it can unmoor mutually entrenched refusals to budge. Most coparenting relationships here do not begin in tremendously healthy circumstances. Thus, degraded romance interrupts bonds with parents behind bars. A simple solution would simply be to invite anyone with kids to have their coparent—and, if desired, children—attend counseling that will soothe the anger that becomes an excuse to keep kids out of touch. Given the major benefits for people beyond this place, this can be tied to increased good time or some other reward designed to reconnect families quickly.

Problem 9: Relationships with loved ones, especially children, interrupted and strained with many lacking skills to strengthen and rebuild them.

We've all encountered it before. Friends or even family members, good people we admire and love, estranged from other good people we love. Maybe it's even us. Often it's behind the best intentions and principles, just laced with stubbornness and coming from different perspectives.

    I recall distinctly a year at the end of high school where I pushed my father away almost entirely over a difference of opinion. He tried to help my sister and I in a way we felt overstepped his bounds. He saw safety concerns, I saw refusal to let us make nearly adult choices and criticism of our wonderful mother. We still spoke—barely, pretty much just small talk and baseball—and it carried over for years where I presumed he didn't understand the deep things I did about the world. This led me to keep him at an emotional distance throughout college and he didn't know how to reach out to bridge it, either. Now, decades later, it turns out that we see the world almost identically in principle and laugh together and share some stuff exclusively with each other. I know how much I wish we'd gotten so close before I came to prison! Oh, how many nights here I lost sleep to thoughts of those lost years, and we never even actually lost contact more than a day. It was the missing moments of powerful connection deflated.

    That was also the reason that I made it a point to instill an unbending commitment to communication and against anger with D since the day he was born. We would not miss a day of closeness because of grudges or differences, I swore.

    And all of that was from a single rough stretch during an enfranchised point in my life, mostly college years, between two men known to be exemplary communicators full of love and positive energy.

Under the best circumstances, with all the resources and positive socialization available, this happens way too often. It gets in the way of the bonds that matter most and build us all up. Now imagine how often such disagreements arise among this imprisoned population. Most of us are here partially because of actions ultimately traceable to being socialized to respond to problems and frustrations in unhealthy ways. As a good friend, Dawid, once astutely noted, "Hurt people hurt people." Add to that the stress of being confined and the lost real-world understanding born of slow years spent as a number in a concrete box while technologies and lives of loved ones move on—as they should and we want, but as we often can't understand. A day or two without a response here feels easily like rejection with nothing else to think of but the roaches beside and the empty years ahead, told we're nothing and will never have a full chance again. Yet that day or two is standard delay for busy people today.

Misunderstandings are endemic to relationships across the prison threshold. It is even more likely in the parental capacity, as our children are especially hurt by our absences, with less support in growing up, and feeling like we have no right to tell them about discipline or homework even as we see it now as even more important. Then simple disagreements can amplify across distance and time while out of contact and frustrated, among those often lacking exactly the resources and training to cope effectively. Often the exact survival mechanisms developed to overcome the challenging milieux provoke standoffish responses to those we love. Often we don't know how to overcome these tendencies. This set up is structurally inclined to create grievances that fester and hinder exactly the bonds that are most important in healing everyone.

When I first entered my new pod at Greensville Correctional Center, KY was the first person to talk with me. About 6'4", 240, tattoos and a well-developed prison mein, I had not even put my stuff away in the cell when he was at the door. Not threatening or asking, he led with a story about another guy in the pod that told me all about his personality and had me cracking up. This dude told whoppers worthy of, well, presidential status. Knowing this was helpful, the tone reassuring. I was incredibly thankful, and we were fast friends despite very different backgrounds. For the next couple years, I listened to his crazy tales of street life, and we counseled each other about everything. When his youngest daughter was able to visit, the first thing he did was introduce us and he put me on the phone with his mom, too. Man, he doted on that girl, set things up so she had great birthdays and knew she was loved. Yet he never spoke to his oldest two children. At all. I could tell it made him sad, but he explained that years prior they had each said something hurtful and refused to listen to the advice he gave—which teenagers are wont to do. He still cared deeply, but he didn't know how to cross the barrier accreted over time.

    Bubba is a peaceful man to the point that many guys call him Buddha now. Appropriate enough, though, as that has become his belief system, specifically because it starts with "Do No Harm." Bubba taught me a little about Buddhism and we spoke extensively and deeply for hours about being positive, restrained people. He was down for a homicide committed thirty years ago, the result of a terrible temper in a man who had been taught to respond with violence. Buddhism and yoga brought him peace decades ago now, and he has been an exemplary leader ever since. Sadly, he has no idea where his two kids even are right now. Before his transformation, he was still angry, and their mother did not want him spreading that when they were toddlers. They are adults now, but he lost contact years ago because he knew not how to rebuild bridges, where to even start.

    LP is one of the greatest leaders I have ever met. Anywhere. He managed to set such a great example among the hardest to reach here that he was made an elder in reentry so every young buck leaving got a dose of his wisdom. He had learned graphic design and then became an instructor in the same, utilizing his skills to support the outreach programs he repeatedly developed independently. He shined so brightly in this darkness that they paroled him after about 30 years on a life plus 80 sentence, almost unheard of in this draconian state. I was fortunate enough to work with him and even get to know him on a personal level, sharing proud stories of our wonderful children. After a while, though, I learned that due to some differences of opinion, he and his daughter had not spoken for over a year, even as he proudly showed me the scrapbook he'd artfully crafted of every key picture, letter, and accolade she had earned. He is a marvelous communicator, a man of deep principle and love, yet they had a stretch where it was only from afar. He is out and working as a community leader and they have been reunited, but what a terrible loss.

Cherokee has been down for nearly 40 years now, and all he does is play role playing games, work at the milk plant, and tell the younger guys grumpy stories of when the system treated us so much better and was full of men with real principles. Certainly not perfect, he started with less than a decade to serve and got into enough fights early on that he ran his time up. He's harmless now and has been for years, but it could have been much sooner. For many years, Cherokee refused to have meaningful conversations with his beloved mother about his anger or anything serious. That finally ended following her cancer diagnosis. He decided he needed to get close with her and change so he could see her again. Too late, she passed away, but the legacy lasted, and he has promised himself permanent reform. Could have happened sooner, saving so much pain for so many.

The list goes on and on. Decent men and their loved ones keep distant because they know not how to reach out emotionally. Often this is a two-way street. In every instance, it is a waste, a lost opportunity to build the connections that strengthen our children, our parents, our partners, our communities, and ourselves. This situation is so difficult on everyone already, all effort possible must be made to avoid and overcome disagreements that block these human connections.

Policy Suggestion 9A: Offer conflict resolution and emotional communication classes with incentives to everyone behind bars.

Nearly everyone behind bars would value the opportunity to get better at avoiding conflict and communicating better. Many of us know that is part of how we got here in the first place, and nearly all of us would welcome the chance to strengthen our bonds with loved ones. Nothing is missed more than those strong connections, even if we know not how to improve them, at the moment. Potential limited cynicism by some about conflict resolution programming could be readily overcome if the course is at least partially taught by people with prison experience. Participation could be maximized by framing the focus on relationships with our loved ones and providing incentives, like extra family time and/or additional good time earned off sentences, for successful completion of courses with scientific evidence of improving social interactions.

The extensive secondary benefits of imparting these skills would more than justify the incentives. Interactions with our children and other family members would improve, strengthening the bonds benefitting everyone. With stronger connections and absent the stress of strained relationships, our children will be happier, healthier, and more successful. We will have greater support upon release, increasing our investment in our families and communities, lowering the risk of recidivism. Many crimes stem from poor communication skills and the escalation of minor disagreements, too. By investing resources in this training, we can avoid life's misunderstandings becoming crimes, saving considerable money and time for our states, and keeping people out of the system and in their families and communities in the first place. Even prisons will become safer, healthier places with everyone taught to express and solve problems gently.

Policy Suggestion 9B: For all parents behind bars, offer contemporary, evidence-based parenting classes and parenting discussion meetings. Include incentives for course completion.

Most every parent here cares deeply about offering the best guidance possible, as evident in these letters. Yet many have outdated and harsh approaches, often learned from their own upbringing. This happens with even the best leaders here. Understandably, too, as ideas about parental and authority roles get ingrained early and are rarely really reconsidered while living decades in this punitive, retributive, non-expressive environment, being treated the same by the nameless system, and most individual officers. Typically, we do not encounter other ideas within this land of toxic hyper-masculinity and devoid of countering evidence, so many of us cling to what we know. We want to be the best parents possible, instill discipline, respect, education, motivation, but we know only stern authoritarianism, violence, and punishment. Not only is this out of vogue today, it has been widely discredited by decades of research. Moreover, it stands to get in the way of strong bonds when today's youth encounter such harsh approaches. Often it is the same reason we rebelled against authority when young that landed us here.

    I am part of a self-started, for us, by us education and leadership group begun here. Ethics, civic responsibility, voting engagement, food drives, we do it all. The best group of men independently working to advance ourselves and our communities I have found in the system. No incentive, we gather, teach, learn, and reach because we believe. Admirable men, true leaders, and good friends all. During one of our breath-visible meetings on the rec yard this November, we were discussing deeply why it's important to change our cultural perspectives on criminal justice. Parenting arose, and one of our cofounders, a brilliant, self-educated man called Red pointed out the criminalization of discipline within communities of colors. His point was valid, and social services and abuse laws are discriminatorily enforced. Yet he had never before considered the fact that the historical attachment to "whoopins" in the African American community is itself a remnant of discipline during times of enslavement, itself a way of teaching violence as a problem-solving method. He announced great thanks the next week for the new perspective someone offered, and we were all enlightened. He just hadn't ever known. The same goes for people of all backgrounds here.

Thus, we will only help our children and enhance our bonds if we commit resources to discussing and teaching better parenting. Being that this topic is often so personal and sensitive, a good idea would be to have open fatherhood discussion groups as a starting point. No judgement, only a facilitator to provide an outside voice and information, but predominantly a room full of diverse backgrounds. Then, parents behind bars could choose to enroll in evidence-based parenting skills classes, led by certified instructors and demanding active learning. Passing these classes, via testing and role playing, should be incentivized with extra visit time with children and even enhanced good time.

At my last institution, I was fortunately invited to the only truly therapeutic group there, one of 10 spots for over 1,000 guys. Muslim, Christian, Atheist, gay and straight, every color of the rainbow, we discussed all sorts of challenges there. What we came back to most was parenthood. It was common ground and mattered most to us all. Tears and fears were shed, and we even organized a full day fatherhood seminar with outside speakers. From sharing ideas and worries, we all grew into brothers, and we all became better fathers. It was exactly that experience that propped up my confidence and helped keep me striving to find new ways to connect with D every day, no matter the difficulties the system placed on it or the challenges of an ex and 3,000 miles. They understood and we helped each other. This works, period.

Policy Suggestion 9C: For any cases where relationships have been strained with children, offer on-site dual counseling for free with subsidized transportation for children.

When things are already tough, we also need a way to help bridge those gaps. Sometimes even enhanced communication skills on our end won't do it, especially when other hurdles exist, and the scars are thick and deep and old. In those cases, there should be resources devoted to third-party assistance in repairing our parent/child bonds. Most people have never had a chance to receive any actual counseling, and clearly it would require mutual commitment. This may therefore be limited, but most people would welcome the chance to have a neutral professional offer calm perspective and advice when nothing else works. By creating a mechanism for allowing those face-to-face discussions that help most and offering a balanced, safe setting, many entrenched difficulties could be overcome. These would be the exact relationships that have the most value in repairing, too, especially if access is subsidized as an investment in the future.

Policy Suggestion 9D: Provide and encourage free parental improvement classes in community centers.

* * *

Even before we get to prison, better parental education should be made widely available. Be proactive and help our kids, maybe even avoid some of our crimes by reorienting our focus to kids beforehand. Parents are the youth's first and foremost teachers, yet many do not know how to have the difficult, honest talks necessary to guide children away from bad choices and social influences that will get them trapped in gangs and prison. Likewise, many parents are not themselves effective models of social and communication skills. Many are unsure about proper parenting techniques for promoting health, and many are too busy and stressed to seek out such information. We can reach the youth early by providing accessible, nonjudgmental parenting classes for free in every community. Make such classes an option for legal diversion when children get in trouble. Make sure they teach about the tough topics and show how to tackle them with kids. Employ those who know from experience so the message is received as coming from people who understand.

Problem 10: Lack of access, awareness, and training in mental well-being techniques for people behind bars and in many stressed communities.

When I got to Powhatan after years at Greensville, a number of old friends reached out via Gin to stay in touch. Many were expected, though some were pleasant surprises, including D, a guy I had instructed in our GED program. He had been making progress when I left, especially in math, and he proudly wrote to let us know that he was passing the practice tests and about to do so officially. Education breeds pride, especially here, I've found, particularly amongst those who were most cravenly rejected by the system in the past. In this case, like in Keith's, much of the pride was due to D's new ability to tell his son he accomplished something. Helping guys get there and seeing them smile has been one of the true unexpected joys in this wasteland.

In this case, though, it was not meant to last. The next time we heard from D, he lamented a terrible new reality. His father had passed away unexpectedly, leaving him with no one to help support him and without his closest confidant. He did not know how to deal with it within the cacophony of prison personalities, either. Afraid he was going to snap, needing some quiet, and told he could not get seen by a psychologist unless suicidal, he felt his only option was to "check in" to solitary confinement to get some time alone. He went to the hole to heal as a last-ditch solution, but that meant losing his job that provided the $23 a month that was now all he had to get deodorant, soap, and toothpaste. He also lost his place in the GED program and his materials to study. When he came out, he was forlorn, too, for he now had no way to afford to contact his son and had failed to finish the school that he had been so excited to show off.

Bad things happen to everyone, everywhere, of course.

Coping skills are important and social networks central to doing so. In this setting, though, the events are often made more stressful for a lack of support and a hectic environment. The setting and confinement would challenge anyone. This is exacerbated further by the fact that many people behind bars, even most, simply have never been taught effective ways of dealing with life. Emotional wellness and communication have not been central to everyone's upbringing or environment, and while the system is beginning to have some basic classes as part of reentry during people's last couple years, most people here go through our time short on these skills.

Worse, the established methods that most were taught and the mentality in this subculture are full of confrontation and toxicity, not healing. Many of our learned behaviors incline us to make things worse, not better, in moments of stress.

In the Victim's Impact class I recently signed up for, we have a productive but limited such environment. Empathy is the goal, and the dialogue is nonjudgmental. However, it is entirely voluntary, brief, requires nothing to "complete," and offers no incentive. Moreover, the discussion often shows how many well-intentioned people here lack skills to deal positively with life's challenges.

"I don't care. If a dude says some slick shit to me, I gotta stand up. In my neighborhood, that's just what you gotta do or else you'll be weak. I don't care if it gets me locked up again, that's my name and my kids also gotta live with that legacy," explained a fellow participant. While understandable and learned, this perspective only hurts him and his kids who need him. It can be taught, but this class is just 13 sessions without actual work required and strictly voluntary. Positive coping skills and alternative cognitive strategies are needed.

I get it, though. I may not have been violent, but once my life unexpectedly crashed, I was determinedly miserable for a couple years. I had been taught strong emotional skills growing up, but this situation took me beyond my experience. I was angry at the world for the injustice and felt defeated and hopeless.

Until, that is, I found purpose and went through some mindfulness training and therapeutic group counseling. It started with just having the social support network needed to give me love and a reason to push. From there, Gin taught me to meditate, and that was a game changer. Dr. William Cook, Jack Doxey, and I read about then conducted ethnographic research inside about purpose and meaning. We all discussed mindfulness, and they—along with my Mom and sister, Rose—had me read some books on the topic and we kept discussing it. I managed to get a precious spot in Dr. Rodney's Therapeutic Support Group, the only actually beneficial program at Greensville. I still have not had a chance to learn and practice yoga asanas from a teacher, but I have read and discussed the philosophy behind it with Gin. I continue to meditate and practice mindfulness techniques, even as it remains sometimes challenging. Days are long and nights lonely here. Yet I go through this wasteland armored now, knowing I have the support and skills to deal with even the most dehumanizing and degrading moments. Mine, though, has not been the standard path and most lack the background and opportunities I have been afforded.

All this happens in a setting where researchers find 15-20% of people have serious mental health issues and the majority have at least minor things, like depression and anxiety, with which to contend. There are no wellness and mindfulness programs to speak of, like meditation or yoga. Nothing to promote well-being just for us trying to stay as positive as possible. Even the traditional mental health counseling for people in dire need is almost nonexistent. The only exception is when self-harm is a proclaimed risk, and that even comes with confinement and punishment under a different name.

As of early 2018, Greensville, the largest prison in the

state and second largest on the east coast, had a total of about 3,500 people there for extended confinement, including about 300 in isolation at any given time. There were only 3-6 mental health practitioners, depending on the month and current intern assignments. Thus, they served almost entirely in crisis management, entirely overworked, and counteracted by administration claiming "security" about everything. They were only able to offer one class of ten people actual proactive, evidence-based cognitive behavioral and acceptance commitment therapy out of 1,032 guys in my cluster. One percent. There was also only a single psychiatrist for all 3,500 people, so even her best meant all she had was five minutes for check in confirmations of "not suicidal" with each person on medication each quarter. No treatment or counseling, even though she wanted to. Just pills and leave us in a warehouse to stew in our worries and loneliness.

Now add to all of this the stressful circumstances, a culture of emotional repression and negativity, and a complete lack of agency in our lives.

We don't just need parents here to learn better parenting techniques and how to get along better with coparents. We need all of us to be happier, emotionally healthier people if we want to fully enhance our relationships with our kids and families. We need to find individual challenges and hang ups and improve those counterproductive patterns endemic to this setting. We need to focus on wellness and train people how to achieve and maintain it. If we help everyone behind bars find mental health, all of our interactions will improve, and our loved ones will benefit in a myriad of ways. Think of the kinder communication with our kids, the example set, and the stress reduced.

Policy Suggestion 10A: Mandatory semi-annual mental wellness meetings that guide counseling and programming behind bars, focused on

treating, coping, and progressing.

What is really needed for the sake of our kids, parents, communities, and selves is a fundamental focus on mental wellness from day one to release. A proactive approach of healthy thinking and feeling, not a reactive approach only once crisis has been reached.

This should start with professional assessments twice a year, during which needs and goals are assessed cooperatively. Everyone should be required to do this, helping reduce the current stigma against seeking help. Based on these assessments, everyone should be enrolled in at least one helpful course each year. Anyone who seeks individual counseling for a specific issue should get it, as should anyone who meets diagnostic criteria or takes psychotropic medication. In all courses and counseling, focus should be on creating individual skills to help navigate this environment and future community and family settings, not just putting on band aids. Proven practices only, led by trained professionals.

Yes, this would be more costly per person per year at first, but completion of benchmarks could reduce sentences significantly, saving much in carceral costs directly while making everyone safer. Longterm savings would be huge because anyone actually engaged in this training is helped, with greater gains for the greater needs often found behind bars. We would make better fathers, partners, sons and daughters, employees, and citizens in a way that would stick. A quick comparison shows that short sentences with this approach across Germany, Norway, Sweden, and the Netherlands reduce reoffending considerably. Dedication to counseling and wellness also has been shown to improve outcomes here, for people behind bars and generally for the children of participants.

Policy Suggestion 10B: Offer widespread group therapy classes with gentle moderation creating a

safe space for dialogue among people behind bars.

My own experience showed me that one of the most effective ways to reach people in this setting was through group therapy. Those of us who stuck in Dr. Rodney's Therapeutic Support Group all benefitted tremendously and learned far more than the basis for the class. Taking a cognitive behavioral therapy and acceptance commitment therapy model, we were encouraged by Dr. Rodney to discuss and challenge ourselves to new ways of thinking about whatever was eating at us. The key was the diverse group and her compassionate, patient leadership, though. We all grew close enough to have leaders from groups labeled as "gangs," devout Christians, and middle-aged teachers and chefs work together to create peer programs outside of class. In class, we learned that our similarities were bigger than our differences and that deep sharing offered healing, even when hard. We learned to support each other and like each other and feel safe and loved and capable navigating a place designed to take all that away. I cannot speak highly enough about the value of this group style.

Part of its value lay in the lack of timeframe or structure or authoritarian leadership. We just came and talked and did a little individual homework practicing new thinking approaches each week. I was massively depressed when I arrived, feeling so very negative, and also convinced no program I would normally be qualified to teach would help me. This broke through.

It was the group dynamic that made it bearable initially and helped me overcome my stubbornness and hesitancy to share in this most vulnerable of settings, new to a gang-run prison with a nerdy pacifist background. The collaborative and free form safe space is a virtue. Yet it is not for everyone, so this should be an optional approach. Many good guys could not get over the sharing in a diverse prison setting. And the compassionate but firm and challenging back seat leadership is a key component. It must be largely amorphous in topic and unscheduled to induce the sense of emotional freedom that best facilitates bonds and learning.

Policy Suggestion 10C: Free yoga, meditation, mindfulness classes made available in all facilities.

I have applied mindfulness and meditation techniques to improve my focus, patience, and coping tremendously in the last few years. Nor am I the only one, as I was advised by my good Buddhist buddy, Bubba, about the restorative benefits of both yoga and meditation. Mindfulness takes many names and forms, but the resiliency to stay positive and productive with no control over our own lives requires some form of being able to be in the moment. My ethnographic research of positive leaders behind bars found it was a common mindset, albeit founded in a range of philosophy, spirituality, and various traditional religions. Point being, this stuff works in this setting.

In fact, given the circumstances the impressive standard benefits are probably amplified. Much research has shown that all three are valuable for dealing with stress and improve mental well-being overall. Meditation and mindfulness practices have also been linked to improved social interactions, too. That is why they are proudly offered as central opportunities in Northern European prisons lauded for rehabilitation and are even starting to be experimented with in limited progressive moments and places in the U.S.

However, these practices are far too rare here generally. They are often framed in ways that seem foreign or "weird" or, worse, "weak" or "feminine." Despite being full of people who have refused to adhere to some norms, such practices are not fully trusted and much traditionalism dominates here.

Thus, these classes should not just be widely available,

they should be encouraged actively. Instructors should be recruited who are relatable and, whenever possible, themselves people with prison experience. Even current residents. Overcome the initial dismissal then have participants vocally describe the benefits. Even allow it to be, like religious programming, a priority that allows for brief breaks from work.

Policy Suggestion 10D: Require communication and conflict resolution classes incorporating both people behind bars and officers.

My "Thinking For a Change" course ended up being actually engaging and helpful, unlike usual, because of a good group of people, leaders selected deliberately, and a counselor who cared and had senses of both humor and patience. An officer always had to be in the room, and it was often the well-liked Shoe. A few times, the best classes, in fact, he got in on the act and discussed topics with us. He had principles and respected the privacy of the room, allowing critical discussion of racist and power hungry officers and administrators, listening as a human, recognizing true injustices. He also shared, gently, alternative perspectives when some guys were being too one-sided or failing to see the "job to do" angle. The room had a palpable sense of revelation those days.

Shoe even suggested that every officer should have to take the same course that teaches thinking before acting, emotional awareness, and empathy. Of course that was popular because, while many are good folks, this job has a tendency to attract exactly the personality types we least want having such unfettered authority: self-righteous, authoritarian, close-minded, judgmental, etc.

I agree with his premise, but it should go a step further. Everyone should take these classes together, officers and residents, with full freedom of expression. Strong, fair moderators would be needed and firm ground rules enforced. Care in selection, too, perhaps a step-up process. Still, the benefits would be undeniable and wide-ranging. Broader perspective would be inherent and diversity fostered. More importantly, especially for our kids, we would learn how to get along with each other in both directions and lose many negative preconceptions. Especially for our children, not only would this make us generally more tolerant and understanding, we would not pass on biases that could hinder their growth. Certainly, I am not defending mistreatment or systemic problems, but even as we strive to change the system, we should help our kids learn the techniques that allow them to thrive despite its issues and help make it more humane.

Policy Suggestion 10D: Subsidized counseling, social skills, mindfulness, and therapeutic classes available in all communities.

For exactly the same reasons that we need to help people behind bars foster mental and emotional well-being, we should do so across our communities. Many of our hang ups began before here, so having those resources available and affordable would help many of our friends and neighbors avoid joining us here, making our communities stronger where our families still reside. Our kids would be able to grow up where wellness is taught and feel better while avoiding trouble and obtaining skills for lifelong success. When we got out, we would be able to maintain gains and have opportunities to continue to grow as parents and people. These are some of the elements of social capital that are lacking in many communities where incarceration is most common and opportunities most scarce. These are some of the elements fundamental to equity. Thus, these are the techniques to promote happiness and well-being equally.

Problem 11: Developmental challenges for kids with parents behind bars, including at school, behaviorally, and socially.

Imagine being a kid again, excited, and believing and hopeful. Your Dad who you do everything with and love deeply suddenly disappears. Now, on top of that, imagine knowing in your heart that he's a hero, a role model, the embodiment of fun and love. Yet, at six or eight, as you are learning how the world works, the world is telling you at the same time that your favorite person has been labeled bad, wrong, dangerous—even though you know otherwise. Maybe you know they didn't follow all the rules or even act perfectly, but your Dad still always gave hugs and love as often as he could. Now, since he's gone, you're lonely and your Mom is always stressed. Money's tight now, so she can't get you the video games your friends have or afford to sign you up for basketball and soccer. Maybe you've even lost friends or teachers after having to change schools. How would you feel about school? How about authority figures? Would you feel really motivated to do fractions or algebra? Would you want to do everything everyone told you even when the world seemed so unfair?

When parents get locked up, no one suffers and is hamstrung more than the kids. The family of my buddy from Greensville, John, provides the perfect tragic example. He is very smart and motivated, having figured out how to do on the fly electronic repair with only cheap fingernail clippers and stationery supplies, a MacGyver kind of guy. He knows science practically and can teach math to anyone, having helped dozens of previously discarded men obtain GEDs with only his support while behind bars. He has three kids who he had to leave behind when he got locked up. He was too angry then, but charges of abuse were trumped up by an angry ex-wife and her parents' deep pockets that paid for a psychologist to claim evidence of physical abuse that the kids even said never happened like that. Still, the courts deemed him dangerous and kept his kids out of direct contact growing up. He channeled all his life into teaching and helping here. He would gather the picked-on guys without support and make big meals at holidays and get birthday cards signed. His heart is huge and mistakes long past.

Given his background and their resources, his children should have succeeded in any endeavor. He left them all excelling in school and socially around 2003. By the time we got close in 2015, his daughters had dropped out, had babies as teens, and ended up in abusive relationships. His son ended up in ROTC but was mediocre in school and challenged socially. None of this would have happened if he had been around; he knew and I can't help but agree.

D has not fared so poorly, thank god, because of the strength of he and his family, his mom's steadfast determination, and my ability to at least stay connected. I'll give the credit mostly to him, but there were certainly challenges that arose specifically because I am gone with nothing being done to counteract that by the system. He was in 2nd grade when I got locked up, bright and forever ahead of all things in school, with a really, really positive outlook. At that age, even as we explained the situation, he didn't process fully time and meaning, only that his best buddy was stolen away. From 3rd to 5th grade especially, he had a hard time adjusting. He grew more quiet and sad, entirely disinterested in school. He expressed feeling so sad and angry that he didn't know what to say. He would be doing great and still had many friends, but would suddenly lash out about small things. Once, he stood up to a bully who was using racist language, punching him for picking on a friend, and he got suspended and ended up being labeled and treated differently by the principal and teachers. He developed a sense of feeling like he couldn't control moments of verbal anger and came to feel teachers didn't like him because they didn't understand. He had a particularly hard time when we had to go on lockdown and

I couldn't call for a week or more. Through it all, his mother and I stayed engaged. Parent teacher conferences she had and I wrote letter after letter, preemptively explaining this factor and seeking assistance. A single meeting with a counselor four years ago, with a promise for more that never materialized is all that happened. Fortunately, Colleen is tough and firm with his well-being and he is incredibly resilient and constantly talked with. He's finally back to feeling confident in school now, but emotional moments still arise and still the school has no active plan to help him deal with it. He has learned to cope by basically pretending it doesn't exist except when we talk. He explained recently that he simply does not mention it to his friends or teachers because it's too sad and they don't understand. That broke my heart. There should be an active support system for this.

The evidence is clear at this point. There is almost nothing worse for a child's chances statistically today than to have a parent locked up, largely because the system takes us so far out of their lives and does nothing to offset or mitigate that loss. Children with parents behind bars are more likely to underperform at school, get in trouble there, end up in trouble themselves with police, abuse drugs, and make less money as adults. Parental absence is an inherent detriment, yes, but it doesn't have to be this way.

D has become an athletic and academic star again recently and leads his friends with positive values, amazingly. Woody Harrelson's father was in prison nearly his whole life. It does not have to be a sentence for kids, too. D still has challenges that feel heavy to him even with our support. Key to avoiding generational sentencing is proactive support for the children. Society must reach out in these moments.

Policy Suggestion 11A: Install mandatory preschool and elementary education models promoting skills that engender desired outcomes: executive

functioning, decision making, role playing, and oral skills.

What is missed academically by kids with parents behind bars is not ability. It is engagement, encouragement, understanding, and interest because maintaining those as children is difficult in the best of times. It is nearly impossible when their entire worlds have been thrown asunder and everyone is stressed. Plus, once feeling behind, it becomes ingrained and difficult to get ahead again, adding mounting discouragement.

But it does not have to be that way. Some recent educational research has found that certain models, applied in key developmental stages beginning in preschool and maintained at least through elementary school, can overcome all the entrenched achievement gaps. A focus on empowerment and executive functioning and language skills early and often has been found to improve academic outcomes for even the most disadvantaged students, with benefits even lasting into income and behavior later in life. In fact, the Perry Preschool Project's application of such showed benefits that transcended generations, even for the poorest students. This would involve teaching with Montessori and dialogic learning elements involving free choice, including active role playing, complex interwoven discussion between teachers and students (talk with, not at), and shifting attention between tasks, ultimately improving choices, impulse and emotional control, and focus. This, we find, is how to help kids become successful broadly on their own, regardless of background. Instituting this widely, starting where kids most often have parents behind bars, will promote opportunity and equality despite this hurdle.

Maybe we could even implement the same educational models here behind bars in all academic, vocational, and social programs. It is, after all, generally the same skills that are underdeveloped amongst us here and the same outcome gaps that would be so beneficial for us, our families, and our communities to overcome.

Policy Suggestion 11B: Dedicated tutoring automatically available for all kids with parents behind bars.

In the meantime, prior and in addition to the implementation of inequality-leveling education models, extra attention is crucial. With one parent locked up, the other one almost always has to work during times that leave homework and studying up to our kids. Private tutors are typically not affordable. When already feeling raw and alone and misunderstood, along with frustrated with a topic in school, asking for personal help after school from a teacher feels daunting. If the time to do so even exists, between needing to get to after school care or other activities. I know all of this stopped D from getting extra assistance when he struggled in school, and even talking daily, I could not show him things over the phone. All students, even the most behind and disheartened, tend to do better with one-on-one instruction, too. My years as a private tutor and college teacher proved this beyond a doubt. For students who feel so alienated by life that comes with a parent behind bars, the personal caring involved adds to the academic benefit.

    Yet schools typically do not offer this. And so the negative effects build upon themselves. Yet a huge leap could be made if districts simply appointed a dedicated amount of personal tutoring time, during school days, if necessary, to any student with a parent behind bars. For free, where they will be anyway. Ideally this would be one-on-one only, and ideally it would allow for after school or at home with certified professionals for the sake of privacy and ease. Even small groups, though, with a tutor working with a few students personally and consistently and indefinitely would build the skills and confidence eroded by the loss of a parent to prison.

If we really want to discourage the breaking up of families except when absolutely necessary, an even better funding source would be the prosecutor's office in a district. If those budgets were forced to account for the secondary costs of mass incarceration for non violent crimes and one-off offenses, they would think twice about meting out such disproportionate punishments that impart generational harm.

Policy Suggestion 11C: Social workers with counseling skills assigned to children of parents behind bars, providing range of support.

If a school knows that a student has a parent behind bars, it should automatically and immediately reach out to that young person emotionally and socially. For anyone to go through the loss of a loved one to prison requires support and nonjudgmental listening. For a child, this should not even be optional. Yet it is simply not done, even when requested, as our experience with D showed.

In fact, his has become the go-to home for other kids with parents locked up partially because there is no emotional support system. He has had two friends virtually live with him for months at a time just so they could have rides to practice and healthy meals when one parent was locked up and the other not effectively coping. One best friend of his had to quit the football team ultimately because his mom was locked up, his dad didn't want to do anything except when convenient, then he suddenly flipped out and took him away for not calling on time one night and he was never allowed to play or talk with D again. No emotional support at school or in social services.

Similarly, D at one point this year brought a hoodie and barely used pair from his sacred shoe collection to give to a nice, shy, unpopular new kid in his math class. This young man had worn the same clothes every day and had a sneaker with the sole coming unglued, so my boy grew concerned he would get picked on. Middle school.

Turns out this young man had a dad behind bars and a mom struggling with meth addiction, so there was no one to get him clothes or worry about his well-being. Such stories are too common, and the system has not reached out to make sure these children have someone to talk with, someone to check in on them and see if they need anything. Instead, D and some others have made a small social group with this commonality, and they're there for each other as adolescents are, socially. But he's told me they don't really talk about anything serious, so it's helpful but also far from enough.

If everyone simply had an assigned, trained counselor they met with at least at school, it would allow problems to be averted early. Someone to listen, to advocate, to care, dedicated to their well-being would help millions of young people navigate parents behind bars without losing out like so many currently do. Again, the averted crimes and costs would be more than worth it, but does it really need to be financially balanced? Children should not suffer for parents' convictions. Invest in the future.

Policy Suggestion 11D: Fund programs that focus on realistic drug education early and ongoing in schools, led by community members and those in recovery.

This is an important issue because drug use or abuse is often the cause for a parent's arrest. There were over 1.6 million drug-only arrests in the U.S. in 2018, over 85% for possession alone. Plus all the drug seeking crimes that lead to arrest. This is part of the lives of many kids with parents behind bars, so it is not surprising that abuse rates are elevated in this group. Often drugs provide an escape from pain, after all, and they are around. While experimentation is often normal and relatively harmless later in life, early and regular use often becomes abuse and contributes to bad grades, trouble, and other hindrances to life. Thus, this needs to be tackled everywhere better than it is.

Not DARE, nor any other Just Say No unrealistic nonsense. Drugs are available and marijuana is low risk and normalized, so do not insult young people with messages that make the truths told untrusted. However, there is a great opportunity now for people who genuinely understand to initiate real conversations about the peer situations that lead to drug use, its appeal, and the severe long-term consequences of abuse. Present real evidence and begin two-way dialogue led by people who are familiar and understood. This can also provide an opportunity for purpose and service for those in recovery, too.

Policy Suggestion 11E: Refuse to arrest or prosecute anyone at school for discipline issues.

One of the biggest things parents behind bars want for our kids, universally, is that they not end up here too. Yet my first cell partner moved out after five days to move in with his father, and I know dozens of guys hanging with dad on the prison rec yard. And that's just those lucky enough to end up at the same facility. All too often, the mixed feelings and many obstacles in the wake of a parent getting locked up bring young people in right behind us. Worse, this is often the product of discriminatory and/or compassionless prosecution following relatively minor misdeeds committed by kids confused and in pain. Too frequently this starts at schools, where budget cuts have left no counselors, only security officers, who start with punishment, not understanding.

Anyone sincerely going to school should feel free from the risk of arrest, even when they make stupid youthful decisions. Criminally prosecuting youth offenses like minor drug possession, small altercations, and truancy only puts people in the system before they have a chance to mature.

San Francisco can be used as a model, as they recently passed policies limiting police actions in schools. Even if discipline must occur or police must be called, the school to prison pipeline so common for children with parents behind bars would be dammed by refusing to criminally prosecute such cases and instead remanding them all to counseling, treatment, and other alternatives. Obviously, there are extreme situations, like shootings, that differ, but all too often today the minor youthful acts of yesteryear are treated as egregious crimes. Make these chances to teach, not punish. See kids that bare hurting as needing help, not entrance into a system that will hold them back for life.

Problem 12: Lack of affordable childcare for many parents with a coparent behind bars.

In addition to all the added stressors related to the incarceration of a coparent, two people's child rearing time must now be covered by one. More work, no help with bills, lonely and angry children, and no one to watch the kids while having to work twice as much.

I know this was the case for Colleen with D on a regular basis. She and his coaches managed to cooperate, but that has often still meant him learning to feed himself and do homework alone while she shows houses in the evenings. He has managed to stay out of trouble lately, but there were a few scary moments of misguided attempts at pranks in those after school doldrums. A hypersensitive parent even turned imitating a horror movie line on social media into a threat to call the cops on an 11 year old. Fortunately, Colleen was stern and fair and we avoided any repercussions, through lengthy learning talks with our boy. I'm sure he still has his own nightmares about all those lectures and "I'm not mad, just disappointed" moments. It could have been way worse, and it would be if he had not grown into the amazing self-cleaning oven that he is, regulating his own study habits and bedtime. Not his volume or attitude, I hear, but he is great to me on the phone!

Even avoiding the worst outcomes of this lack of affordable childcare, interruptions and loneliness hurt our kids already so challenged by the situation. I cannot tell you how many times I've heard, "My daughter has to stay with her grandma now because her mom's gotta work nights and can't afford a babysitter." That means losing both parents and often having to change schools and routines. That means being further from the parent behind bars, often less able to connect. In a number of cases, that is the sole reason that visits and calls don't occur anymore, hurting the kids further.

Affordable childcare is a challenge everywhere these days, it seems, so of course everyone should have such access. In a world of limited resources, though, we should start helping those most in need. The children of parents behind bars face some of the biggest hurdles, and their other parent becomes that much more needed. If we want to do everything possible to help these children, keeping life as stable as possible is imperative. That means making sure that they have somewhere safe and positive to be whenever mom or dad has to work.

Policy Suggestion 12A: Fund and staff community centers focused on youth programming. When possible, hire local youth and people with records to lead.

Keeping kids out of trouble early is key to doing so for life. Especially in working class areas where parents have multiple jobs and cannot be home, one of the best ways to avoid youthful problems is simply by occupying kids' time with positive people and productive activities. This is cost-efficient and social, often including homework, learning, and exercise time. The best programs even add cultural elements, social skills, and even therapeutic opportunities.

D had to go to the YMCA after school for a couple years. No other option, it began, but quickly it became a place of new friends where he wanted to stay later. Not perfect, as this was mostly just time being occupied safely, it was nonetheless a blessing. It was also waitlisted and still cost money and had very limited times open. Most of the kids with greatest need had nowhere to go in his town. And it's typically the only option for parents with a coparent locked up and no family in the area. The price of most after school care there is more than many workers make.

Yet funding has precipitously declined in recent decades for exactly such spaces and programs. This can be seen as an investment not just in these kids, but in public safety. By creating safe space with positive role models who understand, neighborhood centers become community hubs centered around our kids. Social cohesion further reduces crime, and these centers support employment. Much cheaper than prisons, too.

Policy Suggestion 12B: Provide subsidized, income-based home care for children with a parent behind bars.

Not all jobs end at five or six p.m. Especially for those parents working double shifts and extra gig work to make ends meet when their coparent is behind bars, nights and weekends often require childcare. For that reason, at home care should be made readily available at a rate relative to income. A class of dedicated, certified, trained care specialists would be a fantastic investment to support the well-being of kids with a parent behind bars. They would be assigned to particular families to create constancy and build trust, allowing for a chance to do more than just oversee safety. Not for going out and having fun, but they could offer affordable, reliable care for times when the other parent must work or shop and community centers are closed. The chance to avoid generational punishment is more than worth it.

Problem 13: Lack of access, awareness, social support for coparents of children with a parent behind bars.

To endeavor successful, happy lives for our kids, we need their other parent to have as much help as possible. Our bonds will be stronger the better off they are. I know that D does much better, and we get to be even closer when Colleen is feeling supported. That has been a tough row to hoe, however, simply because they are thousands of miles away from extended family and no route to access necessary assistance exists. She needed healthcare for him suddenly when my lost career ended his coverage. She needed help with covering school clothes and sports. She had to seek potential counseling services, if needed. She had to help a kid who experienced about the biggest loss a kid could imagine and keep him going in school alone when his teacher father no longer could do so hands on. The list goes on and on, and it can be even longer for some. She had at least enough income to not have to deal with the bureaucracy of food stamps or housing subsidies. Fortunately, too, my mother was able to give some time and resources from afar, something many in this position do not have.

Point being, there is an enormous amount of logistical problem-solving thrown onto the already stressful situation when a parent gets locked up. Our coparents not only have to pick up our slack and provide double while also serving double duty for our kids who are traumatized, but new obligations and obstacles often appear. Rather than a ready-made safety net triggered by the incarceration, these overburdened coparents often have to tackle these situations blind and alone. This all falls back on our kids, too. I can't count the number of times I have heard from D how stressed and busy his mother has been, and she has echoed that and pointed out the solitary nature of her struggle just as many. All I can do is apologize, try to rustle up a few measly dollars, and ask family to help from across the country. We have moved past the worst now, but it was made worse by a system unprepared to help.

Likewise, I can't count how many times I have heard guys here say, "Man, I wish I could talk with my kid more, but I can't ever catch her momma on the phone. She keeps having to move or her phone gets turned off." Or, sometimes, "She's out there all alone and she's pissed at me about it, so now I can't talk to my boy. I get it, but damn. I'd be out there if I could." Or, "She just couldn't handle our kids without me, so now they're all the way in New York with their grandparents most of the year."

Carl barely gets to see or talk with his beloved daughter because of such logistical overload and a biased court system. A charismatic natural people person and hard worker, Carl loves learning and writing. I met him here when he found out I taught college and wanted some educational advice as he put himself through an associate's degree. Then we bonded over a shared desire to contribute, working on a for-us-by-us educational and civic engagement group founded here solely by residents called Positive Offenders Implementing New Thinking (POINT). A hustler having overcome a history of addiction on the motivation of time with his baby girl. When he first got locked up, Carl's daughter's mom got overwhelmed with the loss of income. They were still super young, and she ended up getting evicted in the early chaos. She had family to stay with but it was not ideal with a young daughter so she felt it would be better for the girl to briefly stay with her father in Pennsylvania. Then he passed away. His new wife, no relation, decided that she wanted to keep Carl's daughter, even though her mother was now on her feet. Never having been in trouble, just that eviction got a privileged lady with a lawyer custody in another state, and she'll only let Carl's pride and joy even visit her own mother for a couple weeks each summer. The rest of the year, she disallows a doting dad from being engaged. Oh, you should see his glow those weeks.

To avoid such tragedies, provide support automatically to the remaining parent when mom or dad gets locked up.

Policy Suggestion 13A: Offer enhanced eligibility and filing assistance for social services for coparents of people behind bars.

The families of most people getting locked up already experience financial duress prior to arrest. With that added loss, usually of the dominant income, those stresses amplify tremendously. Social services are needed even more at those moments than with comparable income without that element. Yet many services are difficult to obtain even for people with degrees and the concomitant experience filling out endless paperwork. For those who most commonly need these services, the bureaucracy is onerous. The result of all of this is stress upon the still-free parent, stress that can be taken out on the children and especially the parent behind bars. Understandable, even, perhaps, but detrimental for the kid when attention is now required for paperwork instead of promoting parental bonds.

Even worse, this can strain relationships to the point that the kids end up without any contact. I know that Colleen felt an extra pinch, and I definitely heard about it. Fortunately, she is capable of navigating bureaucracy and my mother helped track down extra possibilities, while I focused on understanding and apologies. Worse did not come to worst for us because we both recognize the importance of his bond with both of us no matter what, but I know multiple guys for who it has. The intense reactions are understandable, but it is the kids who lose.

Thus, any incarceration of a parent should trigger automatic offers of expedited, enhanced, and assisted social services, as well as optional follow ups from social workers. By reducing financial strain, parents can focus better on working together.

Policy Suggestion 13B: Create support groups for coparents of children with a parent behind bars, including periodic public events to build solidarity and public awareness.

When we set out to write this book, we did so because we believe in the power of universal humanity to overcome differences and stereotypes. We publish it believing that a look at the children and parents affected by mass incarceration will profoundly alter people's assumptions. After all, we are all someone's child and most of us are parents. All it takes is some attention to these parent-child bonds.

But why is no one paying attention yet?

Even in these early stages of progressive criminal justice reform that we are entering, almost no attention is being given to the broader impacts. No one is telling the stories of the kids and spouses and baby mamas and daddies of those treated so harshly with crazy sentences for one-time mistakes. And who suffers more?! Why?

Support groups for cancer are ubiquitous, as they should be. Alcoholics and Narcotics and Gamblers Anonymous are found in every meeting hall. We have Facebook and church groups for the loved ones of vets and people with eating disorders. We have learned how to collect and support those with any worry or need, yet with approximately 10.5 million people arrested annually in this country, over 2.5 million behind bars at any given time, and each of us having parents and most having kids, there remains almost no outpouring of outreach for our loved ones. Informal and isolated instances, sure, but we can do better.

Since every community has jails, every community should commit just a modicum of time and money to making support groups for our coparents. Kids can be included, too, perhaps, but we need a place of understanding and acceptance for those who take on so much in our absence. Clues for navigating social services can be shared. Crucial information that DOC almost never publicizes enough can be networked, making communication and visits more common and tolerable. Most of all, our kids and our bonds with them will benefit because our coparents can feel less stressed and work to help each other out.

Most of the work for such things is done by those involved, so outlay would be minimal. Still, a committed space for free, some community advertising, and a small budget to hold events to raise awareness would bring the widespread participation and broader public support that will help everyone.

Problem 14: Shortage of positive role models and mentors present daily for children with parents behind bars.

When a parent gets locked up, the kids end up missing a role model. Our coparents do their best and are often tremendous role models, but they are now the only one around and often cannot be two places at once. With our coparents often occupied just trying to keep things going, this means many moments with no one to answer questions, no one to teach basic life skills, no one to cure the inherent need for affection that we all feel, especially when young. This steals from our children some of the confidence that comes with just our reliable presence and often leaves them with a hole to fill, seeking unconditional love and acceptance. If we want them to do well and seek to erase the odds against them due to our incarceration, the system must provide additional positive figures to take up some of the slack. After all, humans are social creatures inherently and in adolescence we need to be included. For kids who feel understandably left out and alone, it is easy to fall in behind people leading them to poor decisions. If we head this off, it will help our coparents and strengthen our parental connections while helping avoid generational punishment.

It is not always a recognized gang, like the Skinheads, MS-13, or Bloods, but a gang by any other name remains the same risk. As I have traveled the system, I have hung with all sorts of people with all sorts of crews, many unofficial but just as deleterious for people involved. Lots of different claims of collective identity, from neighborhood to shared hobbies and hatreds. Yet the biggest lesson I've learned, from knowing people still in, got out, and never wanted part, is that the appeal is inclusion and love. For people missing positive role models, either raised with animosity or without strong or complete family units, lacking loyal friends, something is missing. That hole must be filled, even if it means joining a set that involves getting beat in and having to stand up for stupid choices made by a "brother."

The smartest student I taught in my GED instruction here was Ghost. Still in his early 20s, his mom was a drug addled, cold hearted woman and his dad never around. He's friendly as can be and immediately curious and bright, only failing to get a diploma after getting kicked out for fighting. He went out of his way to stand up vocally for principle and refused to pick on the easy targets, rare traits in this place. Yet he was, inexplicably it seemed until learning his background, "gang affiliated." No problem, we learn to get along with every one here, probably more so than anywhere else, such extreme diversity confined in such close quarters. Besides, he asked to work with me on some schoolwork after sharing some intellectual talks. Then, in just a few months, he flew through the entire curriculum. He took the tests and scored higher than anyone else had ever scored at the institution, high enough to earn automatic college credits in science and potentially in math, too. Life on track with only a couple years left to serve, we all felt so proud.

Then, a sudden lockdown hit. Typical of when a fight occurs, often in our gangland building. When we came off, he was gone. Turns out he had felt obligated to take part in a retaliatory beating ordered by a higher-ranking member. Someone not half as smart as him and with none of the loyalty or caring he showed daily. This turned out worse than usual for these situations. The victim in this, though themselves initiating the issue, tragically lost his life. Ghost supposedly got new criminal charges and likely a lot more time and lot fewer chances.

This gang thing is not isolated to prisons either or even to stereotypically rough neighborhoods. D goes to school in a city of about 150,000, itself a suburb of Portland. I lived and taught students in all its districts for years, loving it for being one of the safest places of its size, period. Yet talking with him now, his middle school is full of kids claiming gang membership. Not doing anything serious really, minor drug dealing and petty theft, same as many kids that age. But these kids mob people when disagreements occur and can be dangerous that way, he says. None of them are truly hard, but so many feel the need to be seen that way. He's analytical, though, and we discussed. Turns out he thinks that the reason some of the kids get involved while others don't is the same reason as above: some kids are missing a positive role model and a sense of acceptance.

This is a spreading thing these days, too. Inequality grows, which means opportunities dwindle. Demographic tensions are being stoked by politicians profiteering fear. As fewer people feel they belong and are included and have realistic hopes, everyone else wants to belong and seeks it wherever they can find it. Tribalism is bred, and with mass incarceration breaking up families and ruining unnecessarily so many futures, the kids are often left feeling the need to fill this void.

Positive role models are essential for avoiding these extreme reactions. Positive role models sharing love and stable support are crucial in less urgent situations, too. D never came close to joining a crew, but he certainly had moments of getting picked on and wanting to belong, missing my daily presence. We managed to stay so close, plus his mother is strong and he got involved in football with a coach that took a personal interest. Now that football is in his past, this year has been improved by a phenomenal science teacher really connecting. His confidence is up, and he talks about college and career goals without parental prompting, rare for any teen. And he and I are still as close as any father and son his age. When we keep positive role models in kids' lives, those heroes alleviate doubt and uncertainty that hinder bonds and success.

Policy Suggestion 14A: Actively invest resources in

developing mentorship programs for promising young people with parents behind bars.

Pairing these young people missing key role models in a stigmatized way with successful professionals, businesspeople, and creators will build confidence, demonstrate success, broaden perspectives, and provide social capital not readily available otherwise. This shifts visions of legitimate and mainstream success from the abstract and impossible to the human and known. It provides a constructive focus other than loss and offers stability. Mentorships have been shown to improve outcomes for students facing disadvantages. Success stories from local communities can be especially relatable and reachable while offsetting local negative influences. These interactions can be a source of discussion with parents behind bars.

Policy Suggestion 14B: Develop mentorship programs specifically matching youth facing troubles with mentors who have done time, providing respected guidance from legit sources who are credible and recognized and relatable.

A strong will can be an asset for a kid with a parent behind bars, providing determination to overcome. It can also manifest as a stubbornness that refuses to allow anyone in emotionally, and justifies rejecting norms and authority who took away Dad or Mom who is so loving. This often makes sense and has truthful foundations, given the amount of injustice behind so many convictions. In explaining to D the genuine mistakes and politically-motivated fabrications of my own case as he has asked, he has come to despise corruption and violence among police. We have had nuanced discussions, though, and many parents don't get that chance or know how. Often a child in his situation can conclude with emotional reasoning that getting arrested ain't all that bad a thing.

We learn best from those we know and trust, so there is no one better to show kids at risk of following parents to prison the problems with the road they are traveling than those who have walked it and now bear the scars and stories to share. This would also provide either employment or volunteer purpose for those getting out, and that can help keep them invested and motivated to stay out. One of the most common goals among my peers and friends here is to help the youth avoid this place. Ketchmore has a non-profit that does that work already while he's here. Pairing youth with individual mentors will also provide them an understanding confidant, guidance for tough choices, and an advocate in times of need. Personal investment from positive leaders can help reinforce their good choices. Strong relationships with these mentors will strengthen our bonds by providing fodder for dialogue and a sense of comfort with our situations.

Policy Suggestion 14C: Create programs that specifically teach how to navigate peer pressure and social media. Install these programs early and often in schools and community centers, mandating participation for kids with parents behind bars.

Often youth become involved in crime because their peers are involved, and they don't know how to decline without being shunned. This is especially dangerous where families are already fragmented, reducing counter influence, but it happens in teen years to everyone because we are hardwired to seek independence from parents and seek inclusion with peers at these stages. The facade of social media only exacerbates these pressures.

Likewise, many crimes are rooted in social anxiety or disputes begun in social media, where words are amplified and remain indefinitely as reminders of angst and shame.

Given the amplified social and emotional insecurities resulting from a parent being locked up, our kids are especially susceptible to the heightened anxiety and depression linked to heavy social media use. Social media and friend groups can provide community and belonging, but often a fickle facade of such.

Thus, actively training young people how to successfully navigate these common scenarios so that they can still fit in without behaving in a way that is dangerous will avert bad choices and destructive friendships that can trap them. Being able to stay above the fray while staying friends is a skill that can be taught. Here, too, it would likely be useful to employ those who have made the mistakes and learned the lessons or, even better, have parents behind bars themselves. This would offer legitimacy and understanding in ways that help lessons sink in and encourage better bonds with us.

Problem 15: Lack of productive, positive options for young people to pursue in many communities.

This problem relates less directly to the existing relationships between parents behind bars and our kids. Rather, this is about avoiding this fractured family dynamic in the first place by keeping us from getting locked up. It is also about giving better options to our kids while we are gone that they may avoid the same fate.

Crime does not happen in a vacuum. While many–but not all–people do illegal things that land them here, every adult American has committed at least a minor offense and most do not get arrested. Certain neighborhoods have higher arrest rates for crimes, like drug possession, prevalent everywhere. No demographic group uses drugs more than white kids in college according to self-reported behavior, but this is not who usually gets locked up for possession. Certain crimes are more likely to trigger punishment in certain places. Certain crimes, like homicide and robbery, also concentrate more in certain neighborhoods. There are larger forces that drive both crime and punishment.

No one here committed whatever offense simply for the fun of it, is my point. Perhaps drug possession, but even that usually stems from trauma and addiction when it reaches the level of abuse. Crimes that led us here were a response to life's situations. Not good responses, based on the outcomes, but responses nonetheless. Hurt people hurt people, right? I can't begin to count how many times I have heard my peers here describe how feeling like they needed to stand up for or support a sister, mother, brother, or friend was the thinking behind whatever they did to get here. And often they say they would feel the need to do it again because in their neighborhood there is no other way, no trust for the system or other options to pursue. This leads to some very poignant conversational moments when it conflicts with sincere commitments to not coming back here. I've heard the hardest dudes' voices crack under the weight of this reality.

As I have done my time, the sociologist and humanist in me has sought out an understanding of what has really created mass incarceration on the human scale. I have spoken with hundreds of guys from all backgrounds in seeking to simply listen and honor their paths. In the process, all the explanations and context can be boiled down to two key original factors: hopelessness and pointlessness.

"I had to get some bread and all they had in my town were minimum wage jobs. I did that for a while, but the boss was a dick and fired me for arguing about getting shorted on my check."

"I just did what my older brother did because he had a bunch of dope shit, Jordans, and a car."

"I had a learning disability and most people told me all I could do was get in trouble and be a thug."

"Had to pay rent and get food for my new baby and a job takes too long to get a check."

"I applied a bunch of times but no one real would hire me without my GED. Can't pay bills with a McJob."

"Once I pay my kid's bills and child support, my checks didn't cover the month so I needed something extra on the side."

"Everyone where I'm from gets locked up, so I figured it was no big deal. Besides, I'd see my homeboys inside, I figured, and it was the only way out of the hood."

"Couldn't stay there anymore with my family after what

happened, so I was gonna do whatever I had to do to get us out. No job I could get would do that."

"Where I'm from, there's nothing to do except get high. Factory closed and no one can afford college."

These are but a sampling of typical thoughts that reflect the lack of opportunity often felt by people just before robbing, stealing, or selling drugs. When we feel like there is nothing meaningful for us to do or no way to get the very basics of life, we feel the need to fill that void or escape the stress. American culture promotes the notion that innovation in adversity makes heroes and that masculinity means financially providing. But in many places, urban and rural, there are not enough legitimate routes to these expectations. Having a broader purpose can keep us aligned with social expectations even when poor, but where chances are in short supply, purpose often is too. If we want to avoid people getting locked up like us, breaking up families, if we want to divert our kids from the same, our society must provide everyone with purpose, opportunity, and vision.

This is especially true when it comes to young people, inherently inclined to thinking for immediate gratification and not considering consequences. It is a time to cement perceptions of hope and possibility, not drive people towards the outlets of the hopeless. In adolescence, our views of the world are shaped by our immediate surroundings and social circles, then we enact the reality we have learned. If we are taught survival and success by any means necessary and brute force, so will we act. Learning these lessons behind bars is too late, especially with the way the criminal justice system gives out decades to kids in the wrong place with the wrong crowd, just trying to get by. Many of the best men I have met during my time are 20-plus years down and still only around 40, wise leaders with decades left to serve even without killing anyone. They say, "That was the life I knew. If I had known then what I do now, I'd never be here," as they strive to help others and maybe get out someday.

A good friend here, TJ, is a prime example. As calm and peaceful and respectful a person as you can ever meet anywhere. Never heard him raise his voice. Incredibly strong, yet not an ounce of intimidation where that is currency. He was raised by an abusive, terrible father who forced him to fight and help him scheme. He was taught that only people who cheat get by, and his environs confirmed this. He sought solace in drugs and success in their sale, and this meant violence, too.

Next thing you know, he's 16 in adult prison with something like 60 years to do. Imagine what that looks like from that angle? Doing what he was taught, and his life taken before it began. Somehow, he managed to overcome the fear and distractions of this place and educate himself. He became a quiet leader and reaches out to the community now. He is bright and helpful, even here and facing so many more years. If he could make such good of his life in this context with just the added perspective of years and some books, imagine what he could have accomplished if he had grown up with hope and opportunity.

Policy Suggestion 15A: Create and maintain programs that appeal to the youth's interests and creativity while cultivating their talents and skills and aiding them in turning those into businesses and careers.

We must focus on inspiring the youth, maximizing their vision and potential. This means exposing them to varied forms of success, particularly those not commonly seen or glorified in less advantaged areas where many parents are locked up. They must be shown that success is not one dimensional and extends beyond music and sports.

Such programs need to be established both after school and as part of subsidized summer camps. The goal is to constantly fill their time and channel their energy into productive, creative, positive ventures while expanding their understanding of legitimate lifestyles. Professional success stories in these unknown areas should be brought in as examples, for we learn best from those who know. Often we are limited by a lack of awareness of the possibilities. We cannot dream what we cannot imagine.

This suggestion was written by Justice, a leader of men who would know better than anyone. A smile and a word of advice for anyone, he is one of the two best leaders I have met behind bars. Entirely self-educated here, but oh, the wasted possibilities. He was 19, having only really seen a life of limited opportunities. Not a bad guy, loved his girl, but wanted a little bread and sold some drugs with some friends. That was what the guys did because the shoes and cars weren't affordable otherwise. He had goals, but no means. Never really hurt anyone, either. Then, one night, his friends asked him to drive them after someone threatened them. He did, being loyal and knowing you don't snitch in that area, so they had to handle it themselves. He fought no one. No idea what was going on. Apparently his friends decided to take standing up for themselves to another level while he was out in the car. He got nearly 50 years just for driving his people without any violence or knowledge thereof. He was just doing what seemed normal and right in his world.

Policy Suggestion 15B: Develop programs that expand horizons by bringing young people out of their neighborhoods to see positive things beyond their daily norms. Likewise, actively import external leaders and information into communities.

Many people in the most crime-affected communities lack

the resources or social comfort to travel even outside their zip codes. I was shocked to get to know so many decent, intelligent people who not only had never been on an airplane, they had never been out of the state or even their city. We can only conceive based upon what we know. It is easy to be limited by the boundaries of our understanding. Meanwhile, travel and diverse experiences expand our ability to consider the future and understand the present.

By investing in expanding horizons, we will create young people with world views that extend beyond the petty beefs and seemingly pervasive gangs and criminality that seem like the only options to those who have encountered little else. Give the youth aspirations and build with them creative thoughts as well as well-rounded understanding. That will guide them in the direction that shows that opportunity can be found in decisions we make, not just limited by where we live and certainly not crushed to death by the weight of a parent in prison.

Policy Suggestion 15C: Offer ongoing employment opportunities in challenging circumstances. These should be jobs that develop career and professional skills in nonmenial areas.

Young people are particularly susceptible to being lured into crime in seeking lavish items they cannot otherwise afford. A sense of relative deprivation is exacerbated today by a flood of mainstream and social media images of wealth. Coupled with local experience offering only menial, low paying legitimate work or illicit earning, this leads to short-term decision making by immature minds. The work ethic, confidence, social skills, and self-identity built by early employment are essential to getting socialized into positive attitudes and avoiding criminal habit forming. Broad expansion of such opportunities can be beneficial to employers, too, so government agencies could readily encourage and support such programs.

A small version was recently piloted by our peers at Buckingham, where a group of parents behind bars collected funds to help teens start lawn care businesses. They purchased mowers and marketing. Even better would be tech or creative jobs. If we can do it, the state sure can.

Policy Suggestion 15D: Hold youth-only meetings to engage in positive dialogue with policy makers and officials.

If elected officials, civil servants, and those in criminal justice spent more time engaging the youth who are disproportionately affected by the system and also the most likely to make positive changes, everyone would understand each other's positions better. Develop regular fun, positive, edu-tainment programs specifically to humanize the interactions in both directions, as young people can be more readily guided by those with whom they share enjoyable experiences. Youth often rebel because they feel like no one listens or understands, so this can divert potential problems and broaden perspectives for our kids.

Problem 16: Shortage of support upon release maintains stress and increases likelihood of difficulty readjusting and reincarceration, hindering families.

Upwards of 95% of people behind bars in Virginia will return to communities. It should be much higher since far less than 5% of crimes are homicides and, even for those, evidence shows that life sentences are arbitrary and pointless for public safety. But that's another discussion entirely. Important here is the fact that we are almost all returning to our families, intent on making a positive difference in our kids' lives.

Strong bonds with our kids and their ongoing well-being therefore does not just mean improving things while we are behind bars. It also requires that we stay out there and lead lives with enough opportunity to thrive that we can support them on every level. Unfortunately, there remains an enormous stigma against returning citizens. It is harder to find jobs, living wages, and housing. Many of us also return to communities with even more limited opportunities and with less social capital than overall numbers indicate, too.

And we are all very well aware of these facts. This can easily breed hopelessness. Hopelessness breeds crime and these stresses and shortcomings can poison our interactions with our children.

One of the biggest fears I encounter with friends here, one I struggled with myself, is having no options left when finally getting out. That life is essentially over and meaningless, no one will want us in any capacity, even once time has been served. This causes tremendous anguish. As Smitty struggled with a close friend and girlfriend who was returning to addiction while he was here, ruining their relationship, he worried for her. He also expressed simply, "Who else would ever want me?! I'm gonna be in my 40s, with a dope scarred body and no job prospects because of my record." That same thinking applies to all our relationships and opportunities, including regarding our children.

We may be "convicts" but we're not idiots. Most of us, anyway. I know the stats. I taught this stuff, so when I realized I was going to get prison time, I realized the odds against me. I was absolutely convinced when I first found myself here that life was essentially over. Forget future romance entirely, I would be an overeducated drain on my family with nowhere to stay and no one to teach or help.

So I said so during my intake questioning. States all use questionnaires that link to algorithms that allegedly can predict our likelihood of reoffending. Our answers guide programming requirements moving forward, but I never redid mine for my first six years because I know the actual data. My education and age are high, and my convictions were my first and non-violent. I have extremely strong family support. I figured my risk scores were low. And they were, just not as low as they should have been. My first annual review with a new counselor at a new spot, she for the first time told me that I had a couple that were elevated. She encouraged me to and I redid the questions, now feeling much better about the future but with nothing factual having changed. Turns out a previous counselor had input by mistake that I get no visits, and COMPAS, the proprietary algorithm here, concluded low family support. But the real difference came when I now said that I was very confident I would have a place to stay, being engaged now, and that I would find work, having built some activism connections and knowing better what they want to hear. See, it turns out that simply telling the truth is held against us in predicting our risk rates by a for-profit company's software that has been shown to have marginal predictive accuracy and a strong bias against people of color, predicting unfairly high risks of reoffending. These risk assessments not only guide our requirements here, they are passed on to probation officers and parole boards without context, affecting our treatment moving forward. And we are penalized for admitting the truth, that we are fearful that jobs and housing will be tough to come by.

The idea that job and housing prospects would predict successful reintegration makes sense. But this method of measuring those prospects obscures the real issue. To reduce recidivism and improve community safety and family solidarity, the system should not falsely force confidence to be expressed but actually improve opportunities.

Thinking like my early angst and recent revulsion towards this COMPAS system turns out to be widespread. During a recent class led by the counselors who do these reviews, we ended up in an endless dialogue about how the scores are biased. To a man, every person in the room explained how they are desperately determined to get good jobs and how they all have plans and dreams and determination to never come back. Usually family was the expressed motivation. To a man, though, everyone also expressed how frustrating it is to know how people will stereotype them no matter how well they have prepared. Moreover, everyone was disgusted that when they honestly express reasonable concerns to our supposed advocates, the counselors, they are told to enter it into an algorithm that holds it against us. I add to this that a much better use of this information would be to help us navigate those concerns and find jobs and housing. I'm a fortunate one, though, as most others in the class lack the training, job experience, and social capital I have. I at least genuinely feel more confident, albeit still aware now. These guys know the set up in the impoverished areas where they will return to, both urban and rural realms with lacking chances with a strike against them. It is an unnecessary paradox of determined-to-stay-out-and-support-my-kids and scared-of-no-options.

Policy Suggestion 16A: Install probation/parole

officers with explicit direction to aim for human success, with reincarceration the last option only when a new crime with a victim has been committed.

According to a June, 2019, snapshot of Henrico County Jail, the number one reason for arrest was parole violations and the number three reason was suspended sentences revoked. Not new crimes. What sense does it make to separate families, interrupt employment, and otherwise fracture communities only for rule violations?! Is there not a better use of resources than locking people up for dirty urine tests and missing appointments? A full rethinking of supervised release would provide rewards more readily than sanctions (as evidence shows to be most effective), consider the human circumstances in all situations, and develop tailored monitoring and responses to errors that aim to help people reintegrate successfully. Probation officers should treat successful avoidance of reincarceration as their job, and mistakes should be interpreted as evidence of need for assistance, not punishment. Such supportive monitoring promotes communication and helps maintain the relationships and opportunities that are essential for moving past convictions.

Policy Suggestion 16B: Develop social services and agents dedicated to assisting people released from custody, with prioritization for parents of minor children.

No one should ever have to leave prison without knowing how they will pay bills, find transportation, and offer a place to stay to our kids. No one should ever leave to a situation without support for staying out. This means help navigating social services to get them set up immediately, guaranteeing food, shelter, and healthcare. This means less obvious things, too, but things that cause stress and hinder our ability to feel secure and strengthen parental bonds, like substance abuse treatment for free, counseling services, clothing for job interviews, and a mode of getting wherever we need to go.

A number of small, local organizations already provide elements of such support, but they are piecemeal and fractured and severely underfunded and understaffed. Some things will have to be done at the local scale, where people know each other and local needs. In those cases, let's have dedicated funding to be spread out. Otherwise, let's find the programs making the biggest differences and scale them to other communities. Let's make sure that keeping families together after the traumatic experience of a parent behind bars is the top priority, given funding and person power and executive attention ahead of punishment.

Problem 17: Shortage of employment opportunities upon release that allow parents to help support our families, creating stress and pressure.

Without a doubt, jobs are the number one source of anxiety about our return to society. Even if unrealistic, we feel more confidence about finding somewhere to crash or taking the bus around town. We are usually realistically very confident our love for our kids and dedication will make us good parents. We all stress about future work, though, exactly because it is so important to us to provide for our kids and to be able to afford some fun moments together, to show them we can support ourselves. These worries, once released, have ripple effects. Thus, the ongoing lack of opportunity for meaningful employment has become the biggest reason our lives and our families too often remain stressed after release. My experience here suggests that the most common reason good dads get locked up again, re-fragmenting families, is a disconnect between financial expectations and reality.

This is bigger than individuals, too. A confluence of cultural and structural factors flow down from above, creating a delta of employment insecurity. To start, jobs are scarce that pay enough to support ourselves, let alone that allow us to support coparents and kids. This is especially true in the degraded urban and rural neighborhoods where the most people return. On top of that, studies have shown how commonly qualified people with records are not hired, even when whatever conviction has no bearing on the job. Yet this instant financial independence and provider role is what society and everyone around us expects, including us. Probation officers tell us to find work immediately or they will report our violation and send us back. Exorbitant fines from our cases require payment, often before we can get our driver's licenses back. Child support has officially backlogged thousands while we could not earn, and we want to do even more than that. The cultural standards of rugged individualism and either masculinity or motherhood say provide. The American ethos expects consumerism, amplified by social media and the learned belief that it's our fault if we can't do all this right away, some personal failing, even when no one's hiring people with felony convictions and most of us got warehoused instead of prepared for jobs. Certainly no one amongst the dozens who have directly controlled our freedom to some extent has ever been expected to help us get work.

Thus, some people do get out and come back because they feel the need to make money the only way available. It's disheartening to see, too. Everyone leaves with sincere intent to remain out, especially parents. Contrary to stupid politically-motivated tropes, no one wants to be here. A small portion have been stuck so long as to be institutionalized entirely, but every single person here craves the chance to reunite with and support loved ones. Yet it does happen beneath the weight of these pressures. It broke my heart when one young man left my pod at Greensville in 2015 and then came back to the same pod a year and a half later. "I'm not a man unless I can buy my kid some Jordan's to start school and take my girl out to eat. Couldn't do that at eight bucks an hour and no one would hire me for more. So I started slinging a little again," he explained. Not right to my thinking, but it is realistic and understandable. More importantly, this disconnect between financial needs and legitimate jobs hurts our kids.

My good friend, Dale, embodies just how terrible the current employment prospects are for us when we leave, through no fault or our own. Sure, we have made mistakes perhaps, but we have also served our time, plus some in most cases. Dale was an immediate comrade and confidant when he got to my pod. Hilarious and snarky once comfortable, he was unfailingly polite and generous to everyone around us. He was nearly 50, and this was his first conviction, a single non-violent charge. He was a rule-following professional and we shared a sense of humor. Then he made incredible emotional growth while committing himself to cognitive changes and openness during our Therapeutic Support Group. He only had a couple year sentence, so when he left, I was positive that his recent work experience would outweigh a single blemish.

Boy, was I wrong.

Dale is a trained chef, and he was the head of a multimillion-dollar corporate kitchen when he got locked up. His people skills and work ethic are tremendous. Yet when he got out, the system literally worked against him. He was told by his P.O. that he was not allowed to apply for numerous jobs he had leads on that required a little travel around the state. Nothing in the city was offering a meaningful wage. He kept being rejected following good interviews even when he was overqualified simply because he had a record. DOC even offered an interview for an underpaid kitchen supervisor spot then refused to move the date when they unilaterally scheduled it when he was already required to be elsewhere. His required meetings for probation would conflict with job interviews at other times. After months of this, he got an offer at a middle-class salary, then his P.O. told him he was not allowed to accept it because he would occasionally have to drive 90 miles to do functions in D.C. Ultimately, Dale was forced to spend the better part of a year working the line at a bagel sandwich shop for an unlivable wage. Fortunately, his former partner let him stay in their home and helped out until he eventually got a real gig. Dale also has no children that would add to the pressure. Still, though, he reached the point of telling me he almost wished he could just give up because it felt like he would never get a job, that life had even been less stressful inside where he hated it so much.

And this was a preeminently qualified man with social skills and an excellent work record. Think about the experience of the majority of guys leaving here, many of whom have been down for decades. Never even seen a cell phone or a laptop, as I spoke to guys about when working as a GED instructor. Imagine trying to return to today's society, lacking that comfort. Rather than prepare guys by focusing on computer, smart phone, and internet basic skills, DOC here actively resists any such opportunities except a few dozen spots across 35,000 plus people. No such standard for their alleged reentry. Plus, the vocational classes so sparsely available are often in fields with limited jobs or that require bonding, very difficult to get with a record. Not a single bit of job placement going on before leaving, either. Mostly just, "good luck figuring it out."

Policy Suggestion 17A: Incentivize training, education, and social skill development by guaranteeing employment at living wages to people successfully meeting standards while locked up. Ensure that adequate vocational training and employment opportunities exist to support this, including the incorporation of public agencies directly into programming behind bars.

Quite simply, positive reinforcement is the most effective way to teach. By making it meaningful to develop skills and knowledge, time behind bars can be money well spent and the cost of such programs can be offset by reduced years for completion. As it stands now, such sincere employment preparation is not given a tenth of its due, and this becomes wasted time which sets people further back from peers seeking jobs. As I noted earlier, seven years in and I'm still on the waiting list for my first class. The first step is to dedicate the resources to really creating the training and educational services that are universally available.

Once in place, they will be enthusiastically engaged—but only if they have a real impact on job placement. We here fear not being able to support ourselves effectively upon release, even though we all have abilities and potential to offer. For anyone who knows the stress of prison, a guarantee that they will have a job that pays the bills without risking going back will be all that is needed to motivate. These can be private jobs with tax breaks or even public service jobs that must be done anyway. The point is to orient the training to what the employment needs are. For employers, these living wages can be cheaper than what may have to be paid to others, the workforce would be ensured, and loyalty will be built. More importantly, it keeps us from crimes of need and provides instant legitimate self-identity and income to help smooth the initial transition back. Once reentry is established, it is easy to maintain and communities are safer for all. Even economies improve and examples are set. Most of all, families are stronger for the stability.

Policy Suggestion 17B: Invest in job training and offer low interest, easy access business loans, and dedicated employment support for those who have been recently released.

Extending the idea of training behind bars, opportunity to be self-sufficient upon release goes far to reducing recidivism. Providing dedicated support staff to help returning citizens pursue job security will be well worth the effort. Again, these jobs themselves could be used to employ those with records. Job training and maintaining employment could be a diversion to convictions for minor charges in the first place. Funds could come in lieu of new jails and be earmarked from the reduction in cases prosecuted and jailed, if we shift to a mindset of avoiding that option. Invested, hopeful folks commit fewer crimes.

Policy Suggestions 17C: Make reformed "offenders" into public leaders and mentors after release. Harness the power of experience.

* * *

No one speaks more eloquently or powerfully of the reasons to avoid crime than someone who has been to prison and learned its lessons. Social legitimacy provides deeper impact, so harnessing those who have earned street cred before makes the message stick better. This also provides purpose and leadership training for those reentering society, as well as meaningful jobs.

Policy Suggestion 17D: Employ recovering addicts in treatment settings.

One reason that addiction recovery can be difficult to maintain is because the lost opportunities and stress thereafter can amplify despair. The top direct reason parents initially get locked up is addiction, often in response to structural stressors. Getting high is hard to avoid for those who feel like they have nothing better to do and nothing else to make of themselves. Hence, purpose and meaningful employment are crucial to staying sober, as studies have shown. Many people struggling with addiction express, specifically, that helping others with the struggle is the best way to stay motivated. Employing the sober would keep us that way while avoiding prison and broken families for people we help. Additionally, this can be an incentive to avoid conviction, serve as community service, and help offset treatment costs. Again, most of all, treatment and employment for parents battling addiction are the best thing for our kids.

Problem 18: Criminal justice system over incarcerates, disregarding the secondary impacts of family and community separation, amplifying the negative effects of social problems for many, especially kids.

We are getting it wrong, our collective response to crime in this country. Pockets of progressive action exist, but we are stuck in an outdated, ineffective approach that starts with locking people up. The problem is, the effects do not end there. As we've been discussing, they ripple out and what happens is a traumatic loss for so many children, parents, spouses, and communities. People may get locked up individually, but the experience is shared by everyone who loves us and it hurts everyone who relies on us.

Full disclosure: I have worked diligently for reconsidered approaches to criminal justice since I was in college. As a teacher and activist in the field, my views were solidly founded in decades of data and some interactions with people affected by the system, plus plenty of ethical and theoretical consistency. A lot of people thought I'd become disenchanted with those views as I experienced prison firsthand. After all, I'm a nerdy, white, middle-aged pacifist, so it would be easy for a system full of hardened "inmates" to push me around. Well, I conclude this book passionately, even more strongly in the camp of reshaping our entire prison complex and letting almost everyone out with some training and assistance. My take on all this has been cemented not despite my lived experience but exactly because of it.

I have not been pushed around nor had a hard time at all. To the contrary, I have been repeatedly floored by the decency, intelligence, and principles of people I have encountered here. Repeatedly, the exact "types of people" who were supposed to show me ugliness actually stood up with me in demonstrating community principles. In here! I compile this book, with their voices and in their honor, because what I found here has been true friendship and leadership. Sure, there are frustrating and negative and close-minded people here, but that's the case everywhere, and even those individuals can be readily interacted with. When I get out, I will be proud to say that I am lifelong friends with more people I met in prison than I am again living next door to my family. This experience and the people featured in this book, and some who are not, have taught me tremendous lessons, something I did not expect. I certainly fought before for less harsh sentencing and treatment, but I also certainly came in with some negative assumptions about people who would ever, say, kill someone. Through getting to know people with every possible mistake in their past and finding amongst the same leaders, teachers, and fathers from whom I humbly learned about so many areas of their expertise, I also learned that none of us are defined by our worst day. Thank you, LP, for that turn of phrase. This book is a thank you to everyone who has proven it true.

We must be able to see the human beings in any situation. During this time, I have also learned that almost no one needs to be stuck behind bars for an extended time. I have deliberately interacted with everyone in every pod where I have been, rather than hiding out. Not everyone will be invited to my first barbecue at home, but I can count on one hand the number of guys who I really feel are genuinely a problem to have around, period. Everyone else here simply needs a better shake in life, the training and opportunity to make better choices.

I have had no real problems because my biggest lesson has been that we get from people what we expect and offer. Most—but not all—people who are here did something stupid and even dangerous or harmful, yes. But they did so in the context of pain and fear and a world offering them little hope for any number of reasons. Treated with respect and dignity, that is almost invariably what I have received in return. In a land of deprivation and deliberate indignity,

I have seen terrible things occur because of the context of addiction or pride or degradation or poverty, but I have also consistently seen principled behavior and kindness by people being treated as human. Just like the rest of the world.

Sure, there may be moments and rare individuals for whom separation from society is briefly necessary, but all crimes happen in context before prison, too. While individual decisions are involved, crime is largely a product of enormous forces far beyond individual control. That is why crime rates vary so much between otherwise similar societies and in different places within our society. An individual being poor, for instance, is not statistically more likely to commit crime than an affluent person, but areas of concentrated, ongoing poverty do tend to produce higher rates of crime. Learned behavior where no other options exist for pursuing opportunity and obtaining basic needs or a sense of agency make some types of crime more seemingly logical. "Where my name is all I got, I'm gonna defend it with my life." Like all things in society, violence and theft are learned responses to existing conditions. Just like we all wear pants and sit on couches watching electronic boxes and eat with forks because we have been conditioned to do so and see few options.

Similarly, an educated, wealthy person battling addiction is more likely to have family insurance that covers treatment and support that allows for places to stay and still eat while detoxing. Drug use rates are similar across all demographics, but the need to rob or harm within the throes of addiction is not. It's the situation, not the individual.

Likewise, the way any society responds to the crime that does occur is not set in stone. We have developed an entrenched penchant for lengthy incarceration in the United States, but this is a systemic thing, too. It does not have to be that way. It reflects a long history of punitive, retributive thinking, pain for pain, if not an eye for an eye literally every time. It also reflects a long history of biased enforcement and targeted use of the criminal justice system as a weapon against marginalized people of all backgrounds. Most of all, the reality is that this is not an approach reflecting evidence of success.

If it were as simple as isolated individual choices that are fixed by arrest and incarceration, there would be lower rates of violence and recidivism in the U.S. than in other comparable countries. Instead, nations where people get put behind bars for the least time and in the most humane conditions, like Germany, Sweden, Norway, Japan, the Netherlands, and Canada, have much lower rates of most serious crimes, and people are more likely to succeed after prison. Likewise, states with more rehabilitative programming and briefer sentences generally have less violence, all things considered.

Turns out, this system focused on "tough on crime" that imprisons people as a primary response to social issues is actually counterproductive. States with harsher punishments tend to produce cycles of reoffending after people are warehoused. This tends to have its most concentrated impacts on the communities already most lacking in opportunity, too. Families and generations and role models are lost, and both those locked up and our families are collectively traumatized. This trauma has been shown to manifest itself as an increased likelihood to commit crimes in response to adverse conditions, both individually and collectively in communities. This concentration of incarceration of the needy only exacerbates the exact conditions that push people towards crime and fracture communities in the first place. Again, we tend to get from people what we give.

In the day-to-day world of policing and prosecution, often overlooked are the ripple effects of every arrest, conviction, and sentence. In pursuing charges and time for victimless crimes, substance abuse issues, minor infractions, and first-time mistakes, society is acting in response to one dimensional stereotypes of criminals who are easily vilified and judged. But none of us so discarded are simply evil and the punishment never impacts us alone in a vacuum.

If we want to move forward in a way that honors and strengthens the family bonds so powerfully evident in these pages and so central to the well-being of our kids and ourselves, we must first recognize that every sentence impacts far beyond the sentenced, harming families, job opportunities, education, self-identity, and community. This ultimately produces more crime through numerous secondary effects, too. Rather than start with locking people up, this route should be a last resort and as brief as possible. With law enforcement and prosecution decisions made with human beings and secondary effects in mind, everyone stands to gain.

Simply put, now is the time to end mass incarceration. Lock up fewer people. This counterproductive and inhumane approach to criminal justice brings no justice to the lives of real human beings. It is time that our system switched to doing everything it can to avoid separating families, even where mom or dad has made a mistake.

Policy Suggestion 18A: Hurt people hurt people, so make all decisions with the aim of healing.

Recognize that both direct and indirect victimization create the pain that leads to addiction and other crimes. Often this involves previous familial absence resulting from incarceration. To avoid this, heal rather than punish. Those who are treated with kindness and understanding act accordingly, even behind these walls. Thus, prioritize funds and time for evaluations of the root hurts that led to any crime and respond with therapy, treatment, and assistance that can avoid it in the future. Currently, the only consideration for circumstances comes, very briefly and adversarially, at sentencing, once years are guaranteed.

Before the system gets so far, the root concerns should be required to be considered as part of how to respond to any crime. The vast majority of time, something besides incarceration would be a better way to help everyone, so healing should be the priority.

Policy Suggestion 18B: Always consider the human circumstances and consequences of any arrests, charges, and sentence.

People tend to act as they are treated, so humane consideration of the person involved, and the indirect costs of any sentence should become a mandatory part of charging and sentencing recommendations in all court proceedings. When people are locked up for years and decades in tiny cages, they are more likely to act like animals than when their mistakes are met with human understanding and prison as a last resort. Keep families together and jobs intact as a top priority. Minimize interruptions and generational trauma.

Policy Suggestion 18C: Reorient the prosecutorial mission towards seeking collective justice, not convictions or punishment.

This past summer, the national prosecutors offices in Denmark found on their own and publicly announced that they had used cell phone location data with errors in many cases. Their response and that of the nation's judges was to immediately and voluntarily suspend all prosecutions using such data, reexamine the impacted convictions anew, and reconsider the use of such data entirely. They did so in the name of justice, as they believed any potential distrust outweighed the value of any conviction, period. They prioritized justice over prosecution and yet they have considerably less crime. The social trust in the system is essential for investment of the people in its functioning.

Historically, though, the opposite mindset has dominated American prosecutorial offices. Most blatantly prioritize judgement and punishment without consideration for what is actually fair and just, especially in highly policed communities. Even where recent local elections have given mandates to progressive prosecutors to shift in this regard, traditional mindsets hellbent on punishment have actively resisted. Such has been the case from Philadelphia to San Francisco and here in Virginia in Chesterfield County, yet the choice of what and how to prosecute is historically exactly the prosecutors' province. By being willing to pursue lower sentence lengths, drop charges, and generally aim at justice, they can gain public trust in their offices and the system, in general. When that trust is lacking, problems escalate, and violence ensues. We recognize that there are structural factors here, but a true shift in private meetings and indicators of success—and those of the police—towards pursuing overall justice before punishment would provide a manyfold return on investment.

Policy Suggestion 18D: Incentivize avoiding incarceration for those working in prosecutorial and law enforcement roles. Educate prosecutors and police on the importance of doing so for full buy in.

Currently the root of so much punishment is the 'tough on crime' mindset still so pervasive in most police and district attorney's offices, where arrest and charging decisions are made. Regardless of popular sentiment or political will, this is where laws are enforced and applied and where change must be centered. A deeply ingrained and insular culture exists in this subculture, and the standard approach is punitive in most places. This is understandable, given the closed ranks and confrontational moments encountered, but there generally lacks a full consideration for the human side of an arrest or prosecution.

Rather than an arms race to push for quick plea deals that create streams of the adjudged and stigmatized, create financial and declaratory and promotional benefits for prosecutors who find alternative solutions besides criminal charges and avoid locking people up. Likewise, laud and reward officers who solve problems without arrests or force.

For full investment and to counter existing punitive culture, prosecutorial offices and the police with whom they work must be on the same page eventually. Be willing to use their budgets to make mandatory the treatment, diversity, and conflict resolution strategies that must be the undercurrent to the sea change away from punishment-first prosecution.

Policy Suggestion 18E: Commit to, work with, and encourage non-police problem solving solutions in communities.

We must collectively recognize that while we all aim to improve trust and mindset, there is currently a disconnect between police and many communities. Thus, right now options without police should be applied for overdoses, school discipline issues, and other social service needs. The current over reliance on police as a standard response to an array of social concerns leads to a greater tendency towards escalation and unnecessary arrests. Train and fund other groups to serve needed purposes, as has the Oakland Power Project.

Policy Suggestion 18F: Make community service time without arrests mandatory for all officers and attorneys.

Again, for too long policing here in Virginia, across the United States, and especially its less privileged communities has been almost entirely adversarial. The mindset has been to respond to trouble as a baseline, rather than to approach as community members seeking to help. This breeds distrust and conflict in both directions. Yet we know that simple interactions in a comfortable setting break down barriers. In order to make policing most effective and improve community safety, it must be built in trust, so making part of the job to engage communities as teammates without any possibility of arrest or punishment for a certain amount of time each month will help everyone get to know, like, and trust each other. Events like community basketball games where police participate or having police volunteer within community centers, or police sponsored cookouts—being clear that participating officers will not arrest or punish during those times—can be helpful, along with many other possibilities. The humanizing effect of these interactions will reduce unnecessary arrests more broadly.

Policy Suggestion 18G: Refuse to prosecute "victimless" crimes.

Resources can be more effectively devoted to treatment, education, and proactive approaches if prosecutorial offices simply refuse to spend time or money on drug possession, vagrancy, truancy, prostitution, and other status offenses. Police may not like it, but these are all situations where they could help people instead of persecute them and create better outcomes. Convictions hurt communities and families and cost the state.

Policy Suggestion 18H: Make restorative justice the dominant approach to prosecutorial decisions. Train everyone in police and prosecutorial offices accordingly. Train everyone locked up and offer incentives for successful completion of programs with victims. Be willing to drop or reduce charges

if restorative programming is quickly completed without incarceration.

The cutting edge of criminal justice is restorative justice. This amounts to creating voluntary interactions between people who commit an infraction and the person victimized, with the aim at developing shared empathy and understanding to end conflict in all directions. Recent studies have found that the mutual empathy it engenders not only reduces conflict between those involved in a crime but also helps promote healing for everyone and reduces future criminogenic thinking. Most crimes occur between members of a single community, so retaliation and revenge are inherently likely to perpetuate cycles of crime. The more that such conflict resolution is promoted, rather than simply retributive punishment, the safer communities will become. This also promotes a mindset that gives a voice and a purpose to anyone who has committed a crime, important for rehabilitation efforts, and provides opportunity to actually right wrongs and reduce negative impacts of mistakes in the process, both producing greater motivation for self-improvement than simply being locked in a cage.

For an excellent example of restorative justice in practice, please see the Common Justice program in New York (https://www.commonjustice.org/) and read Until We Reckon, a beautifully written book by their founder, Danielle Sered.

Policy Suggestion 18I: For nonviolent drug possession situations, refuse to arrest in exchange for immediate enrollment in treatment.

A recent snapshot of the Henrico County Jail in June of 2018, showed that possession was the second most common cause for lock up, right behind probation violations. Knowing all we know about addiction now, this is absurd and counterproductive and far too expensive. Incarceration alone rarely ends addiction and creates a cycle fueled by reduced opportunities, despair, and stigmatized self-image. Instead, a very simple offer of immediate treatment should be permanently available to anyone who simply possesses drugs. No charges filed as long as they complete an evidence-based program paid for with diverted funds. Failure should be met with starting over, not punishment. Avoiding criminal records and hopeless time behind bars in consideration of the human side of addiction will avoid erasing the hope necessary to overcome it. Families will be maintained and relationships strengthened.

Policy Suggestion 18J: Fund and divert all possible prosecutions to evidence-based substance abuse treatment programs.

It is not just drug possession cases that are the result of substance abuse. Intoxicated decisions and pursuit of money to satisfy cravings create other crimes. A recent report from Henrico jail found that 87% of people admitted addiction was the root of their arrest. Thus, most crimes can be avoided by making addiction treatment the top priority. By spending the money that decades of incarceration and new jails would cost instead on treatment, the problem can be averted before it occurs.

Policy Suggestion 18K: Create and constantly improve alternative justice models like drug, veterans, and mental health courts.

Of those arrested more than once in 2017, 52% had substance abuse disorders and 30% had serious psychological distress, according to the National Survey of Drug Use and Health data. Two decades plus of research demonstrates that diversion and treatment models are more successful and more cost-effective than traditional criminal prosecutions. They remain imperfect, often still diverting people too readily to criminal penalties, limiting enrollment eligibility too narrowly, and imposing monitoring too restrictive for successful living, but they are already better at reducing the social costs of crime and its punishment than simply getting time.

During grad school, I was part of an extensive independent analysis of one of the first drug courts, in Clarke County, WA. We found many areas of potential improvement, but I was also struck at the time by how much better it was than simply criminalizing the lives of these thousands of participants. Not all succeeded, but many were able to avoid convictions and family separation. Many people I spoke with were endlessly thankful, and many of the judges and attorneys involved took pride in actually helping people as people. The biggest factor was a collective meeting before all court proceedings, where social workers, prosecutors, judges, and advocates for addicts worked as a team. Continue and broaden the creation of these courts in conjunction with ongoing independent monitoring with the collective aim at avoiding prison and it will bolster economies, families, and communities.

Now what?

"Great! Now I've ridden a roller coaster of emotions, from sad to touched to outraged. Gee, thanks! But what am I supposed to do about all this?!" you're very likely thinking. Maybe you're even carrying a heavy heart or holding a slightly used tissue.

I apologize for the feelings that the stark nature of the system's reality often elicit. Even Gin, my wonderful partner and cofounder of The Humanization Project, has expressed how draining this work can be and how small bites are all she can handle at times. I certainly concur, and I am grateful for the fortitude and principles displayed by everyone who read this far.

Even being a lifelong activist for criminal justice reform, researcher, and sociology teacher, I went through the emotional wringer as I encountered the system personally on a human level, meeting the people and learning their stories. Particularly when it came to the family side of things, exacerbated by my own separation from my beloved son, D, I live that poignant tension daily. Sometimes I can only stay productive by hyper-focusing on my purpose. It is devastatingly sad to me still, even accustomed as I am.

But that is the only way to get things to change.

Because often the things we need to read most are those most uncomfortable to digest. Because I hope and believe that, faced with the reality of human beings and families limited by an archaic systemic culture and obsolescent structure, you will add the one other emotion that I've experienced with this awareness: determination.

I wrote this book because I had to do something, to try to change the narrative and make a difference. So at least the years D and I lost could mean something. Drowning in my own loneliness amidst the contrast between active disregard and the well-glossed lip service to family values and personal growth worn on DOC's public face, I believe that change will come from good people learning the truth about the dads, moms, brothers, sisters, grandparents, even great grandparents, all the people, especially the kids.

Since you're still reading now, you are almost certainly thinking at least a little differently and deeper about the human beings affected by the system, so that's already a win. But that's not enough, and I'm hoping that you have been inspired to want to do more. Not nearly everyone will read this for a variety of reasons, including bias against authors with convictions, limits of a small organizations, and a general tendency ingrained in our culture to dehumanize people behind bars. So those who do read it—those of us in any way aware of the human side of all this—must do just a bit more with this awareness.

Lucky for your feelings and the hopes of so many thousand families, a difference can be made in this realm. Even better, I've compiled a humble list of suggestions of how to contribute.

1. Rethink your assumptions.

Now that you've heard the voices of so many good, loving parents behind bars and thought about their kids as individuals, elevate this humanizing perspective whenever you read or hear something about someone who has been convicted of a crime. This is the smallest, easiest thing to do, but if everyone considered everyone else as a human being, everyone would be treated more humanely—in this and all other realms.

Rarely is a conviction as straightforward, "good-vs-evil" as prosecutors say and the press prints. The situation is almost always embellished by police, lawyers, and media to sell outcomes that match stereotypes and myths. Even when someone is fully guilty just as described, they are always so much more than their crime. I mean, is your entire identity defined by your worst mistake? Would you want society's conclusions about you to be based on the moment you did worst decades ago? If nothing else, think of it always as what is best for community, family, public safety in the long run, permanent one-dimensional disenfranchisement for those who have harmed or three-dimensional human opportunities to show improvement?

2. Seek further info.

This book covers just one sub-realm, family, within a much broader criminal justice system rife with inequality and dehumanization. And these are just the accounts, voices, and facts able to be collected and described by a single person handcuffed and muzzled within that system without internet access for nearly a decade (though I did study, teach, and write about the system nonstop before my personal submersion). Point being, there's a ton more information out there about virtually any aspect of the system you wish to see improved. Seek out more whenever you are moved by an issue. An informed citizen demands and affects the most progress.

Within the limited resources of a prison library and fellow activists behind bars, I can recommend some deeper dives. Danielle Sered's *Until We Reckon* compellingly describes the rationale, structure, and evidence for a restorative justice-based system that prioritizes keeping families and communities intact while actually righting wrongs. Shaka Senghor's *Writing My Wrongs* and Chris Wilson's *Master Plan* offer powerful personal accounts showing the importance of familial bonds to rehabilitation and the possibility of growth. Michelle Alexander's acclaimed *The New Jim Crow* epically describes the discriminatory effects of an intentionally designed injustice system. Reuben Jonathan Miller's *Halfway Home* explains the Himalayan obstacles faced today in returning to a dehumanizing society, highlighting the need for better rehabilitative support. And everyone who cares should just generally read Ibram X. Kendi's *Stamped from the Beginning* and *How To Be An Antiracist*, Howard Zinn's *A*

People's History of the United States of America, and Mosher and Akins' *Drugs and Drug Policy: The Control of Consciousness Alteration.* Though the first three are not specific to criminal justice and the third's technically a textbook (that I once helped pen), they deepen understanding of injustice.

3. Humanize to others.

Simply put, spread the word about what you have learned here. Virtually everyone who lives in some disadvantaged, over-policed neighborhoods knows someone behind bars as a human being, making a human understanding inherent there. But the very same structural disadvantages and biases that make it much likelier people committing the same crimes there will end up behind bars make it so that such enlightenment has limited clout in policy or mainstream public opinion. If we want sea change on the way the system functions, we must first get the average privileged voter to understand and care, on principle and because of the indirect ways it affects them even when it does not do so directly.

All this requires that people who would not typically encounter anything but a stereotyped, HBO- or evening news-based misunderstanding of people with convictions encounter and actually engage humanized portrayals. And who better to bring this than those they know? We digest most new info presented to us by trusted sources so share this book, its lessons, and any other dialogue or posts or journalism that force a full-bodied consideration of people behind bars and the ripple effects of an unforgiving system in an unforgiving society.

The first three above are excellent steps, very important, and anyone can do them at virtually any time. And they should be part of daily life, really, to change the collective narrative.

But they are not enough.

Real change will occur when we take direct action. Not every day, not every week, but consistently. Today's social media-driven understanding of social movements allows for small sparks to become national conflagrations of attention quickly, but it also lacks much structure and consistency. When social movements are merely millions sharing and liking and posting, they bark loud but have no bite. Politicians know they can just say platitudes and do nothing till tomorrow. It is when we take some real time and put in some real energy, even just a few fours here and there, that things really happen. That is what separates a moment from a movement.

The rest of these are simple steps to engage on the next level.

4. Help the little organizations.

While some big, well-known organizations certainly make an outsized difference, the vast majority of actual change work in criminal justice is done by just a few local organizations. They typically have meager budgets and an entirely volunteer staff of just a few people. Or less.

A number of factors contribute here. First, nobody has much time in today's bustling world, period. Second, this issue is not easy to make "hot" because helping people behind bars, even if it saves taxpayer money, assists families, and reduces crime, runs counter to decades of stereotypes. Third, it means helping those individuals who have been long stereotyped and are, on top of that, now actively judged as "wrong." Even when the actions were but the person good, this is tough to overcome. Finally, we have a cultural tendency towards regressive, punitive responses towards crime. Even groups claiming generally progressive values, like RAINN, have actively worked against evidence-based reform here in Virginia that would have helped reduce the number of future victims.

As a result, the biggest limit to more progress is a

shortage of committed volunteers and funds. With almost no budget and only three to five consistent contributors (two of those behind bars), The Humanization Project has in three years managed to draft and lobby and rally the passage of two meaningful reform bills in a Southern state. It could be so much more in the future if we had more people and funding to help us out.

The good news is that it is very easy to get involved. Those who are involved are typically down to earth, helpful people. And we all know each other. Go to one website or one rally, have one conversation or send one email, and anyone who wants to can readily find a place in the network. You can easily get involved with a welcoming group, doing whatever you think you can contribute best on pretty much whatever issue you are passionate about. Please, reach out to some smaller organizations and find your role!

5. Vote purposefully in state elections.

The next most impactful thing anyone can do to reform criminal justice anywhere is to vote in all local and state elections for candidates explicitly running on promises to make specific changes. In terms of these issues raised here, it's particularly important because, while federal policy gets much more attention, around 85% of those incarcerated are in state prisons and local jails. That means that the laws dictating the conditions and extent of confinement in each state are what impacts nearly all people behind bars. Plus, the federal prisons already have much higher standards for constitutional and budgetary reasons.

In fact, any criminal justice issues matter most at the state and local levels. Your local district attorney decides what crimes are focal, what charges get pressed, and which get dropped—and often which get stacked to force plea deals if you don't elect reform candidates. Sheriff elections determine the spirit of the policing that lands people behind bars. State legislative elections especially, though, guide prison, state police, and sentencing policies, while also potentially allocating the funds for programs that may actually help. Best of all, your state representatives are politicians but not year-round and they are willing to meet directly with people and constituents who are persistent. After all, elections on the state level often get overlooked by many and come down to just a few dozen votes either way. So go out to primaries and promote candidates who promise this issue will matter and then make sure to hit the election itself and support whomever is better on these issues. It literally can change whole lives.

Proof that this state election strategy can have an impact can be seen here in Virginia, too. For decades this was a very Confederate place, Alabama in a suit in terms of its criminal justice system, with the second most executions in modern time and the second most people locked up in the past ten years despite a very low violent crime rate. With extremely discriminatory patterns, too. Nothing changed, either, until there was a statewide political reckoning in 2019, with Democrats taking both chambers of the legislature following a huge organizing effort including around criminal justice issues. Not nearly enough has been done yet because it's a new majority and Republicans have relied loudly on fear mongering to block the biggest stuff. Still, besides being the first Southern state to legalize marijuana and abolish the death penalty, at least 50 new laws reforming our system have passed in under two years and more are on the way. The Humanization Project and POINT (a for-us-by-us educational and community engagement organization I'm part of in here) worked tirelessly to get out voters and educate legislators, who can actually be met with personally at the state level, and things are actually changing for the better, albeit with mostly small steps first.

I don't mean to sound partisan. I am not myself a Democrat, either. Criminal Justice reform is not a fully partisan issue everywhere, but it certainly plays out that way in Virginia (and many other places). There are a few libertarian-minded or economic-geared Republican groups who helped promote reform here, and credit to them, but the record will show that nearly every big reform bill that reflected a humanized perspective has been unanimously opposed by Republican legislators here except those outlawing strip searches of minor visitors. In a few other states, some Republicans have helped some reform pass, and I hope we can find bipartisan support for more in the future here. There are also a number of Democrats who do poorly in this area, as cultural stereotypes are heavy to lift. Still, if these issues really matter to you as a top priority, the most helpful candidates tend to be progressive Democrats. The only way to change things then is to either elect them or be part of a very vocal constituency prodding other state and local officials to make specific policy changes. After all, helping families stay connected and providing educational and therapeutic opportunities to everyone should not be a partisan issue.

6. Speak loudly to legislators.

That brings us to taking your voice beyond just the ballot box. Whenever there are criminal justice reform bills coming up for votes on the state level (which happens primarily the beginning of the year in most states), make sure you know what they are. Then email and call whoever represents you repeatedly, expressing your support as a voter in their district. Then get everyone you know to do so, too. Because they want to keep their jobs and, thus, their power, state elected officials tend to respond fairly well when even hundreds of people from their district directly support a particular bill. We have seen some long shots pass following vocal drives, and we have seen some expected winners falter because not enough actual voters made it sound important to them. A direct voice spoken to your representative really does matter.

Similarly, if you want to see an idea become a bill, talk to elected officials directly and ask them to sponsor it. Even try drafting it yourself. I did, and it worked, while I was behind bars still. As noted, many state legislators can be engaged in person fairly readily, too, particularly if you volunteer with an organization. Even just as an individual, though, you can establish relationships that lead to actual policy change affecting millions. All you have to do is speak clearly, passionately, and repeatedly.

7. Give second chances yourself.

Finally, you can help directly by giving others second chances whenever you have an opportunity. If you have a business or make any hiring decisions, offer a job to a qualified person with a past conviction. Hire someone for an odd job even. Beyond jobs, offer some time to volunteer with the children or families of people behind bars. Tutors and childcare and job training are in perpetual need. At the least, donate some money to a group that directly helps in any of these areas.

Estimates suggest there are over 100 million people fighting the stigma of a conviction, so you are likely to know some yourself. Because of extreme structural racism in the criminal justice system, this is especially true for people of color. And all of those people have tens of millions more kids and partners and parents. Someone you encounter around you will fit in these categories this year, probably this month. Move forward with the conscious intention to help make life a little more humane for those individuals whenever you have the opportunity.

Thank you

"Wow, there sure is a lot to be done!"

I know. I agree entirely, and that is why we reform activists are inclined to end this book with such a laundry list of requests. The scope of it all is why we are compelled to act ourselves, too, I promise. When the need for change is evident, it requires that all who recognize it participate. The Nazis never had more than 38% of voter support in an election, but it was the acquiescence of the majority that allowed them to keep power and continue enacting such policies. In no way am I equating policies, only pointing out that discriminatory, harmful policies are maintained by inaction. Luckily, though, this book is but one in a growing cacophony of voices spreading awareness and inspiring action.

Encouragingly, the more people who take on even minor roles even occasionally, the lesser the load and resistance.

Which is why I must end by thanking you, Reader, for taking this journey, for sharing your time and opening your mind to these voices of parenthood behind bars and the needs of the families who love us. As everyone involved in the reform movement knows, none of the items above are easy to accomplish. As we at The Humanization Project are particularly aware, the widespread perception is stigmatizing and changing that is the first and, perhaps, vanguard priority.

Hence, we thank you for taking the time to learn and listen because even that is progress. It is not easy, either, because these voices are poignant and sad. It is not easy to bring an open mind, either, because you have been inundated your whole life with media and political messages reducing anyone with a conviction to dangerous, unidimensional stereotypes of "criminal," "convict," and "thug." And those of us who actually did the things for which we were convicted did not help by acting as such so many years ago. But that has never negated or outweighed the many layers of our humanity, and certainly not that of our kids and families. As with any effective mediation or reconciliation, the first step is listening, so we end this book simply by thanking you for thus being an essential part of this healing process necessary to strengthen and make safer all our communities.

Acknowledgements

First and foremost, we must begin at the beginning, by thanking D. The bond that I have shared with him since the day he was born is initial inspiration for this entire project. The letter I wrote him, heartbroken but determined to continue being a positive influence while behind bars, is the entire foundation for this project. He is almost 16 now, and he has grown into the most kind, reasonable, principled teenage guy I've ever known despite having to spend many years with his father only available on the phone. His strength and resiliency are a testament to his incredible heart and character. And he just dunked for the first time, still shy of six feet tall, so he's kind of badass, too. I could not be more proud of you, son.

Next, we must thank all the men and women behind bars who contributed their words, offering the world a glimpse at their family bonds in hope that we can strengthen those of millions in the future. It was dialogue with so many fathers who, regardless of their convictions, are dedicated and loving, just like parents everywhere, that led us to realize that the world would be better to see this humanizing side of life behind bars. All you mothers and fathers have written beautiful, heartfelt letters belying so many stereotypes and deserving of the admiration of your children. Your ongoing efforts to stay connected and help raise your children continue to inspire us daily.

Likewise, we thank the children of all our participants and those of every one of the 2.3 million people behind bars in this country. Your patience, strength, and unconditional love are beyond what anyone could expect. You are the foundation of all our hopes for a more humane future.

We also wish to offer endless thanks to Dr. William Cook and Jack Doxey for their guidance, input, and philosophical support. This book and our entire organization, The Humanization Project, came to life as an extension of the work we all did together to "think dignity" for all people, including those confined in our jails and prisons. Had it not been for your encouragement and belief, we never would have had the courage to begin any of this. Without your wisdom shared, these ideas never would have percolated.

Next, a giant thank you to Sonee Singh and Donna Yates Ferris, two amazing authors in their own right, who kindly lent their eyes and editing expertise. This book would not have been finished without you both. We appreciate you so much!

A hearty thanks goes out to everyone involved in the astoundingly tight knit, remarkably perseverant, powerfully determined community of criminal justice reform advocates in Virginia. As The Humanization Project expanded and this book was refined, we stepped blindly into directly advocating for legislative and executive change on the state level. It was daunting at first, but we were quickly welcomed and offered a seat and a voice by many who have been doing this hard work for years, even decades. There remains a lot to change, as this was once the capital of the Confederacy and the culture remains regressive from many resisting change. "Alabama in a suit," it was aptly called a few years ago. However, the state has enacted dozens of reform bills in the past two years, thanks to emboldened progressive leadership, indeed, but primarily because of the endless efforts of this small cadre of dedicated volunteers and professionals. We still have a long way to go, but we have made progress few only dreamed of even five years ago, and we are honored to be part of the effort and touched by your inclusiveness. We will continue to press for humane change by your sides until equity and community are elevated everywhere.

Among this group, we have developed particularly strong bonds with many who we now call friends. A particularly heartfelt thanks goes out to Shawn Weneta, our legislative liaison, who has elevated our organization and the whole movement since his release. Likewise, we send deep gratitude for the endless hours of cooperation and camaraderie to Kari Anderson of Restore Justice in Virginia, Johanna Gusman of NAACP Loudon, Mateo Gasporotto, Ashna Khana and everyone else at the ACLU of VA, Bryan Kennedy and Justice Forward Virginia, Jana White of The Virginia Coalition for the Fair Sentencing of Youth, Tony and Linda Brown, Valerie Slater and Gary Broderick of Rise for Youth, Rebecca Keel and everyone at Southerners or New Ground, Shannon Ellis, Wyatt Rolla, Yohance Whitaker, Luis Oyola and all the lovely people at Legal Aid Justice Center, Sheba Williams of NOLEF Turns, Richard Walker with Bridging the Gap in Virginia, Kimberly Jenkins-Snodgrass and David Smith and everyone at the Virginia Coalition on Solitary Confinement, Paul Taylor, Prince Bunn, and many others who have worked with us, promoted bills with us, and spent their time and effort trying to change this crazy criminal justice system.

Of course, as we all fought for and continue to seek change, we spent a lot of time with state officials and legislators, many of whom were incredibly welcoming and supportive. On behalf of the movement and ourselves, we would like to offer considerable gratitude to those who helped offer us a voice and who actually listened to us, on principle alone, no money to offer. In particular, Jennifer McClellan, Kaye Kory, Don Scott, Patrick Hope, Chap Peterson, Kelly Thomason, Adrianne Bennett, and Joe Morrissey, you have bravely led the Commonwealth towards a more fair and humane system.

Among those we have encountered in our reform efforts, an extra heap of gratitude goes out to Fletcher and Mary Fran Lowe, Jack Doxey, and Seth Watson, all of whom generously offered financial support without which this book would not have come to be. Writing a book from behind bars is difficult, and the stigma involved leaves most publishers automatically disinterested. To publish this ourselves and provide all participants and relevant state leaders with the copies we believe can help humanize and inspire direct change required more than we could offer alone, especially as one of us makes but 45 cents/hour. Thanks to you, this book will finally reach the hands of those who need to read it.

We absolutely must thank the two most supportive families possible. Howard Haft, Kathi Jane Alvarado, Boyd Lintecum, Gale Lintecum, Luis Alvarado, and Beckey Haft, our collective parents, have listened, promoted, and helped us both out at every turn in life, and especially as we set off together on our relationship and this seemingly Quixotic—at first—effort to prompt change in Virginia. Extended family and friends, especially Marigot Miller, Nikki Giovanni, Jason Stubbs, Seth Watson, Sam and Trisha Wright, Anna Morgan, Liz Immel, Lauren and Auren Monosov, Steve Larkin, Abby Steketee, Bunny Young, Jordan Albright, David Winber, Victor Martell, Dylan Brenneman, Keegan Brenneman, Slade Brenneman, Kane Brenneman, Tori Haft, Sadie Haft, Mark Haft, Joan Stubbs, and Scott Grooms have offered us the levity and unconditional love to keep smiling and know that we will always have good people around us. We shine only reflecting your light.

If we have forgotten anyone in our list of thanks, please know that it was not intentional. The chaos of the past year or so with the pandemic and countless zoom calls for legislative sessions and special sessions may have caused us to overlook some important people, so if you know you contributed in any way, thank you.

Lastly, of course, we must thank each other. Neither of us ever thought that a storybook love was a possibility in this lifetime, but after a friendship of almost 20 years, we found it and in one of the darkest places imaginable—the U.S. prison system. We can never thank each other enough for our love and for being partners in so many ways. This book wouldn't have happened with our love and so that love is the note we must end on.

Want to learn more about people behind bars and how to help?

A great place to start is with our recent peer-reviewed paper which contains many other good references:

Mahon-Haft, Taj Alexander, John Doxey, and William J. Cook, Jr. "Meaning, Purpose, and Hope: Reflections on Religion, Spirituality, and Life of Leaders Behind Bars," *Journal of Religion & Society* 21 (2019): 1-23.

If you want to get even more involved, please reach out to us via our website:
www.thehumanizationproject.org

Requests for speaking engagements and podcasts interviews, please email:
gin@thehumanizationproject.org

Made in the USA
Middletown, DE
22 March 2022